IMAGES
of America

EARLY PASCO

On the Cover: The Riverview Social Improvement Club was loosely organized in 1913 to promote a sense of community. Meetings consisted of community speakers, local entertainment, dances, and refreshments. This building was constructed in 1921 on property donated by the Pasco Reclamation Company. Seattle photographer Asahel Curtis took this picture shortly after the hall was finished. The picture was used to promote the social aspect and benefits of living in Pasco. (Courtesy of the Washington State Historical Society.)

IMAGES
of America

EARLY PASCO

Susan Davis Faulkner

ARCADIA
PUBLISHING

ISBN 978-0-7385-7103-4

Published by Arcadia Publishing
Charleston, South Carolina

Printed in the United States of America

Library of Congress Control Number: 2009920418

For all general information contact Arcadia Publishing at:
Telephone 843-853-2070
Fax 843-853-0044
E-mail sales@arcadiapublishing.com
For customer service and orders:
Toll-Free 1-888-313-2665

Visit us on the Internet at www.arcadiapublishing.com

For Payten Lynn Henderson, my first grandchild. May the passion of history run in your blood and in the blood of the generations that follow.

Contents

Acknowledgments

Writing Images of America: *Early Pasco* has been one of the most enjoyable experiences of my life. This project is the result of the efforts of many individuals who have a love of the history of Pasco. Through their assistance and encouragement, I have learned not only about this local history but also about the passion of history that stirs in so many historians.

Without the understanding and encouragement of my family, this book would have never begun. Late nights and "fend for yourself" dinners were taken in stride while I met with various people and burned the midnight oil. Family members (David, Brian, Maxwell, Merit, Krystal, Natania, and Jane) listened and asked questions that sparked ideas for more research.

I want to thank my closest friends, Elaine Wasil and Lisa Lovejoy. Elaine made herself available as a traveling companion and nurtured me to do the best I could throughout this project. Lisa applied her thorough understanding of grammar and gave me her opinions with brutal frankness.

While writing Images of America: *Early Pasco*, I met many wonderful people who I now count as history buddies and good friends. Kennewick mayor Tom Moak and Dan "the Postcard Man" Stafford shared my passion for local history and freely gave of their thoughts, ideas, and knowledge. Mike Huntington became my mentor and challenged me to consider ideas and historical points that would not have been addressed without his assistance. Frank Pontarolo personally shared his memories and allowed me to sit at his feet while we walked down memory lane.

The collection of photographs and information that was made available to me by the Franklin County Historical Society (FCHS) was tremendous. Sherel Webb and Gabriele Sperling listened to my questions and poured through resources to help me find the right photograph or narrative to provide the correct answer. They encouraged me while proofreading draft copies and offered their expert writing abilities as alternatives.

More than anything, I want to thank the people of Pasco. Many doors were opened and many lives exposed to share the history of this town.

INTRODUCTION

The confluence of the Columbia River and Snake River appears in an arid terrain in southeast Washington. Natural indigenous vegetation consists of sagebrush and bunchgrass. There are no great mountains or eye-appealing wonders, with the exception of the mighty and untamed rivers that boil through the desert.

For these very reasons, the Northern Pacific Railway selected this location to build a bridge that would be part of the last spur of the transcontinental railroad. The bridge across the Snake River would connect the transcontinental railroad to Portland, Oregon. Without this bridge, railway traffic could only travel as far as the rivers. Once the rails met the mighty rivers, the trains would need to be disassembled. Groups of railroad cars would then be transported across the rivers on large steamboats.

In 1879, the Northern Pacific Railway began building the Snake River Bridge. Lumbermen from the state of Maine were recruited to fell the timber of the Cascade Mountains and then transport the lumber to the construction town of Ainsworth. Robert Gerry, Danville Page, and the Gray brothers—Alvin, Charles, Will, and Lon—were some of the expert lumbermen who came to Washington to take on this daunting task. They stayed and served the community for many years.

The town of Ainsworth continued to thrive. Its average population was 400 to 500 citizens, but the population spiked to 1,500 people when particular tasks of building the bridge took additional manpower. Ainsworth was a rough town with no official law enforcement. Vigilante forces attempted to tame the town but to no avail. Saloons, brothels, and opium dens were prevalent.

Franklin County was formed from a portion of Whitman County in 1883. Even though Ainsworth was known for its unlawful living, it was selected as the county seat for this newly formed county. At the time, Ainsworth was the largest populated community in Franklin County.

The Columbia and Snake Rivers were commandeered by the captains of various vessels. Sternwheelers and ferries were necessary to transport building materials, railroad cars, and people from one side of the river to the other. Capt. William Polk Gray and the transport sternwheeler the *Frederick K. Billings* became prominent in the area. Captain Gray, who was no relation to the Grays from Maine, had been a man who lived upon the river but soon became one of the area's largest promoters.

The railroad bridge over the Snake River was completed in 1884, and the next year, the Northern Pacific Railway started building the railroad bridge over the Columbia River. The new bridge would be located 3 miles west of the Snake River Bridge and would connect the infant towns of Kennewick and Pasco to the existing track. A town site was platted, and building materials were moved from the old construction town of Ainsworth to the new construction town of Pasco. This created a large migration as government offices, businesses, and families all made the move to the new town. Buildings were literally picked up and moved 3 miles to the new town. Buildings that could not be moved in one piece were disassembled and reassembled in their new location in Pasco.

This new town brought hope for a better life. Some of the men who had worked on the railroad in Ainsworth became official law enforcement in the new town of Pasco. There appeared to be a permanence and pride associated with the new town that never developed in the construction town of Ainsworth.

The railroad bridge over the Columbia River was completed in 1888, nine years after the Snake River Bridge construction started in Ainsworth. By this time, Pasco was known as a railroad town and a major depot. Rudyard Kipling and Frances Fuller Victor were just some of the well-known travelers who passed through Pasco. The activity of the railroad brought many people to stay in Pasco, drawn by Northern Pacific Railway employment.

Even after building the bridges, riverboats were a necessary form of transportation in the southern part of Franklin County. Their presence was mighty, and their existence was necessary. Harvested crops, freight, livestock, and individuals were ferried across the two rivers. Many of the riverboat captains held an important role in the development of the area.

In 1895, the U.S. government granted 1.5 million acres to the Northern Pacific Railway. This land was to be used for the growth of the railroad. Land was either to be used for building new tracks or to sell to prospective farmers; it was a win-win situation. The government would acquire more transportation routes, the railroad would build its wealth and pay its debts, and prospective farmers would be assured that transportation was available to haul their products. Once the land was granted to the Northern Pacific Railway, land agents found buyers for the land the Northern Pacific Railway had acquired.

Boosters and Northern Pacific Railway land agents were busy selling Pasco land to individuals in faraway places during the 1890s. Captain Gray and Louis Frey took the slogan "Keep Your Eye on Pasco" to cities such as Cincinnati and Chicago in an effort to provoke interest in the wonderful city that was developing at the confluence of the Columbia and Snake Rivers.

These efforts were not in vain, and Pasco began to grow. The river was an active transportation route as products were hauled from nearby farming communities to the transportation hub of Pasco. The railroad was vital in transporting these crops to markets. Social clubs were established, and a feeling of belonging to a community began. These social clubs gave individuals an opportunity to congregate and contribute to the town where they proudly belonged.

As Pasco continued to survive and grow, it began to thrive. Celebrations were enjoyed by everyone, and people would travel to Pasco to take part in the festivities. The "Open River" celebration of 1915 was a large event that many river towns along the Columbia River enjoyed. The Open River celebration was a time of rejoicing. The Dalles-Celilo Canal was completed, which provided continuous river navigation from Lewiston, Idaho, to the Pacific Ocean. With the new "open river," riverboats would be able to compete with the railroads for agriculture transportation.

Pasco's first hospital was established in the refurbished Montana Hotel in 1916 and renamed Our Lady of Lourdes Hospital. Necessary equipment and sterilization were improvised using existing facilities. Pasco was hit hard during the flu pandemic of 1918–1920, and it became obvious that a new hospital was needed. The new Our Lady of Lourdes Hospital was built in 1921.

Sheep ranching was an important industry in Franklin County, and dry-land farming was attempted. The dry and warm climate made sheep raising a booming industry. Dry-land farming was a challenge, however. The mighty rivers contained more than enough water to make farming successful in Franklin County's succulent soil nearby, but the rivers were not tamed. Many attempts were made at developing an irrigation system. Farmers like the Schunemans, Gantenbeins, and Harrises were successful because they created individual irrigation systems and did not wait for a unified district. Several attempts were made to create irrigation companies. One attempt after another went bankrupt as unforeseen circumstances blocked the attempts. Construction costs were prohibitive. The desire for irrigation water was so great that the individuals of Pasco pulled together to ensure the success of the Franklin County Irrigation District.

Engine power swept the nation in the early 1920s. Automobiles could be seen along Pasco's roads, also used by bicycles, horses, and pedestrians. The Pasco-Kennewick automobile bridge, also known as the Green Bridge, was built in 1922. Before this bridge was built, riverboat ferries had been the major form of transportation across the river from Pasco to Kennewick or Richland.

The first contract airmail flight originated in Pasco in 1926. Varney Airlines, which later merged with other airlines to create United Airlines, won the contract and was commissioned by the U.S. government with orchestrating an airmail flight from Pasco, Washington, to Elko, Nevada. The community was excited, and festivities were enjoyed. The flight to Elko was successful, but the corresponding flight from Elko to Pasco had its difficulties. Lessons were learned from the challenges of the day, and airmail traffic became an important part of Pasco. This placed Pasco as one of the early aviation communities of the country.

During the Depression, Pasco continued to be promoted as an agricultural haven. Families from dust bowl states flocked to Pasco with hopeful hearts. Pasco, however, was not immune to the effects of the Depression. A federally subsidized transient shelter was established. Transients were given meals and, if available, short-term jobs to help the community. The Works Progress Administration hired many unemployed individuals for various community-needed jobs.

Pasco would continue to face challenges yet thrive and grow. Pasco's early years experienced the building of the railroad and the importance of the riverboats. It was challenged with the need for irrigation water that appeared all too plentiful yet hard to obtain. Unlawfulness was a way of life as the community experienced growing pains, but social clubs and a desire for a stable community prevailed.

Today Pasco is a community of undying foresight, courage, and hope. Since its beginning, Pasco has never believed its dreams were too large or unattainable, and no matter how many plans have been thwarted, Pasco continues to reach for the next accomplishment that will keep her on the map. In 1883, Henry Villard, president of the Northern Pacific Railway, stated that a large city would grow at the confluence of the Columbia and Snake Rivers. The hope, pride, and hard work of Pasco's inhabitants have continued to work toward this goal.

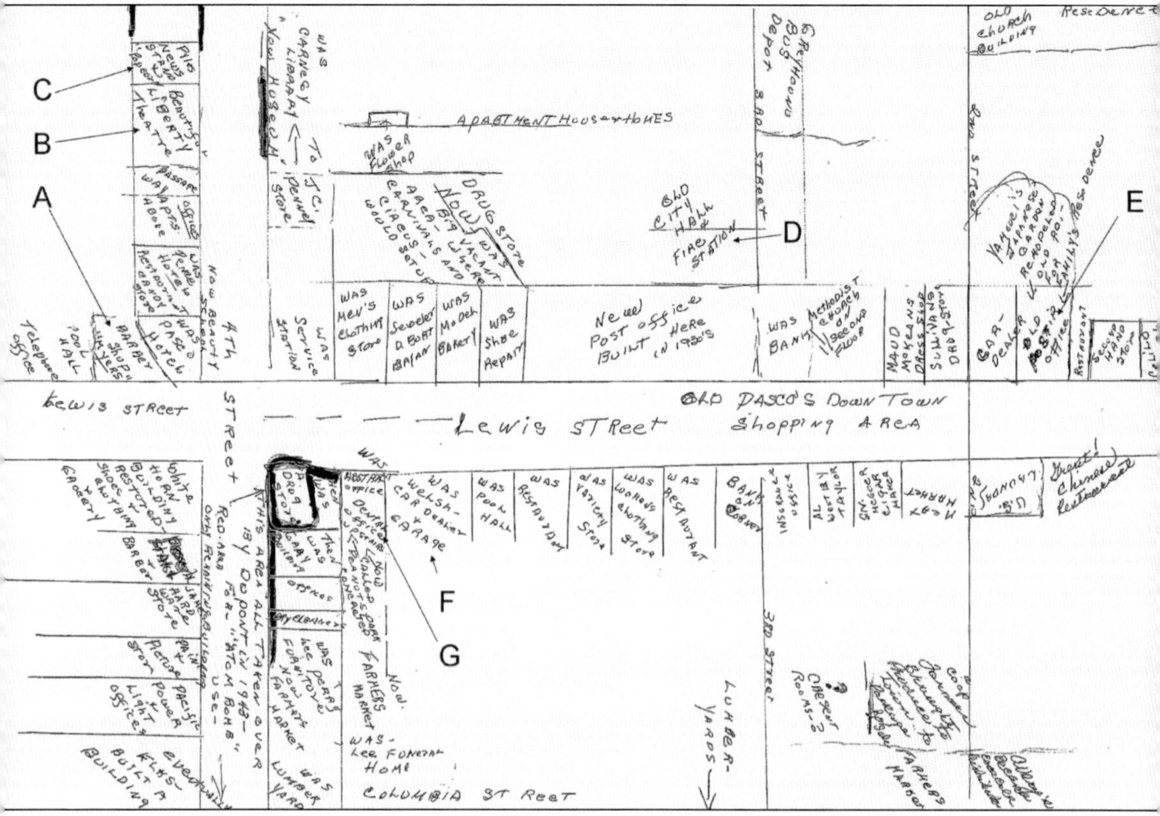

In 2008, Dorothy (Myers) Miller drew the above map of historical downtown Pasco. Dot was born in Pasco in 1918. She spent many of her adult years in Connell but grew up in Pasco and returned upon retiring. While living in Connell, she visited her parents, Carl and Adah Myers, who continued to live in Pasco. Lewis Street, the major artery of downtown, started at the railroad tracks on the far right and was intersected by First, Second, Third, and Fourth Streets. Many of the locations on this map have information on the following pages of this book. Point A was Carl Myers Barber Shop, page 83. Point B was the Liberty Theatre, page 90. Point C was Pyles News Stand, page 96. Point D was Pasco City Hall and fire station, page 78. Point E was the M&M Café, page 58. Point F was Welch Motor Company, page 108. Point G was the Title and Trust Building, page 68. (Courtesy of Dot Miller.)

One

Before There Was Pasco
1800 to 1885

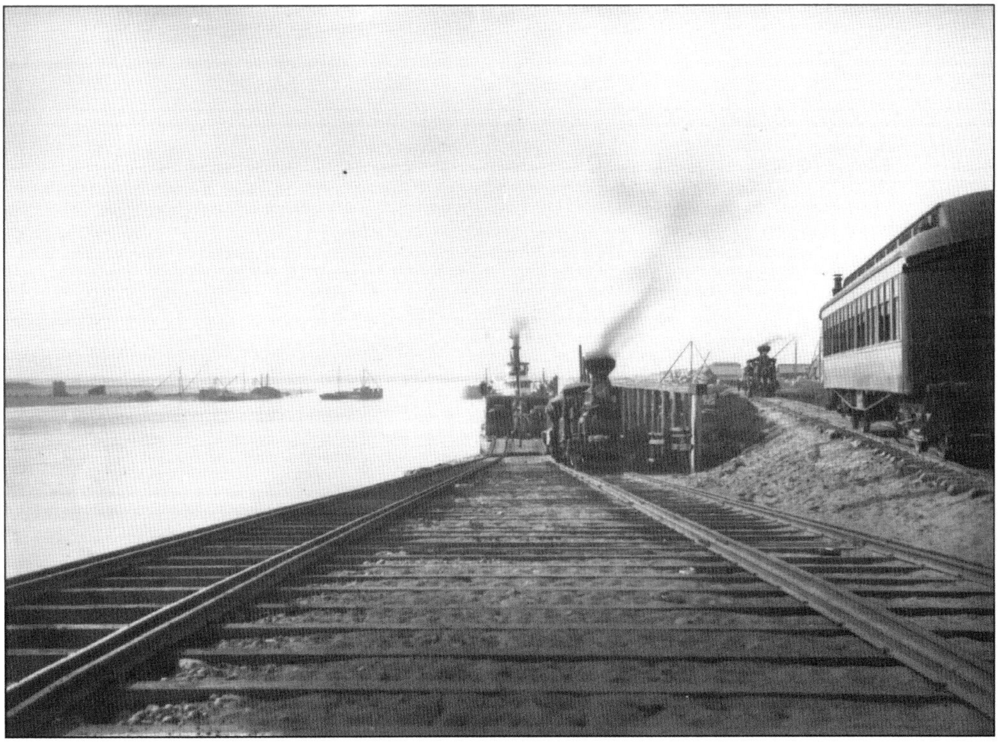

Before and during construction of the Snake River Bridge at Ainsworth, railroad cars were loaded onto steamboats and hauled across the river. The *Frederick K. Billings*, captained by William Polk Gray, could hold up to eight railroad cars in one load. In this picture, the Snake River Bridge is under construction in the background. The town of Ainsworth is shown to the right. (Courtesy of the Washington State Railroads Historical Society.)

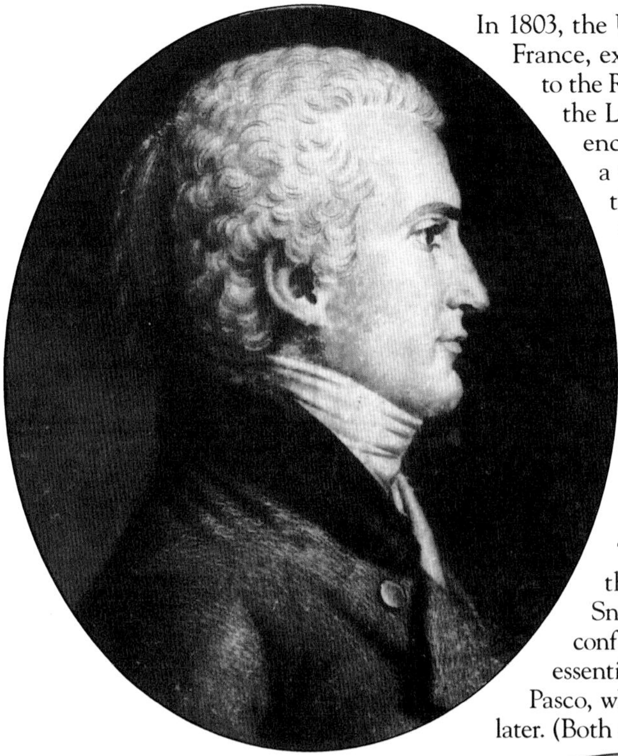

In 1803, the United States purchased land from France, extending from the Mississippi River to the Rocky Mountains, that was known as the Louisiana Purchase. This acquisition encouraged the United States to find a waterway that would extend from the Atlantic Ocean to the Pacific Ocean. President Jefferson selected Capt. Meriwether Lewis (left) to lead an expedition to study several aspects of the land between the two oceans. Lewis was selected for his military leadership and cartography (mapmaking) skills. Lewis selected a former army comrade, Capt. William Clark (below), to co-lead the expedition. Clark was selected for his knowledge of Native Americans. The expedition team camped on the riverbanks of the Columbia and Snake Rivers on October 16, 1805. The confluence of these two rivers would become essential to the community later known as Pasco, which established itself there 80 years later. (Both courtesy of the Library of Congress.)

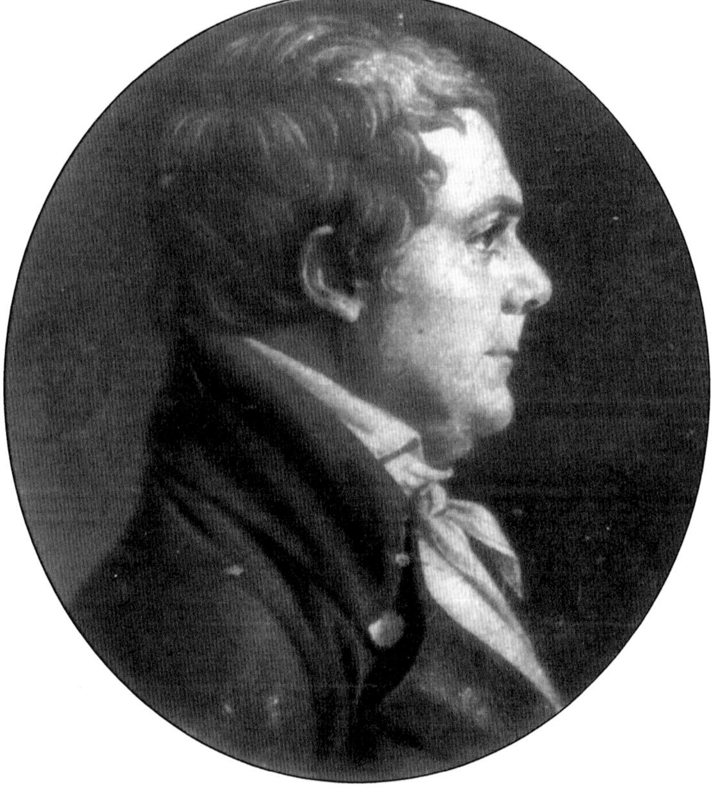

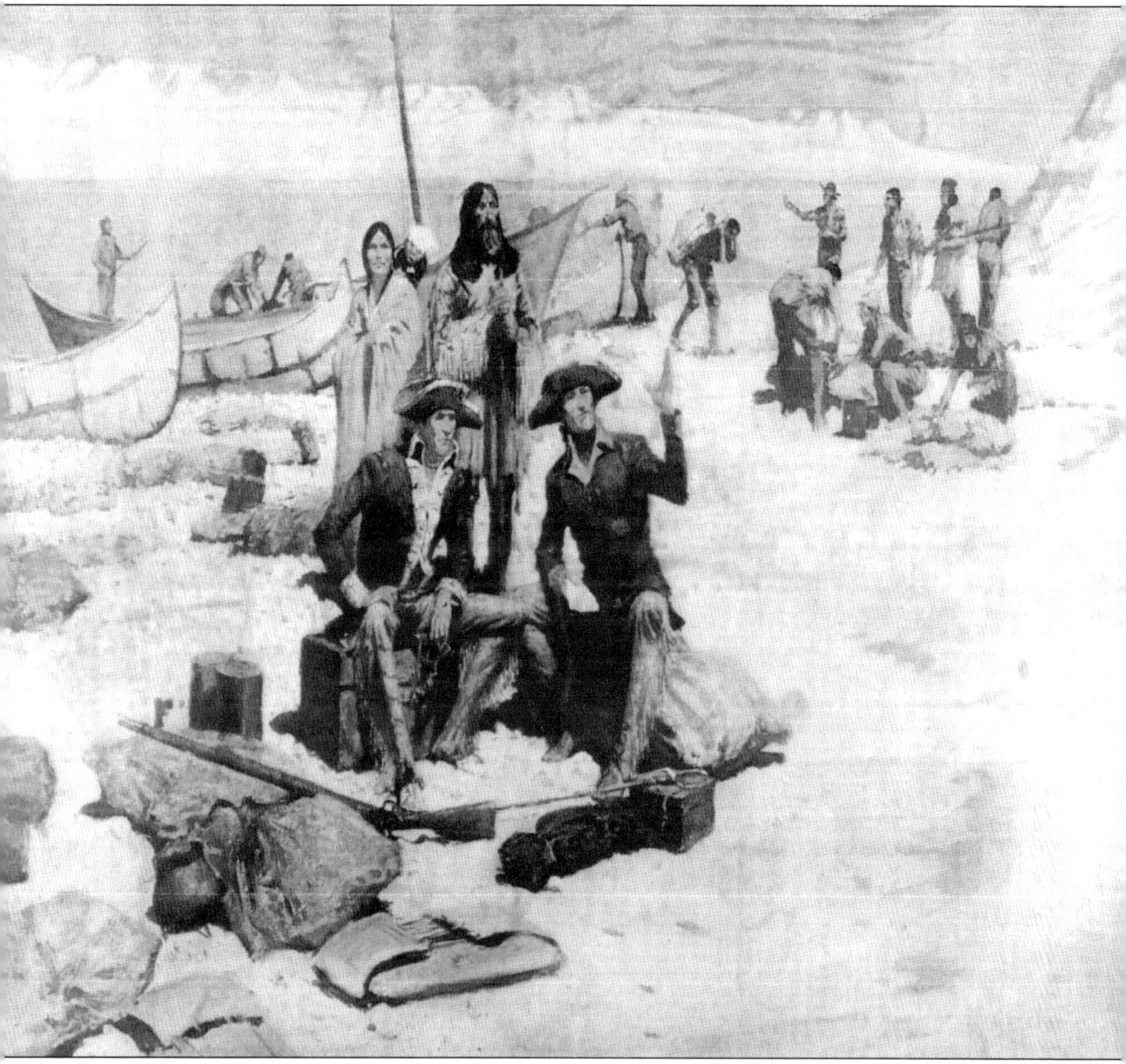

Toussaint Charbonneau was hired by Lewis and Clark as an interpreter in March 1805. Charbonneau was a French Canadian trapper who spoke the Indian language of Hidatsa as well as French. His wife, Sacagawea, also joined the expedition team as a guide and an interpreter. Sacagawea was a survivor from a Shoshone/Hidatsa war and had been taken in by the Hidatsa tribe. She could speak Shoshone and Hidatsa. Captains Lewis and Clark did not speak French, so Pvt. François Labiche was called upon to translate French to English. Many times, interpretation required a chain. The captains would speak to Labiche in English, who would speak to Charbonneau in French, who would speak to Sacagawea in Hidatsa, who would speak to the Shoshone in their native tongue. Sacagawea was six months pregnant when she joined the team. She was the only woman on the team and was well remembered for her levelheaded thinking and team-building skills while on the trail. (Courtesy of the Library of Congress.)

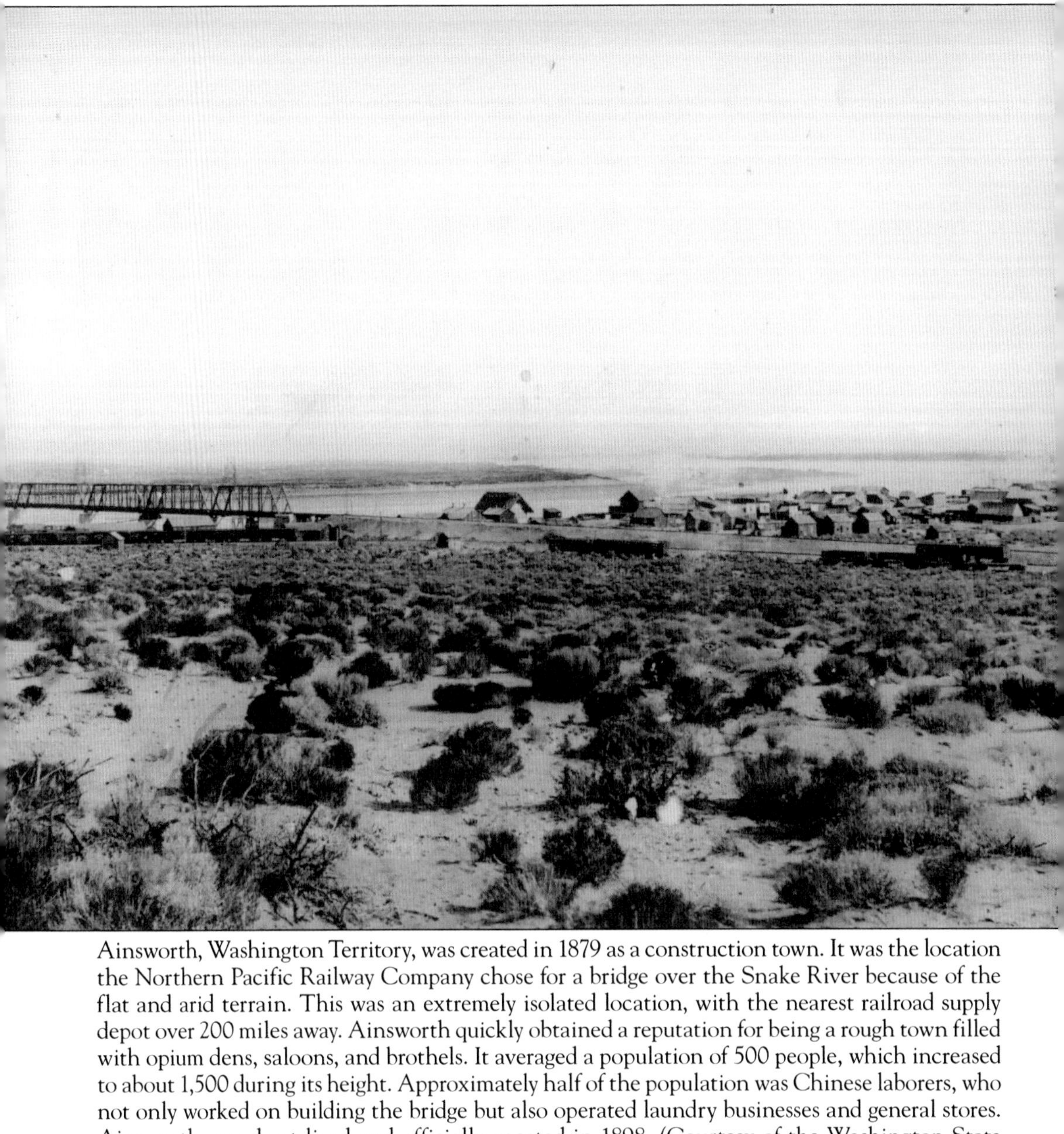

Ainsworth, Washington Territory, was created in 1879 as a construction town. It was the location the Northern Pacific Railway Company chose for a bridge over the Snake River because of the flat and arid terrain. This was an extremely isolated location, with the nearest railroad supply depot over 200 miles away. Ainsworth quickly obtained a reputation for being a rough town filled with opium dens, saloons, and brothels. It averaged a population of 500 people, which increased to about 1,500 during its height. Approximately half of the population was Chinese laborers, who not only worked on building the bridge but also operated laundry businesses and general stores. Ainsworth was short lived and officially vacated in 1898. (Courtesy of the Washington State Railroads Historical Society.)

It was common to name a place after a prominent person, and the railroad town that built the Snake River Bridge chose the name of Ainsworth. John Commingers Ainsworth was a well-known steamboat captain and president of the Oregon Steam Navigation Company in the late 1860s. Interestingly, Captain Ainsworth was never reported to have spent any time in the town of Ainsworth. (Courtesy of FCHS.)

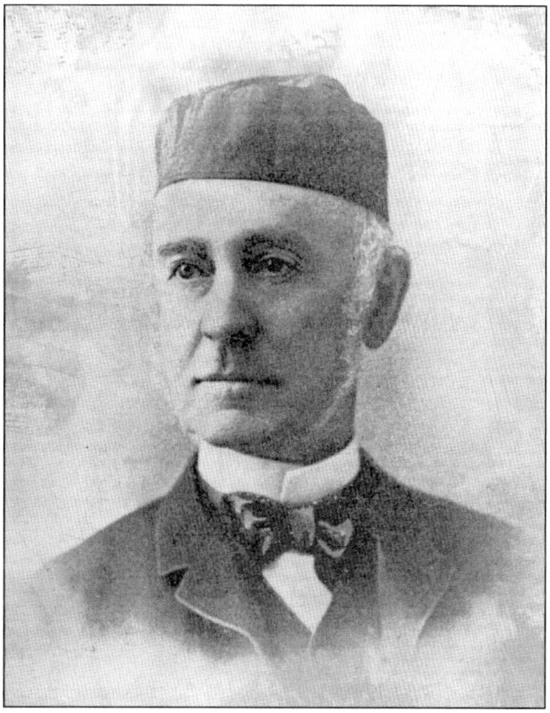

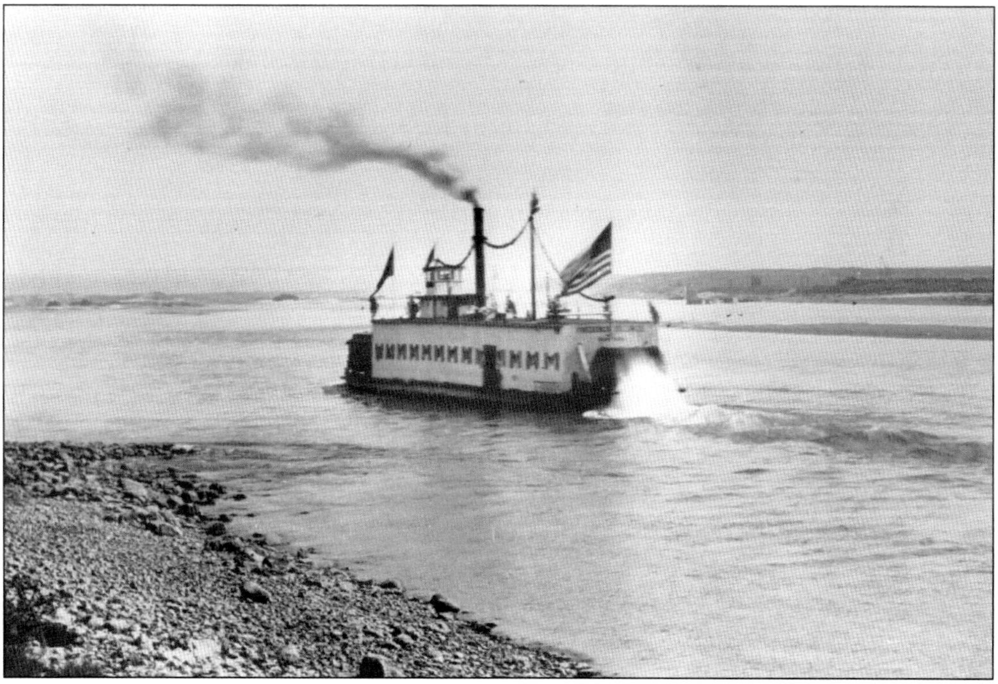

The *Frederick K. Billings*, named for the Northern Pacific Railway president, was the first transfer sternwheeler built by the Northern Pacific Railway. It was built in 1880 for the purpose of transferring railroad cars over the river during the construction of the Ainsworth bridge. The sternwheeler was rebuilt to hold almost twice its original capacity and was used during the railroad bridge construction between Pasco and Kennewick. (Courtesy of FCHS.)

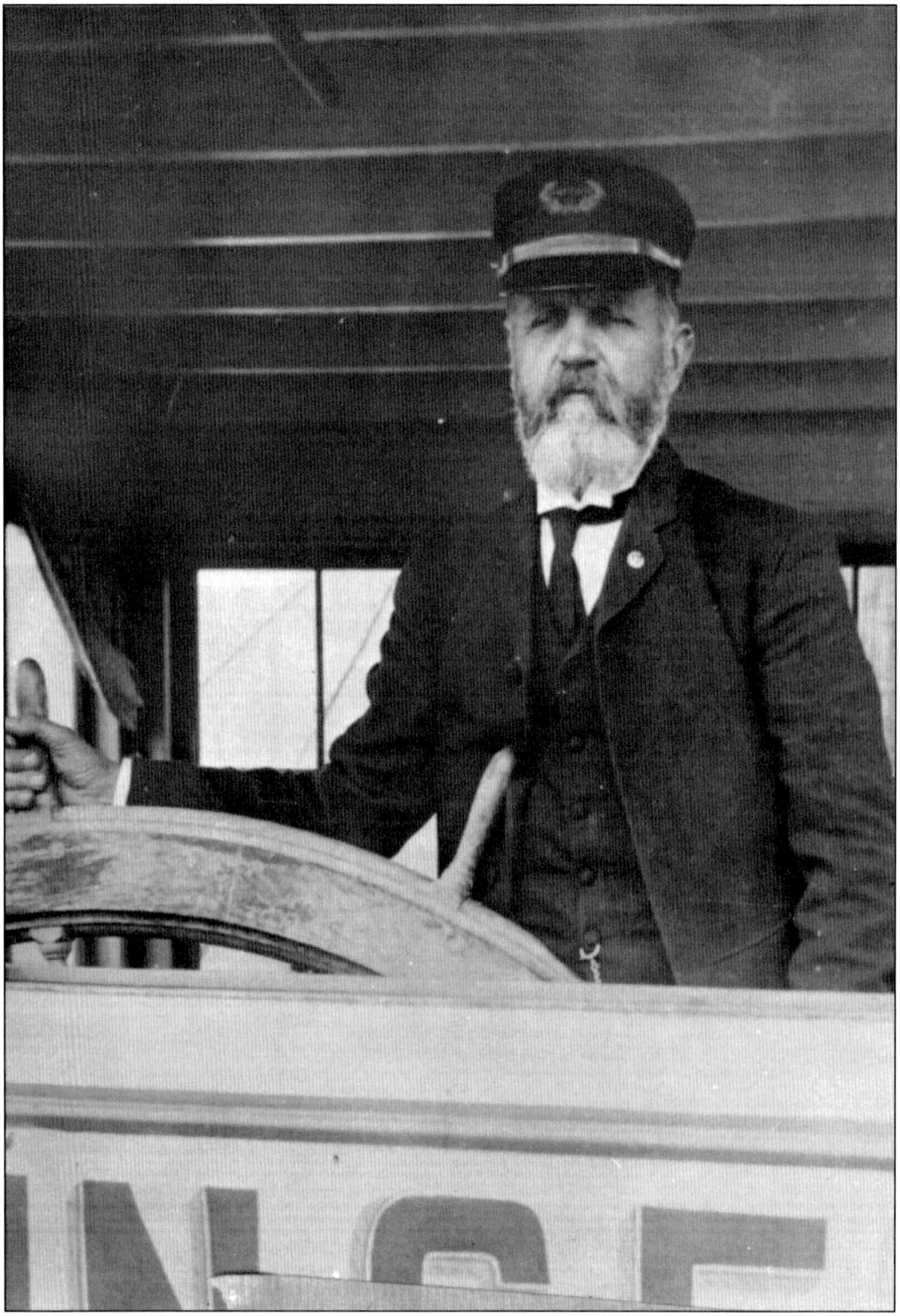

William Polk Gray was born in Oregon in 1845. He learned the ways of the river at a young age, helping his father build a boat, from raw materials, that was launched in 1861. Between 1861 and 1877, he commanded boats on the Columbia, Snake, and Willamette Rivers. He was also commissioned by the U.S. government to survey the Columbia River. Capt. W. P. Gray became well known for his river navigation abilities. By 1880, he was hired by the Northern Pacific Railway to captain the *Frederick K. Billings*. (Courtesy of FCHS.)

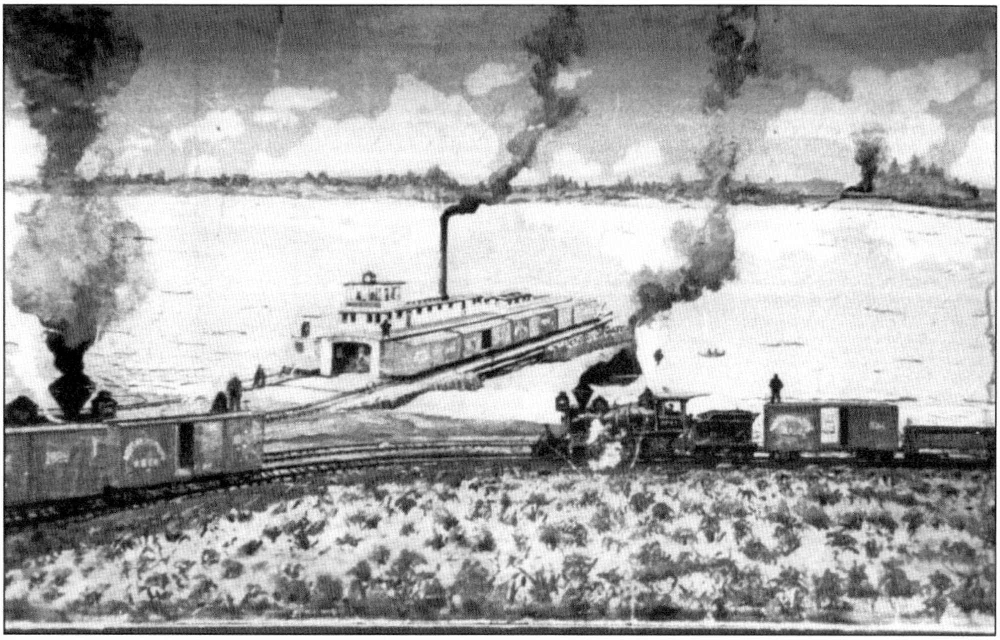

Before the railroad bridge was built over the Snake River, railroad cars were ferried across. There were railroad track inclines on both sides of the river. This painting shows the activity necessary to load railroad cars on the *Frederick K Billings*. Ainsworth, the railroad construction town, was a hub of activity during the building of the bridge. (Courtesy of FCHS.)

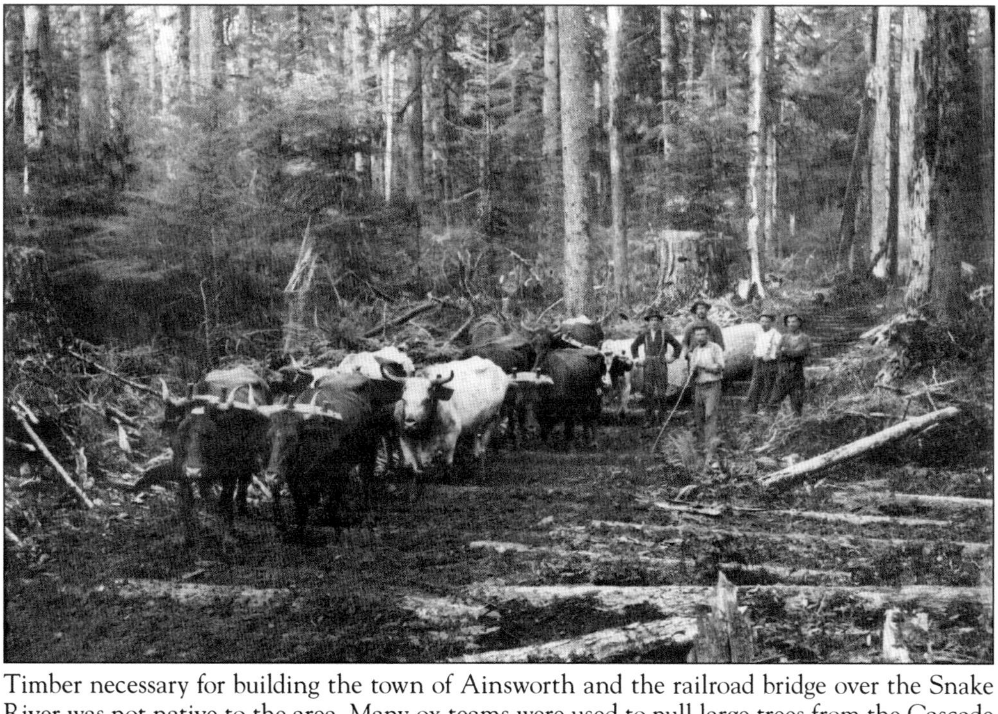

Timber necessary for building the town of Ainsworth and the railroad bridge over the Snake River was not native to the area. Many ox teams were used to pull large trees from the Cascade Mountains to the Yakima and Columbia Rivers. Logs were then floated down the river to the Ainsworth sawmill. (Courtesy of FCHS.)

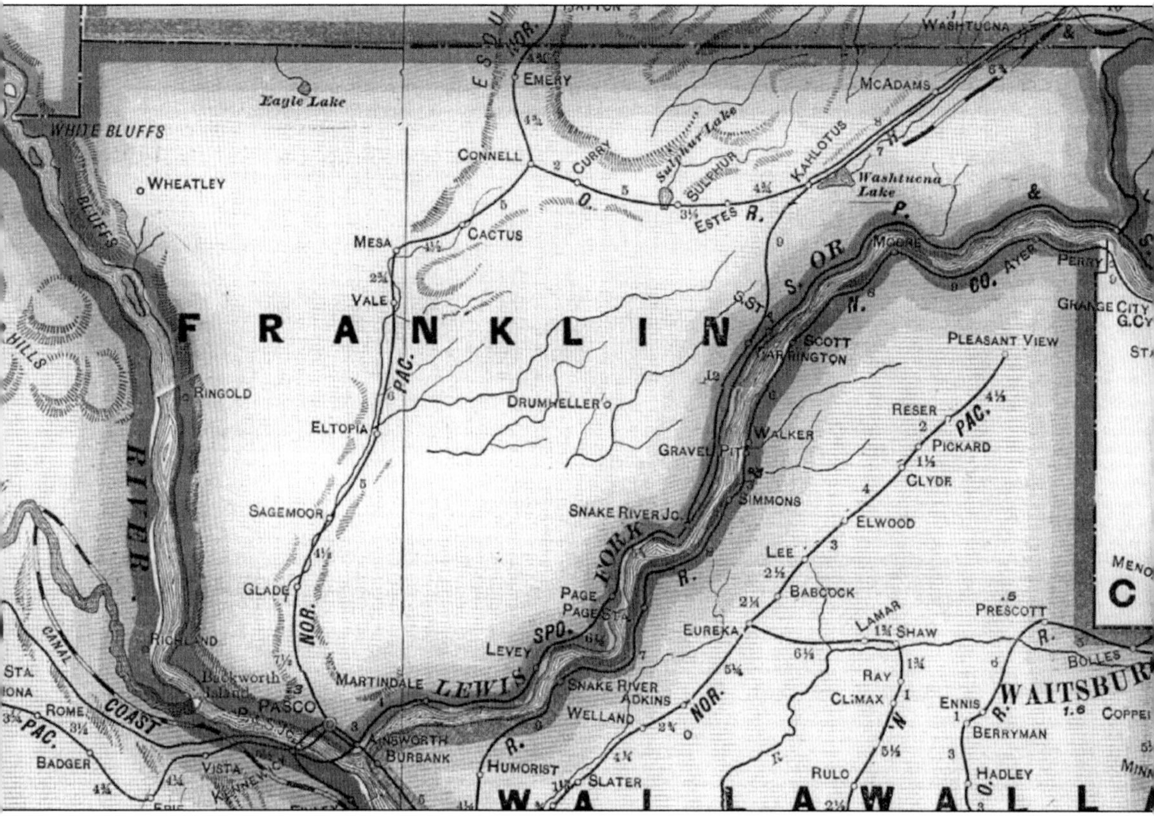

Whitman County, Washington Territory, was divided into three separate counties in November 1883. The northwestern portion of the county became Adams County, and the southwestern portion became Franklin County, named after Benjamin Franklin. The largest populated area of Franklin County at that time was Ainsworth, which became the county seat. This map shows Franklin County in 1909, with Pasco at the confluence of the Columbia and Snake Rivers. (Courtesy of Cram's Superior Map of Washington, 1909.)

Recording of legal documents was not always a time-crucial exercise in the 1880s. Ainsworth was officially created in 1879; however, it was not platted and recorded with Whitman County courts until 1881. The plat was officially certified in 1884. By 1898, Ainsworth was "vacated, set aside, and annulled" by the Franklin County commissioners as petitioned by the Northern Pacific Railway. (Courtesy of the Franklin County Auditor's Department.)

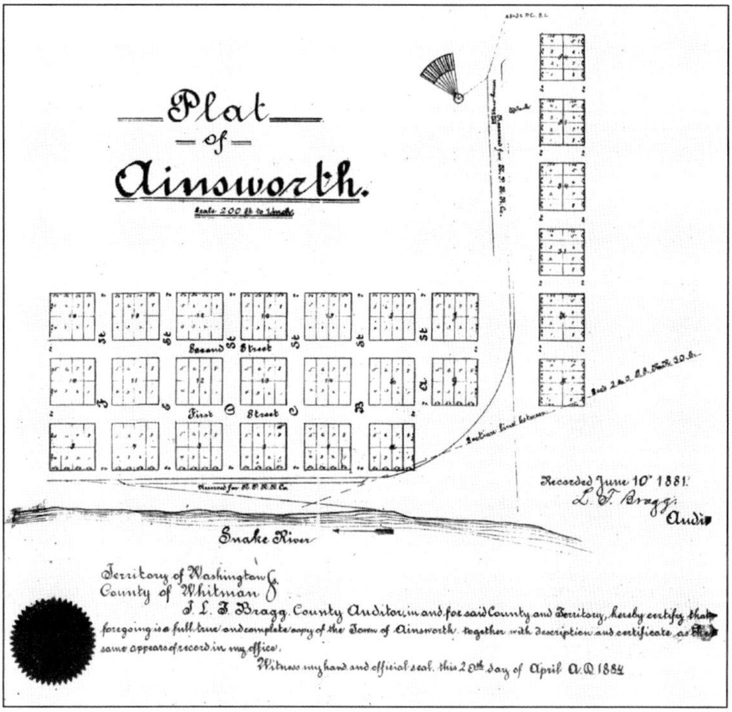

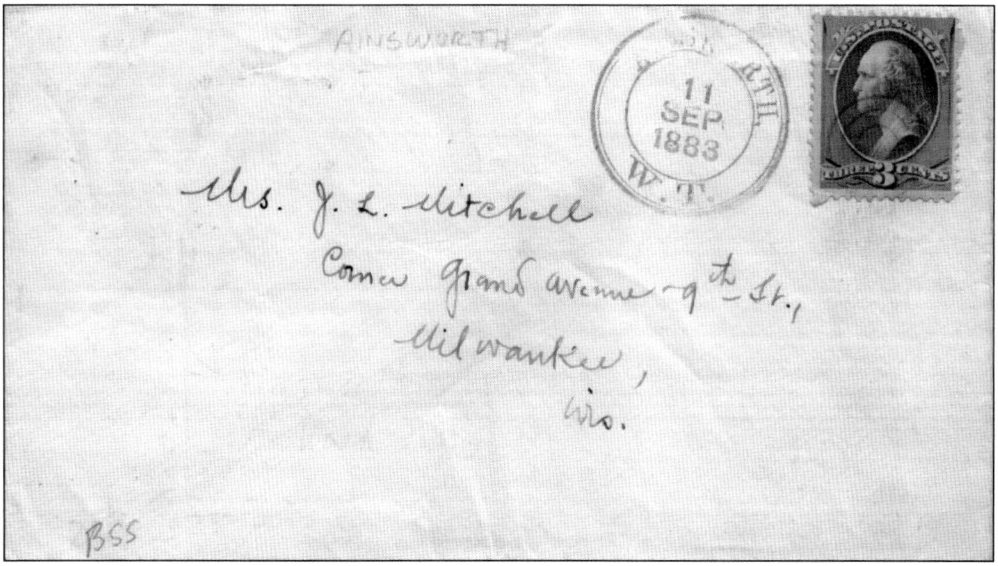

Ainsworth, even though short lived, supported an average population of 400 to 500 persons. At its peak, 1,500 people were reported to have lived in the railroad construction town. Business establishments and government services were necessary to support its population. This envelope shows the Ainsworth, Washington Territory, postmark dated 1883. (Courtesy of Dan Stafford.)

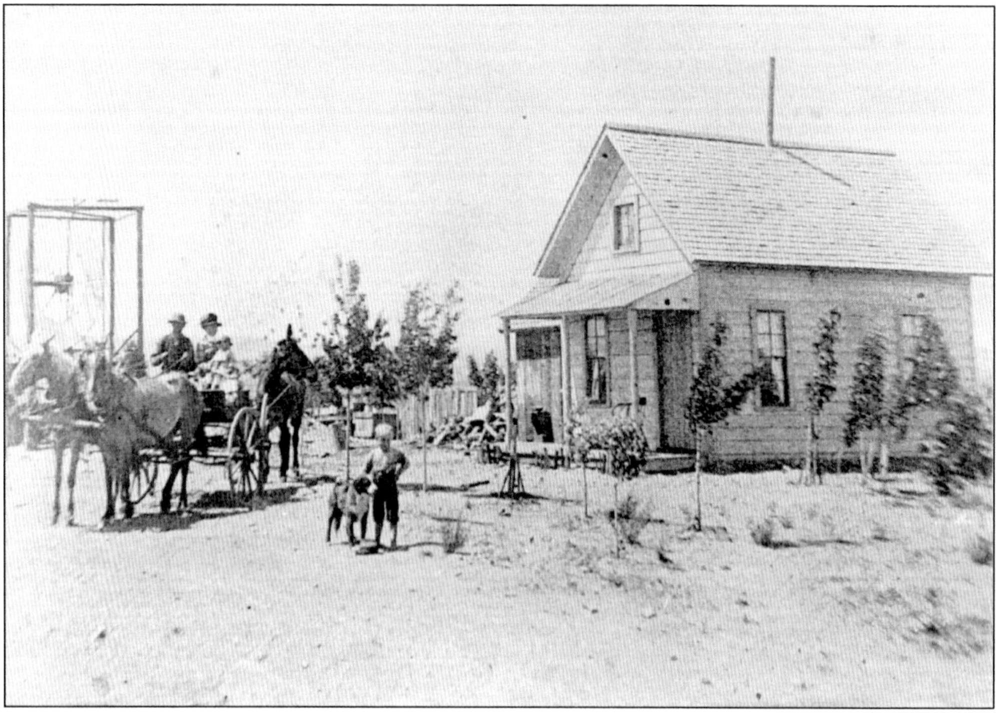

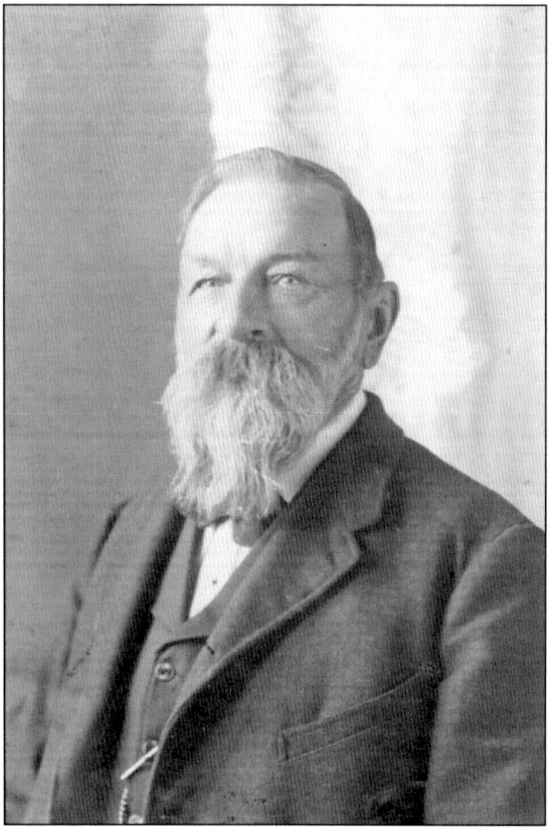

Henry Gantenbein Jr. was a farmer who homesteaded land near the confluence of the Snake and Columbia Rivers. In 1884, he moved his family and their house from Ainsworth to the area that would soon be Pasco. This picture shows Henry, his wife, Mary, and daughter, Ella, in the wagon. Emery is standing in front of their house in Pasco in 1885. (Courtesy of FCHS.)

German-born Frank Schuneman was one of the first blacksmiths of Ainsworth, arriving in 1879. He homesteaded and purchased property that eventually totaled over 900 acres along the Columbia River. Here he grew a productive orchard and raised over 20,000 head of cattle. He also imported 200 Chinamen to pan for flour gold on his riverfront property. (Courtesy of Duff and Pat McGinnis.)

Two

The River and the Rails
1886 to 1900

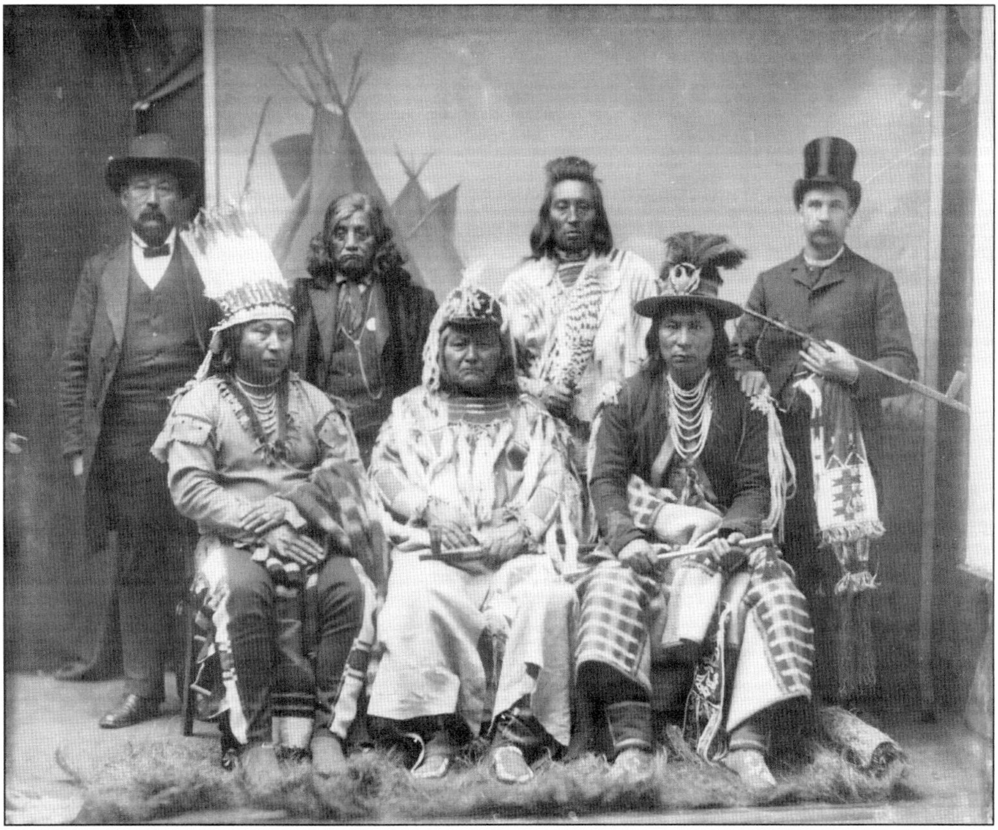

In 1889, a delegation from the Cayuse and Shahaptian tribes of Washington, Oregon, and Idaho went to Washington, D.C., to meet with the commissioner of Indian Affairs. They are shown here from left to right: (first row) Chief Peo (Umatilla), Chief Hamli (Walla Walla), and Chief Young Chief (Cayuse); (second row) John McBain, Chief Showaway (Cayuse), Chief Wolf Necklace (Palus), and Lee Moorhouse (Umatilla Indian Agent). (Courtesy of the National Archives.)

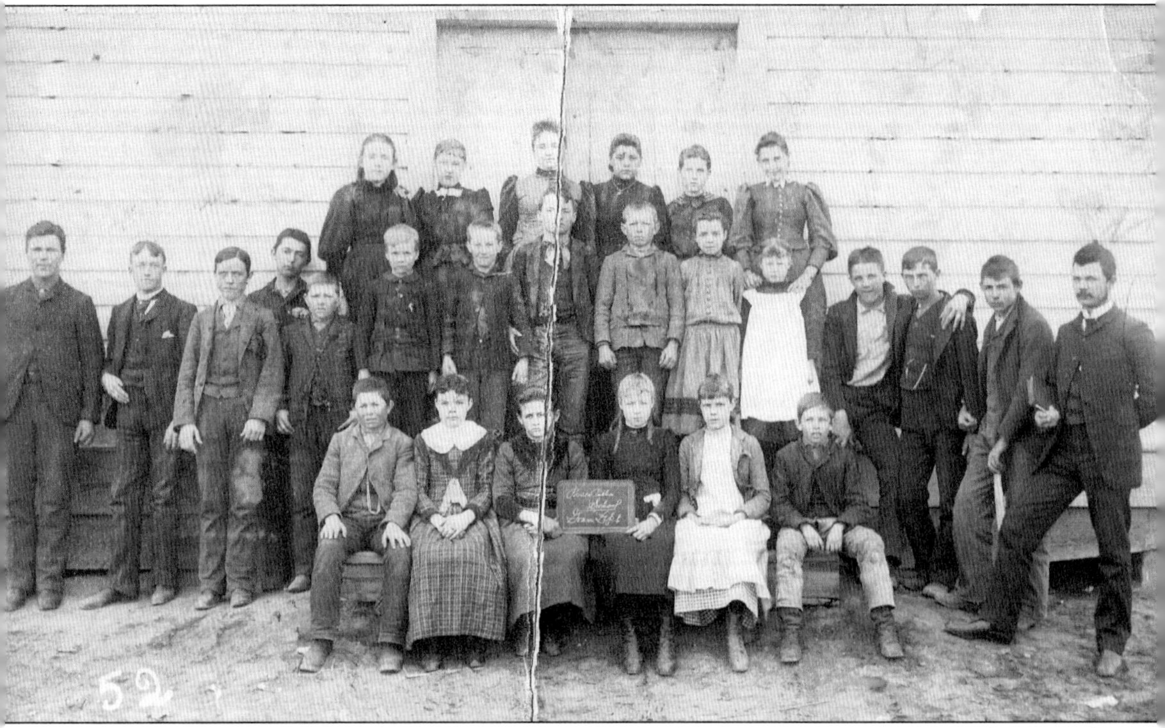

The Ainsworth school building was moved in 1886 and became the first Pasco school. Pictured above are the students who moved with their school to the new town of Pasco. The sign held by the two girls in the first row reads, "Pasco Public School—Gram Dept." From left to right are (first row) Chris Gantenbein, Elizabeth Farley, unidentified, Grace Coleman, unidentified, and Criss Moltin; (second row) Chris Shaffer, Will Burns, Burnett Farley, Clement Wilkins, Fred Schuneman, two unidentified, Archie Wilkins, Duff Schuneman, unidentified, Maud Coleman, Alf Buchanan, Edd Sparks, Alex Jones, and teacher J. S. Burndall; (third row) Eva Osborn, Ollie Strumph, Lizzy Graham, Zora Johnson, Willetta Gray, and Ida White. (Courtesy of FCHS.)

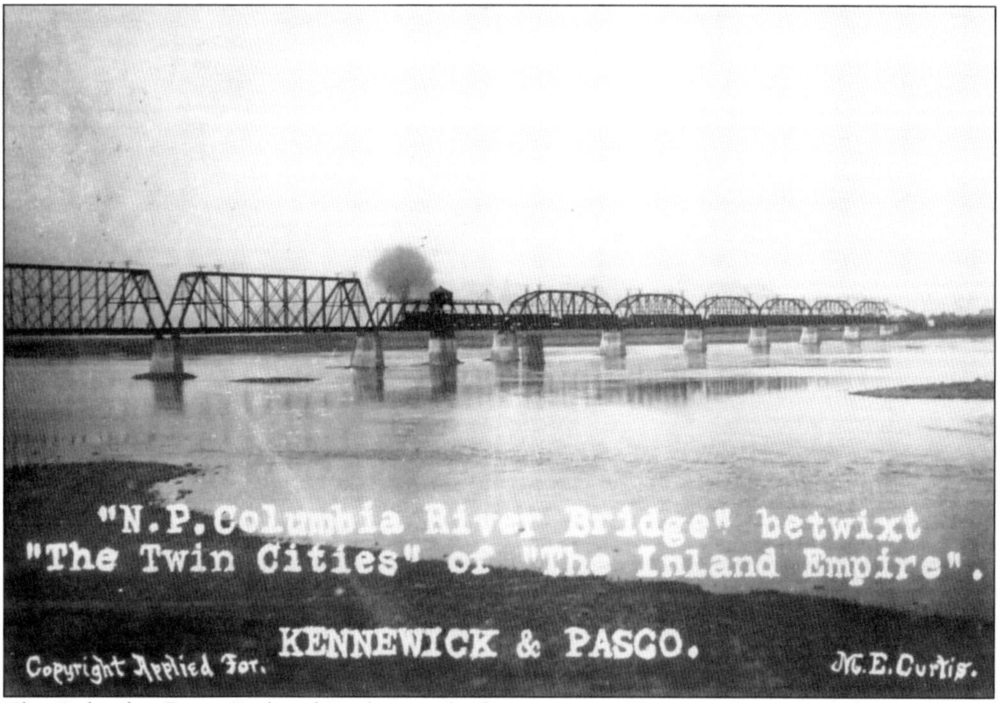

The Columbia River Railroad Bridge was built to connect Kennewick on the left to Pasco on the right. It was completed as a temporary structure, with the first train crossing on December 8, 1887. Ice jams swept a portion of the temporary bridge away in January 1888. New material was brought in and the bridge was rebuilt, in permanent form, by September 20, 1888. The completed bridge was the first to span the Columbia River. (Courtesy of Dan Stafford.)

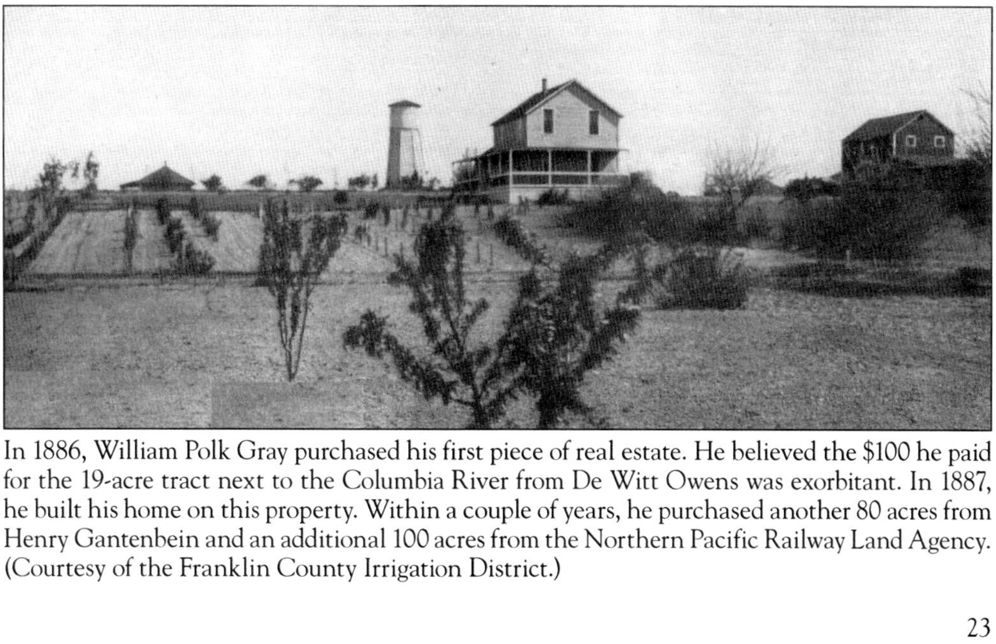

In 1886, William Polk Gray purchased his first piece of real estate. He believed the $100 he paid for the 19-acre tract next to the Columbia River from De Witt Owens was exorbitant. In 1887, he built his home on this property. Within a couple of years, he purchased another 80 acres from Henry Gantenbein and an additional 100 acres from the Northern Pacific Railway Land Agency. (Courtesy of the Franklin County Irrigation District.)

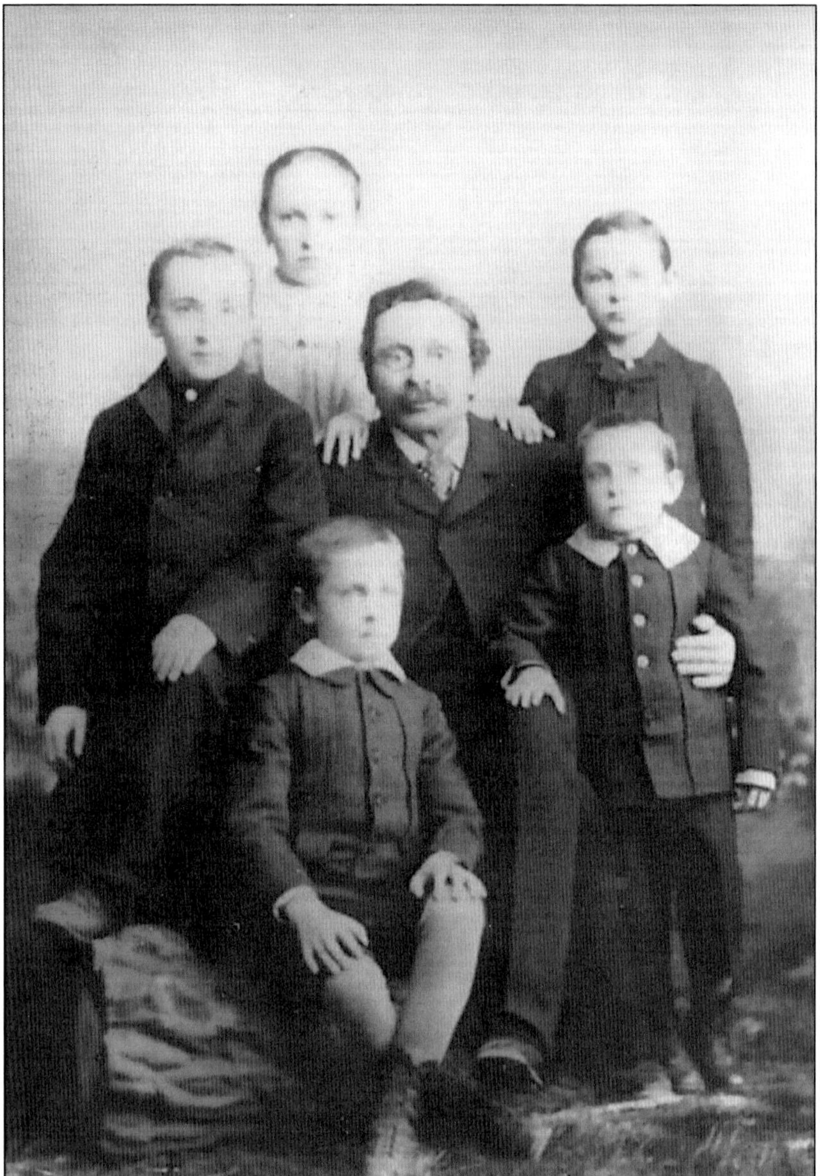

Dieu Donne Sylvester was an Ainsworth blacksmith originally from Canada. In 1887, his beloved wife, Margaret (Nixon) Sylvester, passed away, leaving Sylvester with five children. Being a devout Catholic, he took the children to St. Joseph's Catholic School in Vancouver, Washington, for their care. While the children were in the orphanage, Sylvester homesteaded 160 acres, much of which became the central business district of Pasco. Many of the streets in Pasco were named for members of the Sylvester family. By 1891, he married Ruben Densmore and they went to Vancouver to retrieve the children. Each of the children became active and contributing members in Pasco. This photograph of Sylvester and his children was taken in approximately 1888. Ainsworth Sylvester, named for the town in which he was born, is sitting in front of his father. The other family members in this photograph from left to right are (second row) Arthur, Dieu Donne, and John Henry; (third row) Aurelia and Norbert. (Courtesy of FCHS.)

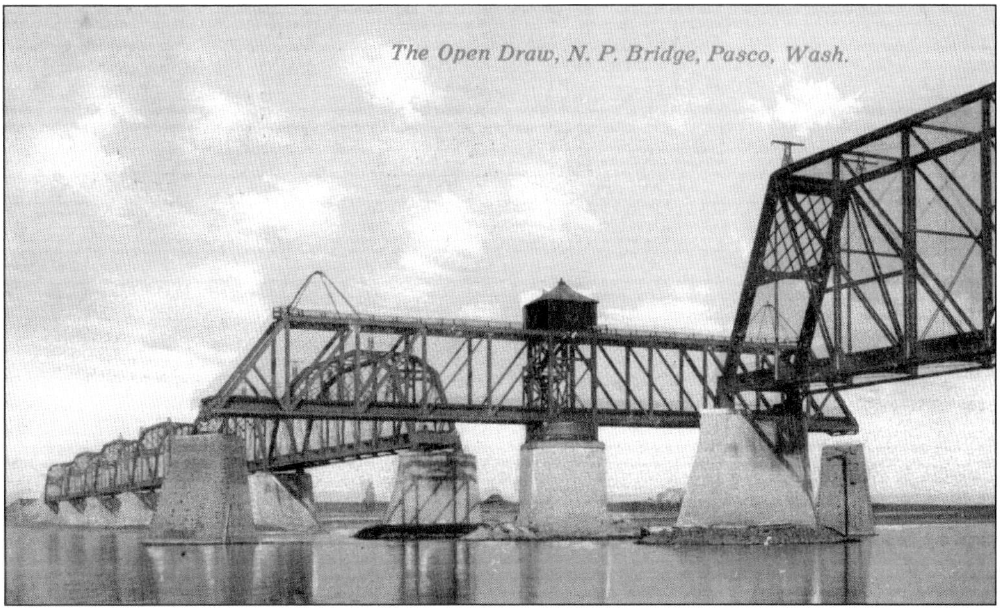

The Northern Pacific Railway's need to build bridges over the rivers that surrounded Pasco brought workers and their families to the area. The rivers were vital to an existence in the desert terrain. Bridges had to accommodate the many steamboats and sternwheelers that dominated the river. The Columbia River Bridge was built in 1888 with a swing span that would spin open, enabling boats to pass. (Courtesy of Dan Stafford.)

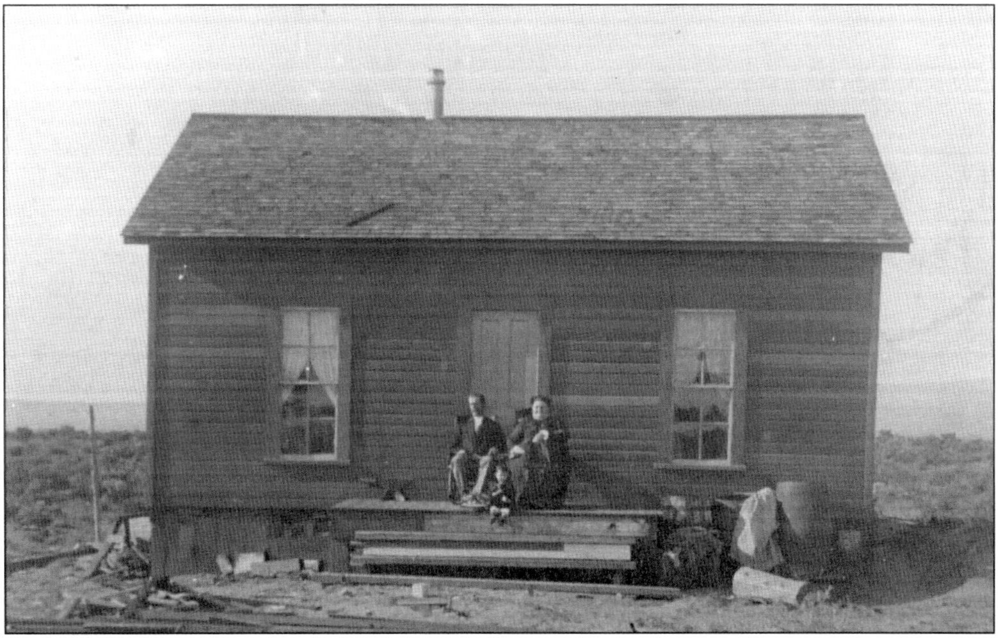

Alex Gordon moved his family, including grandson Fred Harris, to Pasco in 1889. Housing was not available, so he purchased a recently vacated building in Ainsworth. He disassembled the building and built his new house on East A Street in Pasco. This picture shows Gordon, an unidentified woman, and grandson Fred Harris on the porch of their reassembled house. Unused lumber is seen in the front yard. (Courtesy of FCHS.)

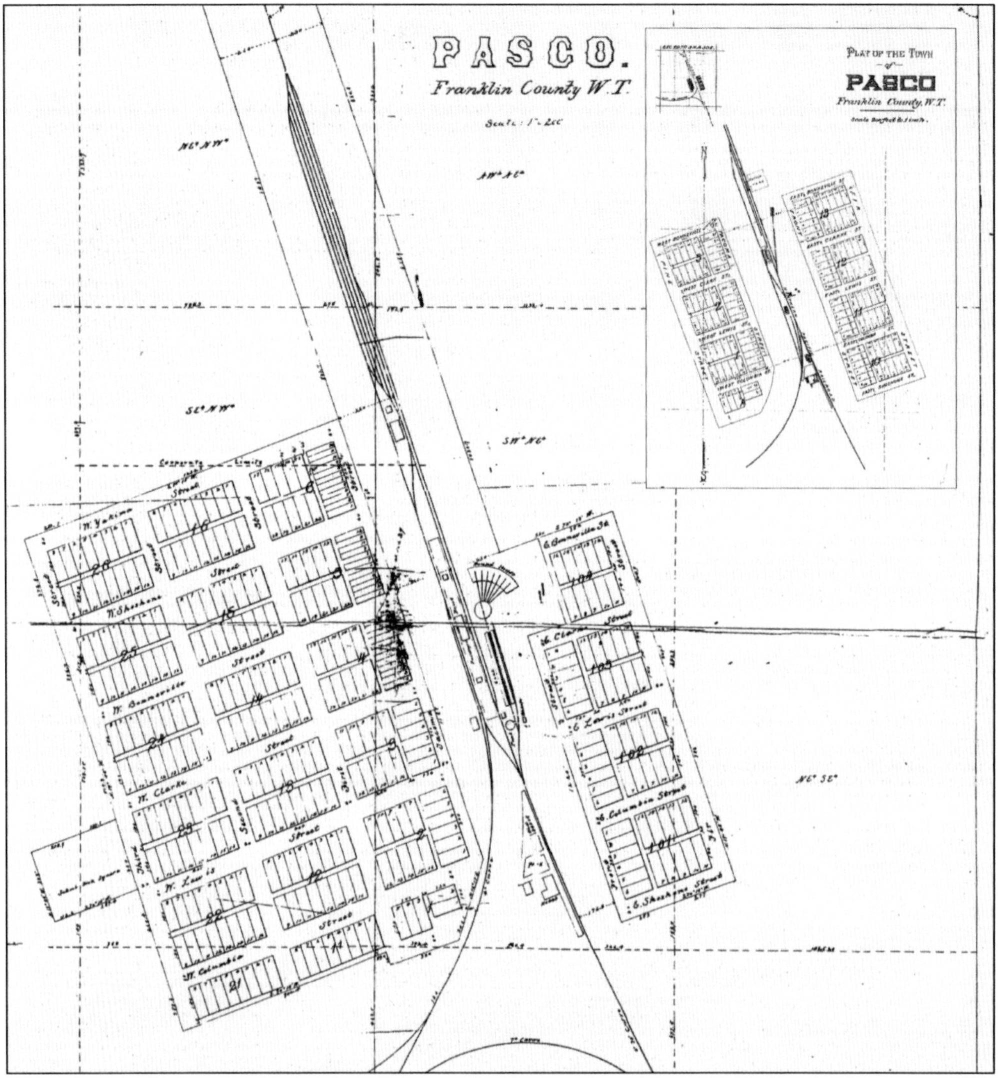

The Northern Pacific Railway laid out the new town site of Pasco 3 miles up the Columbia River from Ainsworth in 1885. The post office and courthouse were soon moved from the old railroad town to the new town. A migration of businesses and homes followed. The large map shows Pasco in 1889, when Washington became a state. The inset is of 1885 Pasco. (Courtesy of the Franklin County Auditor's Department.)

Chief Wolf Necklace, also known as Harlish Washshomake, was a spokesman for the Palus tribe during the meeting with the commissioner of Indian Affairs in Washington, D.C. The Kasispa village, of the Palus tribe, was situated at the junction of the Snake and Columbia Rivers at Ainsworth. Chief Wolf Necklace was a prominent resident of Franklin County in the 1890s. (Courtesy of the National Archives.)

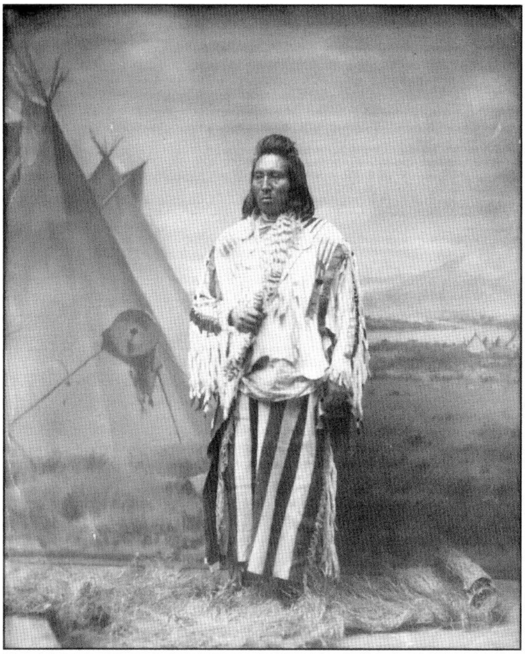

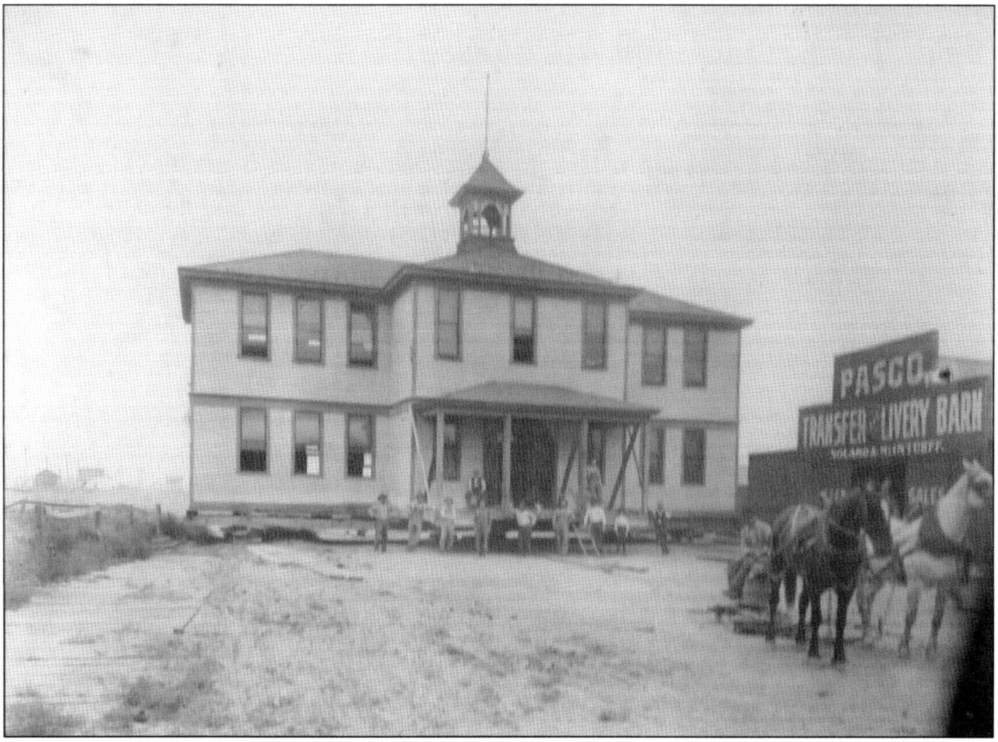

Building supplies in the late 1800s were scarce. This southeastern part of Washington Territory did not grow trees, so the majority of lumber was brought down the Yakima River to the Columbia River from the Cascade Mountains. When Ainsworth's residents moved to Pasco, they took their buildings with them. If the buildings were not dismantled, they were placed on logs or skids and relocated to their new destination. (Courtesy of FCHS.)

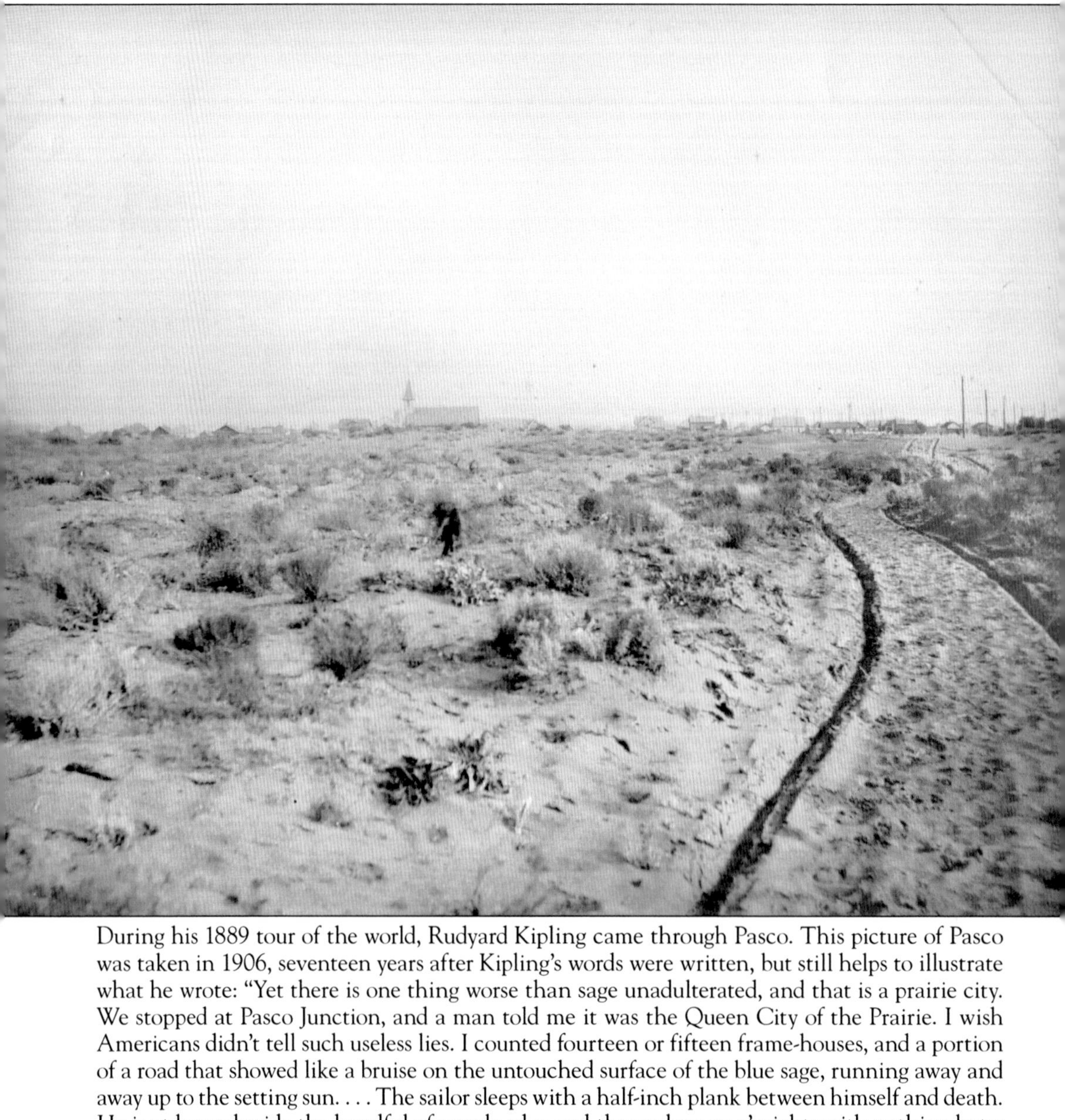

During his 1889 tour of the world, Rudyard Kipling came through Pasco. This picture of Pasco was taken in 1906, seventeen years after Kipling's words were written, but still helps to illustrate what he wrote: "Yet there is one thing worse than sage unadulterated, and that is a prairie city. We stopped at Pasco Junction, and a man told me it was the Queen City of the Prairie. I wish Americans didn't tell such useless lies. I counted fourteen or fifteen frame-houses, and a portion of a road that showed like a bruise on the untouched surface of the blue sage, running away and away up to the setting sun. . . . The sailor sleeps with a half-inch plank between himself and death. He is at home beside the handful of people who curl themselves up o' nights with nothing but a frail scantling, almost as thin as a blanket, to shut out the unmeasurable loneliness of the sage." (Courtesy of the Washington State Railroads Historical Society.)

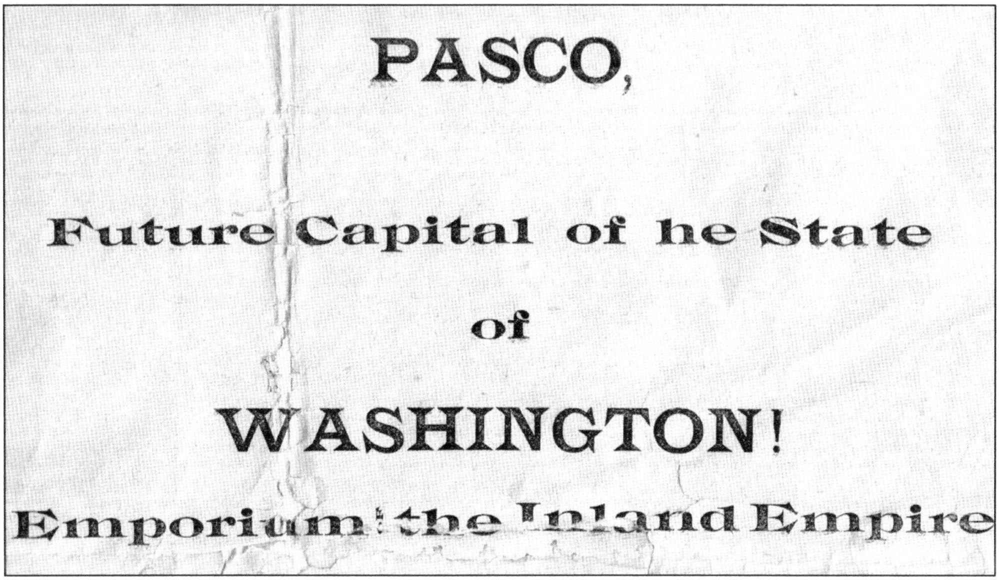
PASCO,

Future Capital of he State

of

WASHINGTON!

Emporium the Inland Empire

Congress passed the Enabling Act for Statehood in February 1899. This act established requirements for Washington to become a state. On the same day Congress passed this act, the *Pasco Headlight* ran this feature article explaining the benefits of making Pasco the new state capital. Pasco promoters I. I. Muncey and W. P. Gray continued to express statehood desires until Olympia was selected to be the state capital in November 1899. (Courtesy of FCHS.)

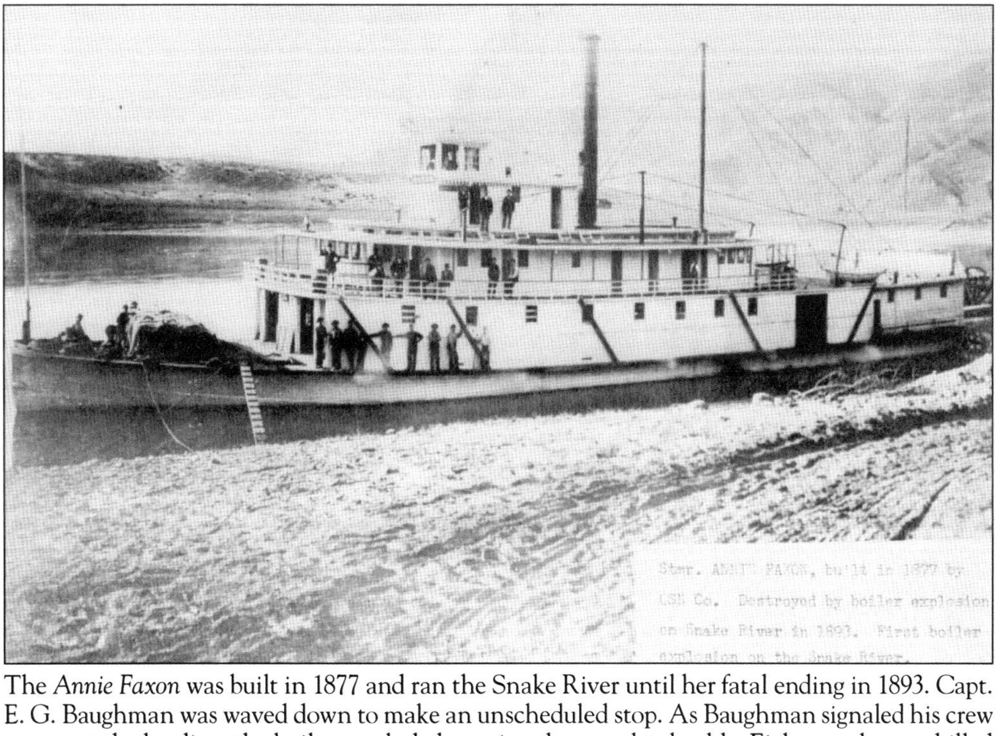

The *Annie Faxon* was built in 1877 and ran the Snake River until her fatal ending in 1893. Capt. E. G. Baughman was waved down to make an unscheduled stop. As Baughman signaled his crew to stop at the landing, the boilers exploded, causing the vessel to buckle. Eight people were killed and another 11 were injured. Baughman walked the necessary 12 miles to the nearest town to obtain help. (Courtesy of FCHS.)

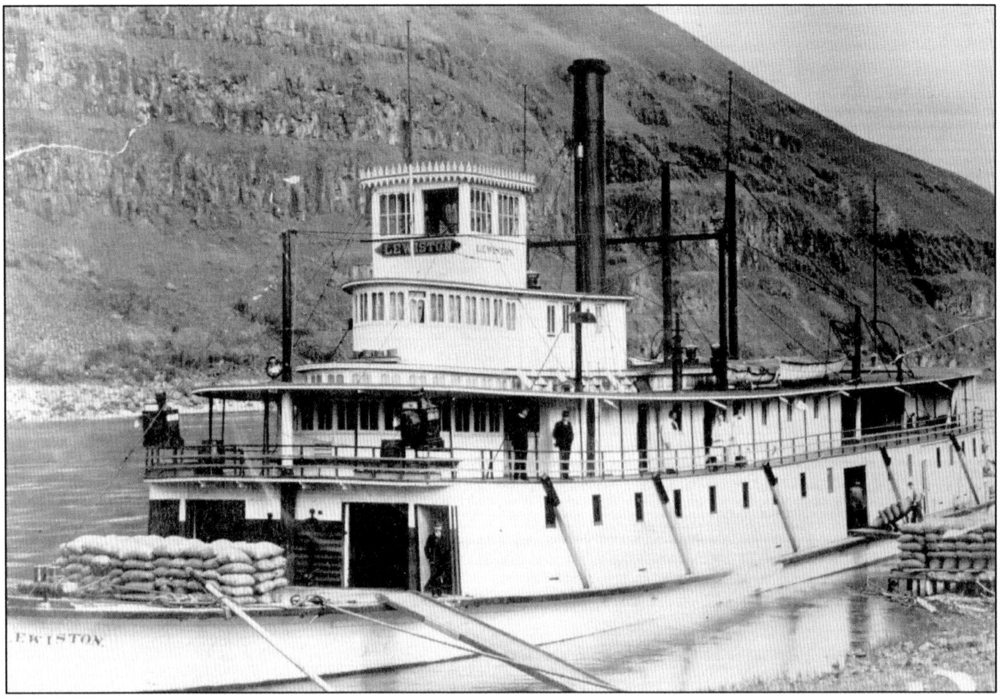

The *Lewiston* was originally built in 1867 in Umatilla. She was used to haul freight and individuals up and down both the Columbia and Snake Rivers. The *Lewiston* was rebuilt three times. The first time she was rebuilt was in 1894, and the hull of the destroyed *Annie Faxon* was used to double her size. (Courtesy of FCHS.)

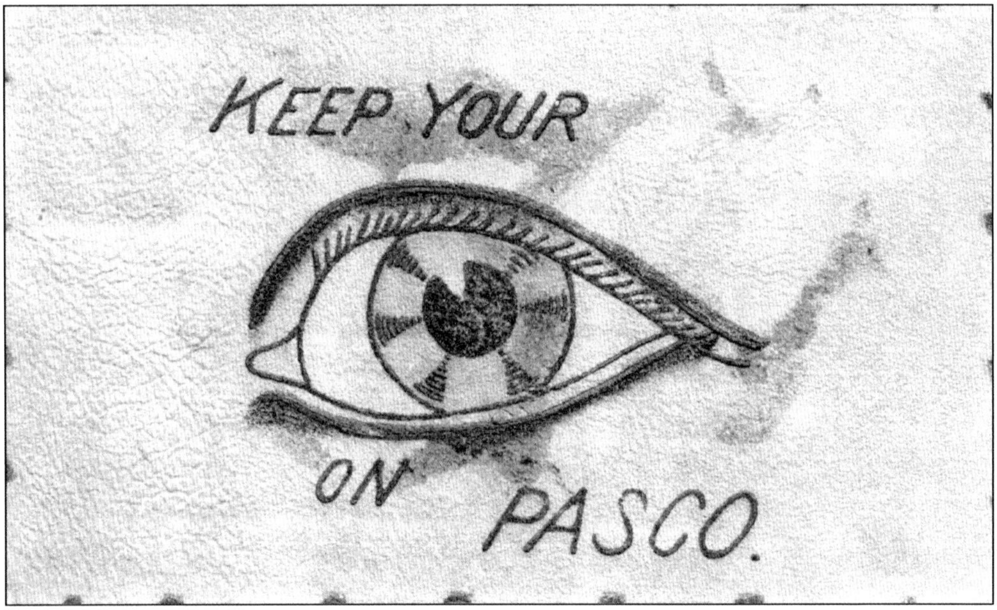

"Keep Your Eye On Pasco" was a slogan used by the Pasco Land Company to promote the growing community of Pasco in the late 1880s and early 1890s. The Pasco Land Company was formed in 1888 by Louis Frey and William P. Gray. They not only sold land to local prospects, but they also traveled to areas in Illinois and Ohio to promote and sell Pasco. (Courtesy of Dan Stafford.)

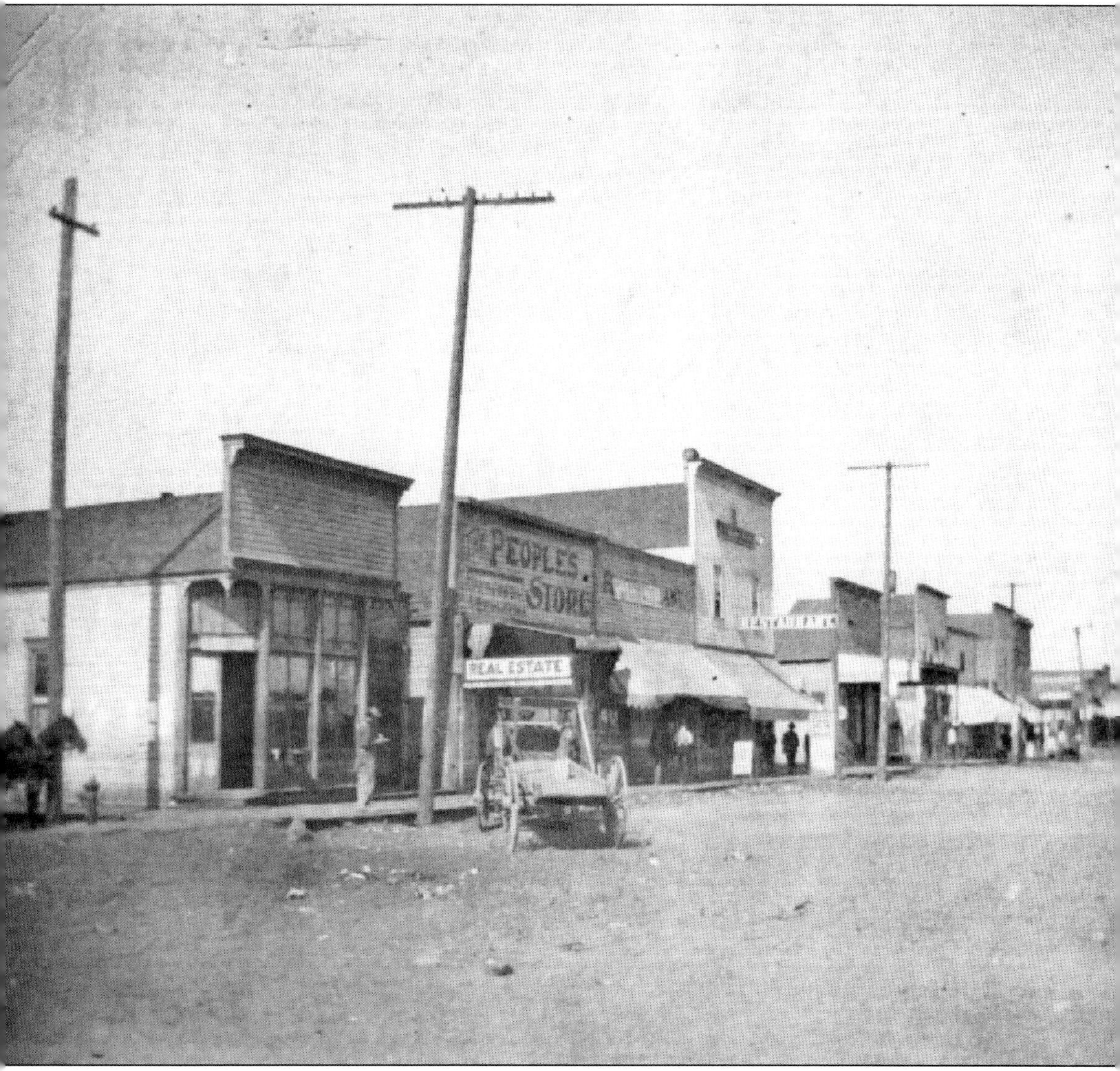

Frances Fuller Victor, acclaimed author and one of Oregon's first historians, wrote about Pasco in her 1891 book titled *Atlantis Arisen*: " 'Keep your eye on Pasco!' is the injunction which meets you in newspaper and handbill advertisements, making you curious to behold it, as if it were the What Is It. When you arrive, you look about you for something on which to keep your eye, which being blown full of sand refuses to risk more than the briefest glimpses thenceforward." One of the earliest photographs of Pasco's streets is this one, taken about 1899. Individuals who did watch Pasco watched an incredible amount of growth and change to the community. Victor went on to say, "Merely as a location for a city, Pasco, or Ainsworth, which is a couple of miles beyond, at the crossing of Snake River, either, or both together, are fine town-sites. Mr. Villard, it is said, has remarked that a large city must some day be built up at the junction of the Snake and Columbia Rivers." (Courtesy of Dan Stafford.)

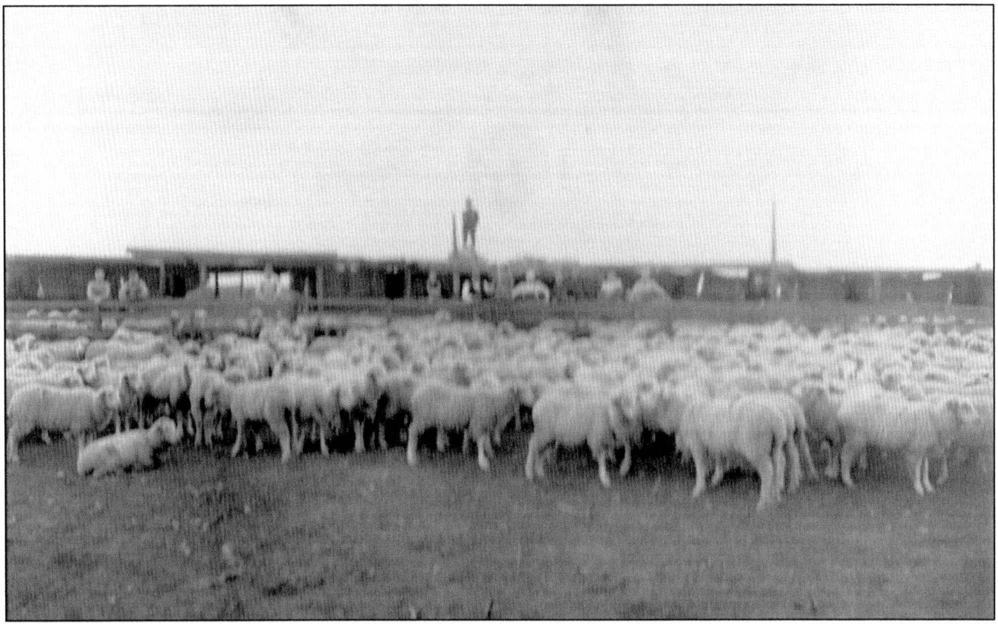

In 1893, the State of Washington passed a law impacting the transportation of livestock. This law made it mandatory to feed, water, and exercise animals that were confined longer than 48 hours while being transported. Pasco was a major railroad hub and hired the Hales Sheep Company to maintain a stockyard to abide by this requirement. (Courtesy of FCHS.)

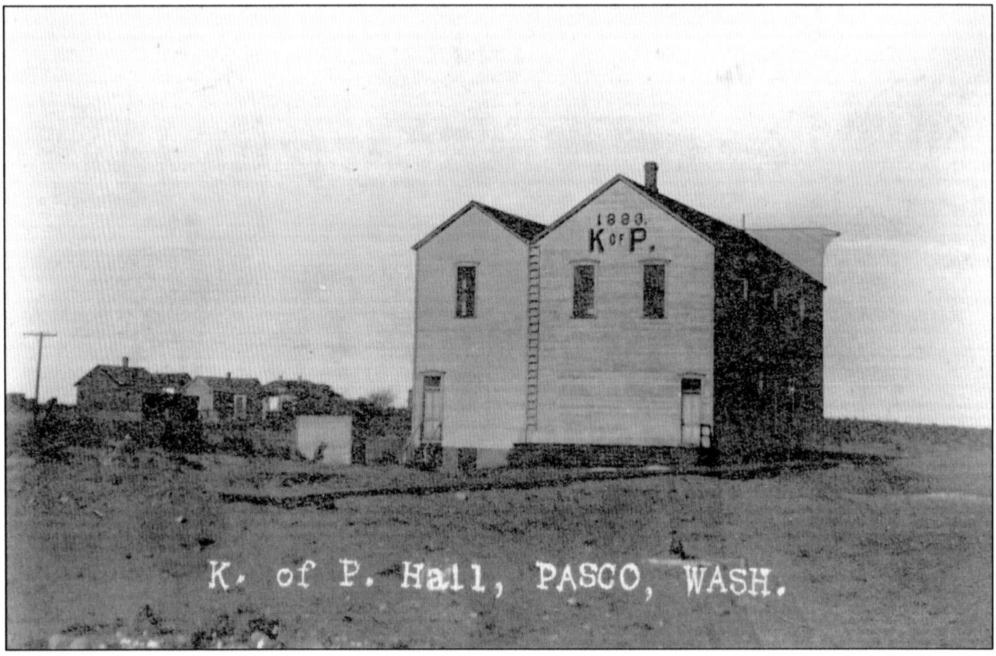

The Knights of Pythias, which began in 1864 in Washington, D.C., was a societal club that was based on the principles of friendship, charity, and benevolence to promote universal peace. The Franklin Lodge No. 60 was organized in 1893. This lodge built its hall, shown here, on the east side of the Northern Pacific Railway tracks in 1894 and proudly displayed the date of organization on the building. (Courtesy of Dan Stafford.)

Isham Davis was one of Pasco's first law enforcement personnel. This 1894 photograph shows him with his wife, Emma. From 1899 to 1902, he served as sheriff, and from 1902 to 1903, he served as marshal. Isham Davis left Pasco and law enforcement. His stock buying business moved him to Montana, where he died in 1932. (Courtesy of FCHS.)

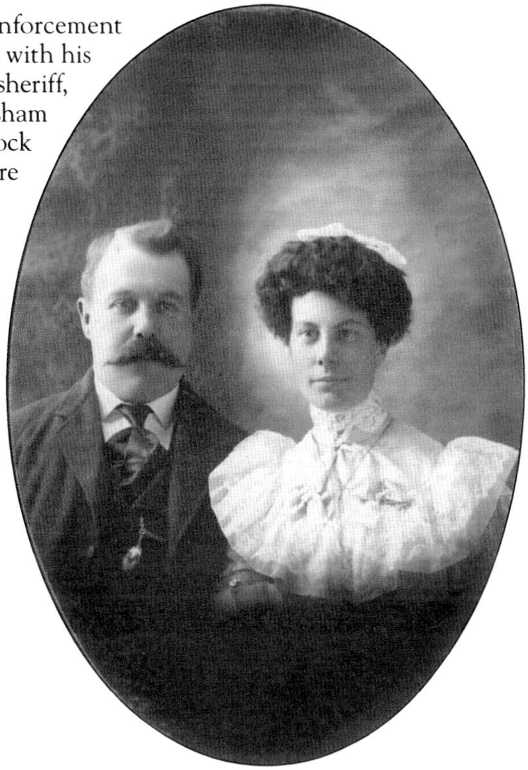

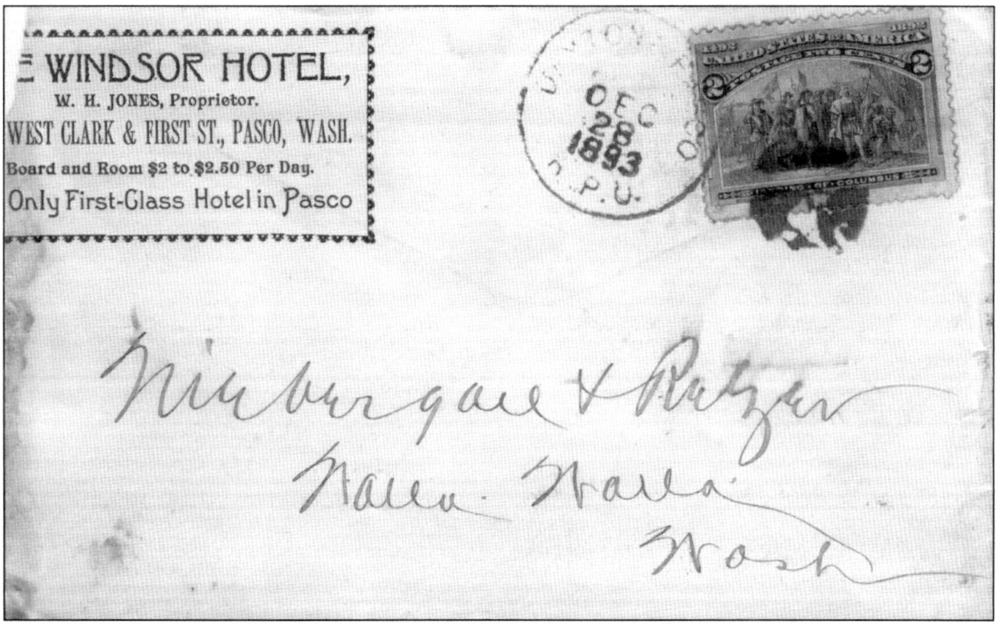

There were many boardinghouses in Pasco in the late 1800s and early 1900s. By this time, Pasco had a large population of railroad travelers who needed accommodations. The Windsor Hotel, built in 1893, was one of the first elegant hotels. Not only did their letterhead boast their location and proprietor but also their rates of $2 to $2.50 per day for room and board. (Courtesy of Dan Stafford.)

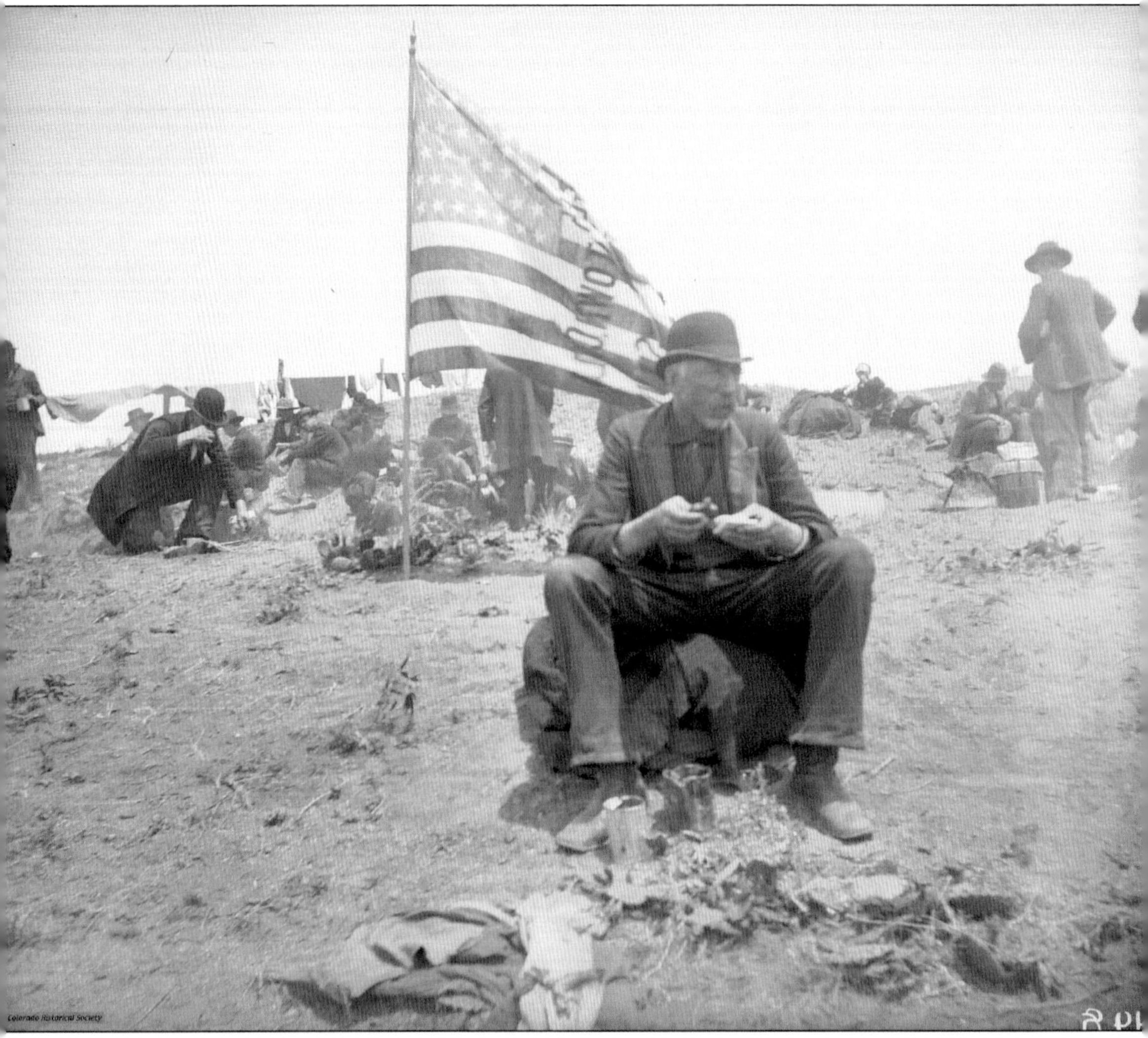

The depression of 1893 created an outcry from the unemployed for relief from their plight. Jacob Coxey formed a group to march from Ohio to Washington, D.C., with the purpose of urging the U.S. government for assistance. This group was called Coxey's Commonweal Army. Unemployed, including recent railroad strikers from the northwest, decided to join Coxey's Army and formed their own division called the Northwestern Industrial Army. In 1894, over 650 unemployed persons marched out of Seattle, in military style, with intentions of going to Ohio to join Coxey's Army. A portion of this group came to Pasco and created a hobo jungle near the railroad stockyards. Here a remnant of the homeless and unemployed Northwestern Industrial Army shared their lives, including what food they could obtain from residents of Pasco. (Courtesy of the Colorado Historical Society, Buckwalter Collection, Scan No. 20030902.)

In 1895 and 1896, the U.S. government gave every odd-numbered section of land to the Northern Pacific Railway. The amount of land granted totaled over 1,500,000 acres. This land was sold to individuals, and the money was used to fund the building of the transcontinental railroad. Sections numbered 16 and 36 were granted to the State of Washington for the purpose of agricultural research and education. (Map by Dann Borden, manager, GIS Division, Franklin County Information Services.)

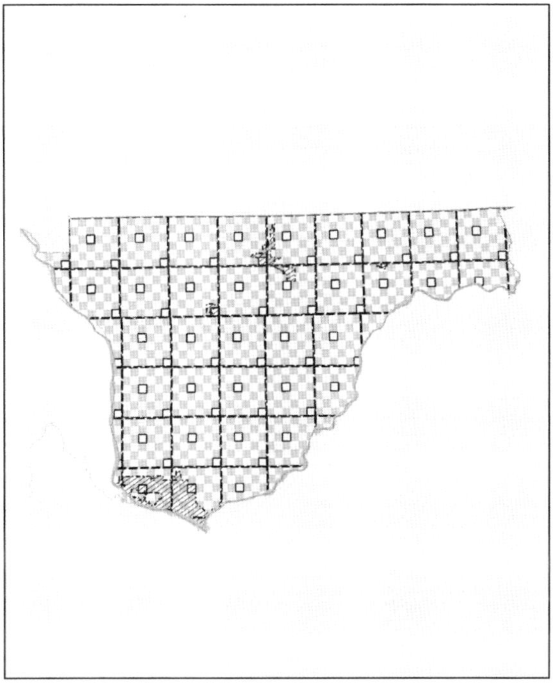

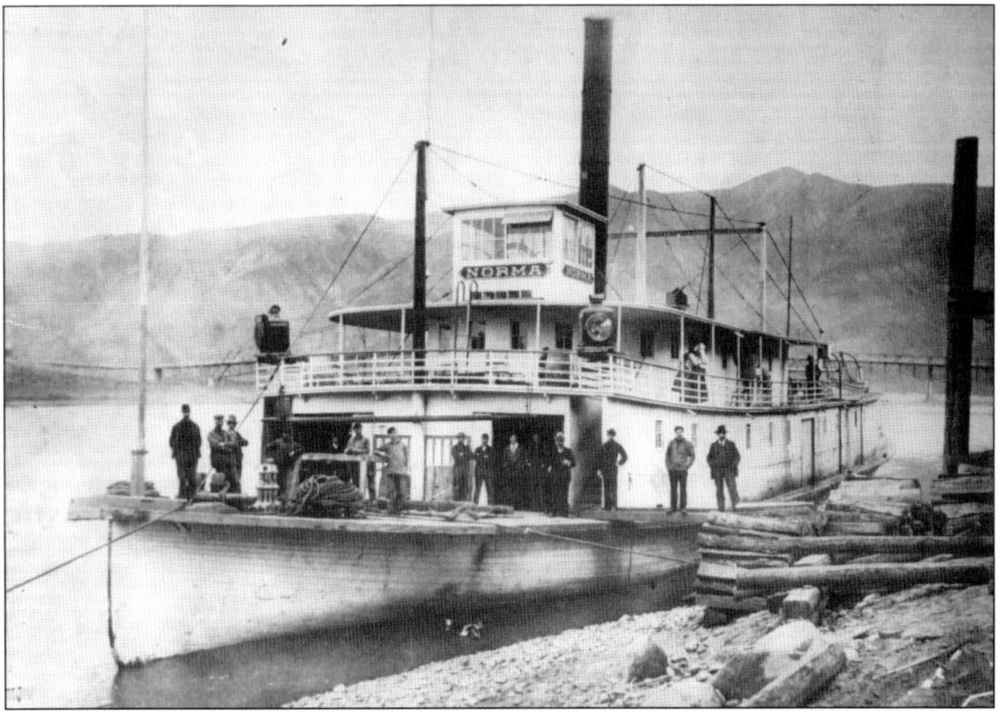

The *Norma* was a sternwheeler that not only transported people and crops but was also used to push barges full of railroad cars. In 1895, Capt. William Polk Gray brought her through Hells Canyon, a feat that was said could never be done. After this monumental event, *Norma* was used primarily to haul wheat between Lewiston, Idaho, through Pasco to Celilo Falls, Washington. (Courtesy of FCHS.)

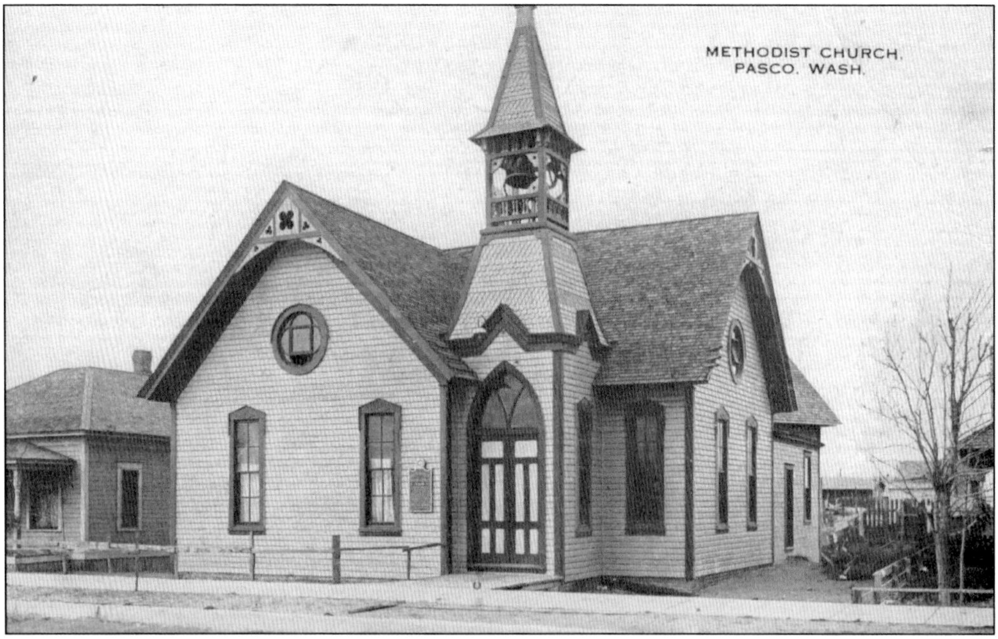

The first church building in Pasco was the Methodist church, which was built in 1891. It was used for a variety of gatherings, including school activities and public meetings, as well as serving as a church. The church was built and supported by many individuals in the community, regardless of their pronounced faith. (Courtesy of Dan Stafford.)

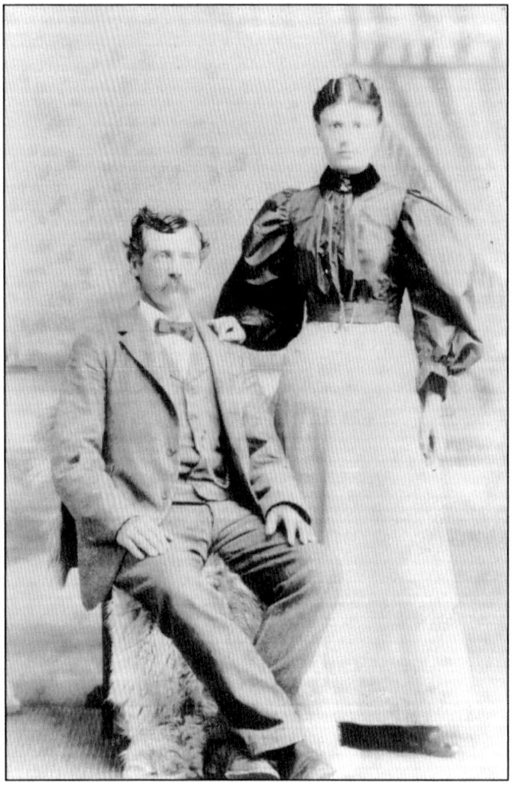

August Edward "Ed" Timmerman was best known for the *Timmerman Ferry*, which his family operated from 1894 until 1931. The Timmermans resided in Richland, across the Columbia River from Pasco. The *Timmerman Ferry* was important to Pasco, as it provided the most traveled route to cross the Columbia River. Timmerman is shown in his wedding picture to Mary M. Sohl in 1891. (Courtesy of FCHS.)

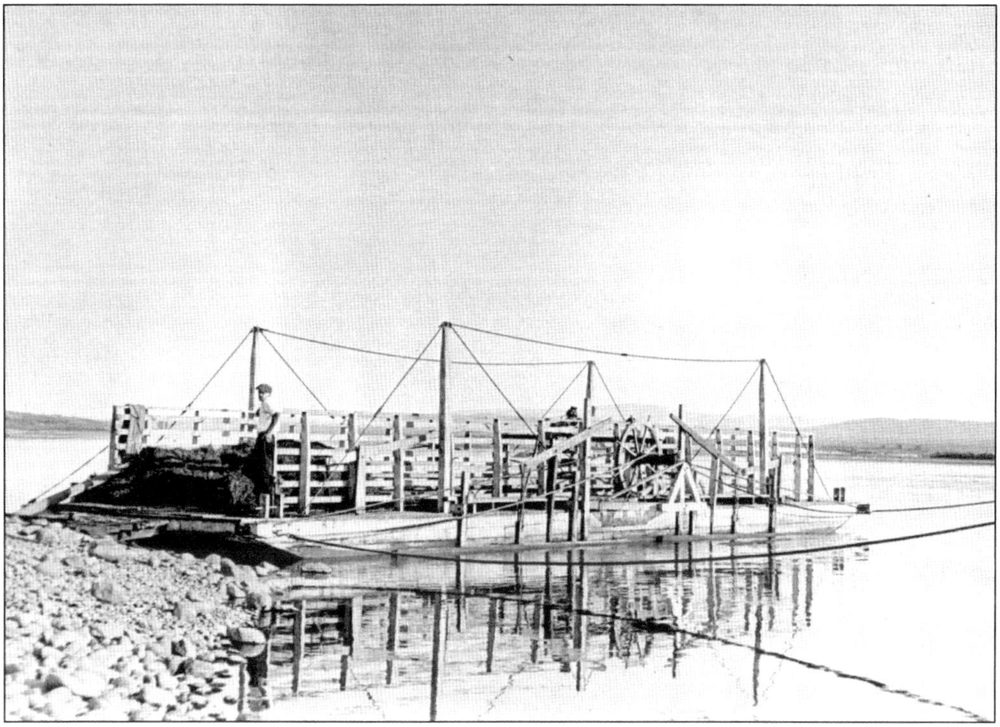

The *Timmerman Ferry* was owned and operated by August Edward Timmerman and his family. Three thousand feet of ¾-inch cable were strung from towers on either side of the Columbia River to guide the ferry across the untamed waters. The *Timmerman Ferry* was used to transport animals, livestock, and people across the river from 1894 to 1931. (Courtesy of FCHS.)

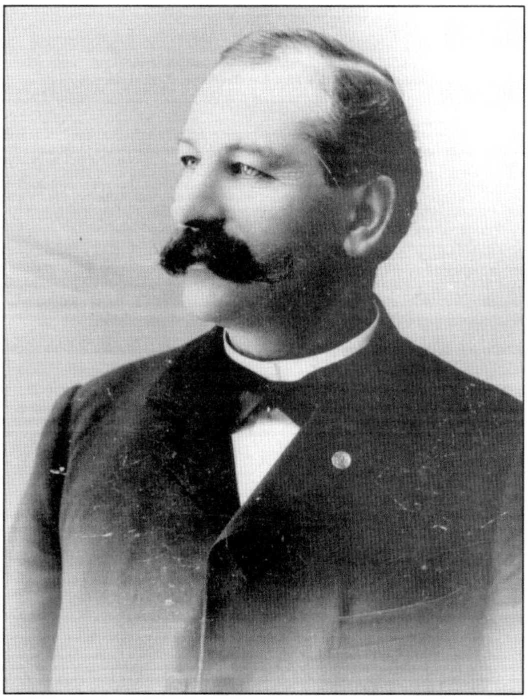

William Byron Gray was an experienced lumberman who was recruited by the Northern Pacific Railway to help build the Snake River Bridge at Ainsworth. Gray became Franklin County's first sheriff from 1883 to 1888. He took the office again in 1895. He also served as assessor and postmaster. When he died in 1905, his wife, Margaret K. Gray, assumed the office of postmaster. (Courtesy of FCHS.)

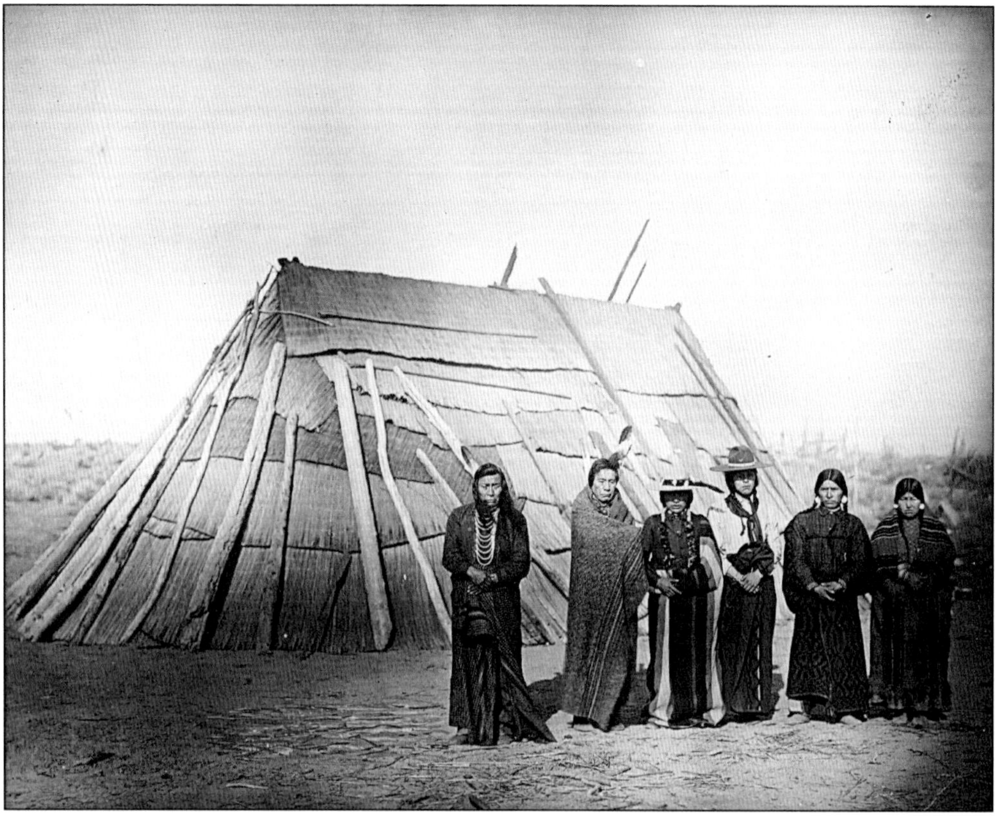

Palus Indians lived in the Kasispa village, near Ainsworth, in the 1800s and early 1900s. The Palus were one of many tribes listed in the Yakima Treaty of 1855, which attempted to band many Indian tribes into one nation and provide a reservation for their existence. The Palus never recognized this treaty and declined to live on the reservation. (Courtesy of the Yakima Valley Libraries.)

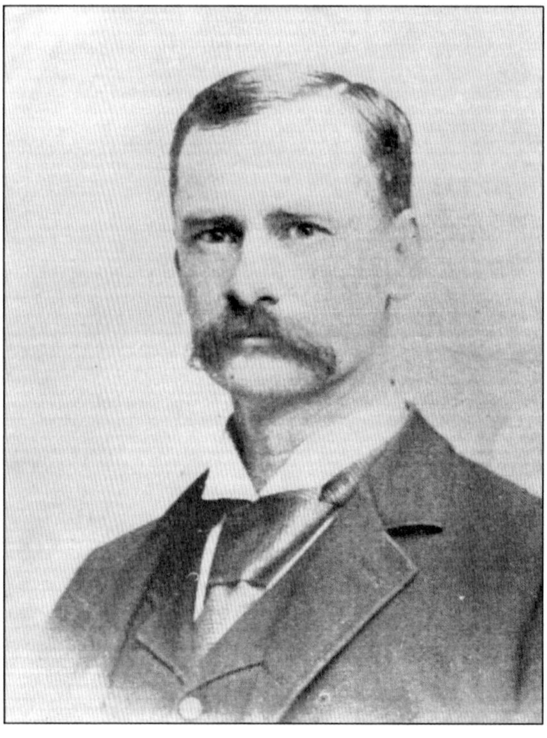

Capt. E. G. Baughman was a riverboat captain whose family lived in Seattle. His presence was well known along the Columbia River as the captain of the *J. M. Hannaford*, the *Eliza Anderson*, the *Annie Faxon*, and other riverboats. His boats and crew were instrumental in bringing necessary building supplies and lumber to Ainsworth and later to the new town of Pasco. (Courtesy of FCHS.)

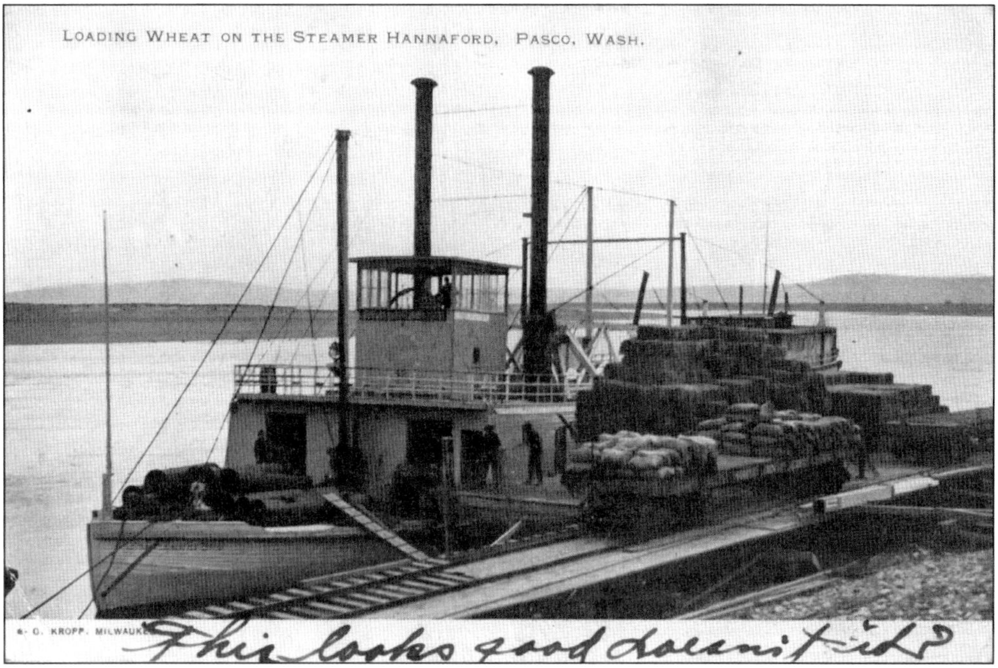

The *J. M. Hannaford*, named for Northern Pacific Railway president Jule Murat Hannaford, was built in 1899, weighing 746 tons with a length of 169 feet. She was the second largest sternwheeler on the Columbia River, next to the rebuilt *Frederick K. Billings*. Capt. E. G. Baughman was in command until 1906, when she was dismantled. (Courtesy of Dan Stafford.)

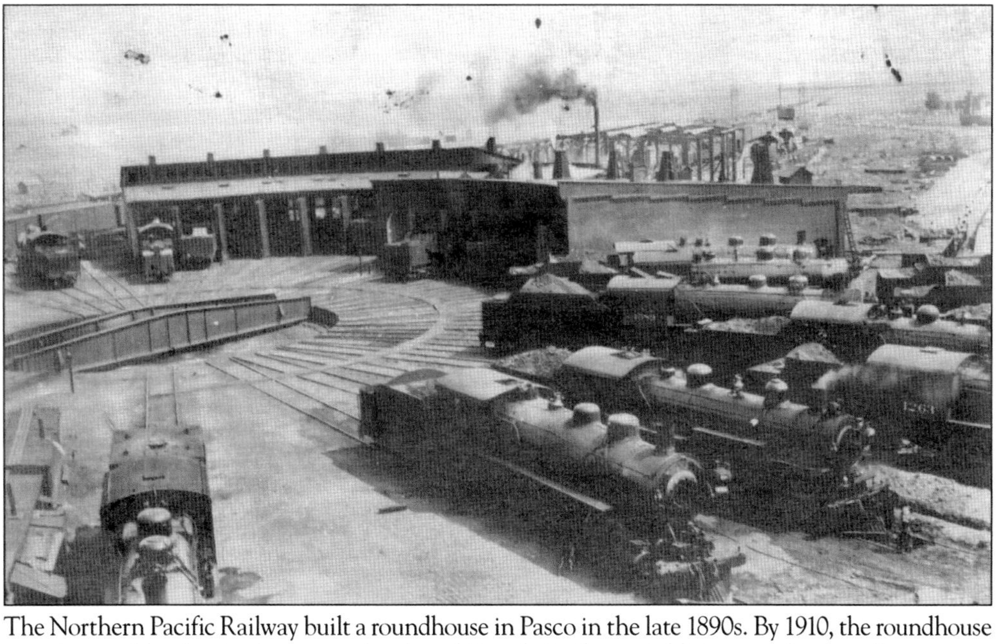

The Northern Pacific Railway built a roundhouse in Pasco in the late 1890s. By 1910, the roundhouse was also used by the Spokane, Portland, and Seattle Railway. Additions to the roundhouse were necessary because of the increase in traffic. Traffic at the Northern Pacific Railway roundhouse peaked from 1910 to 1930, at which time the roundhouse structure formed an almost complete circle. (Courtesy of FCHS.)

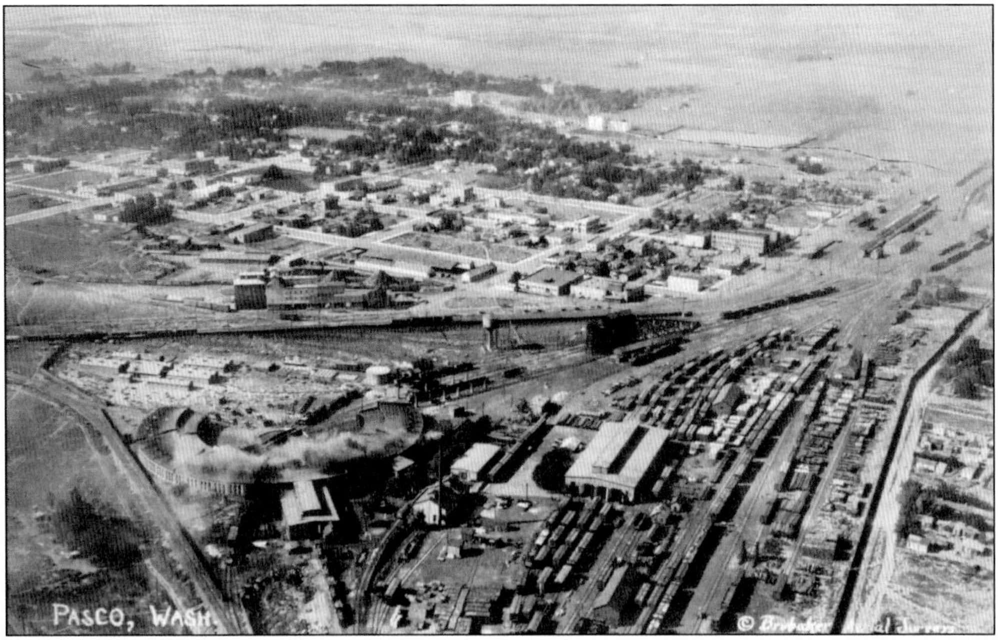

The circular building surrounded by steam in the lower left-hand portion of this photograph is the railroad roundhouse. Roundhouses were used as repair garages for early steam locomotives, which typically only traveled forward. When repairs were necessary, a locomotive would be parked on a turntable, which would align the locomotive to the proper bay. (Courtesy of Dan Stafford.)

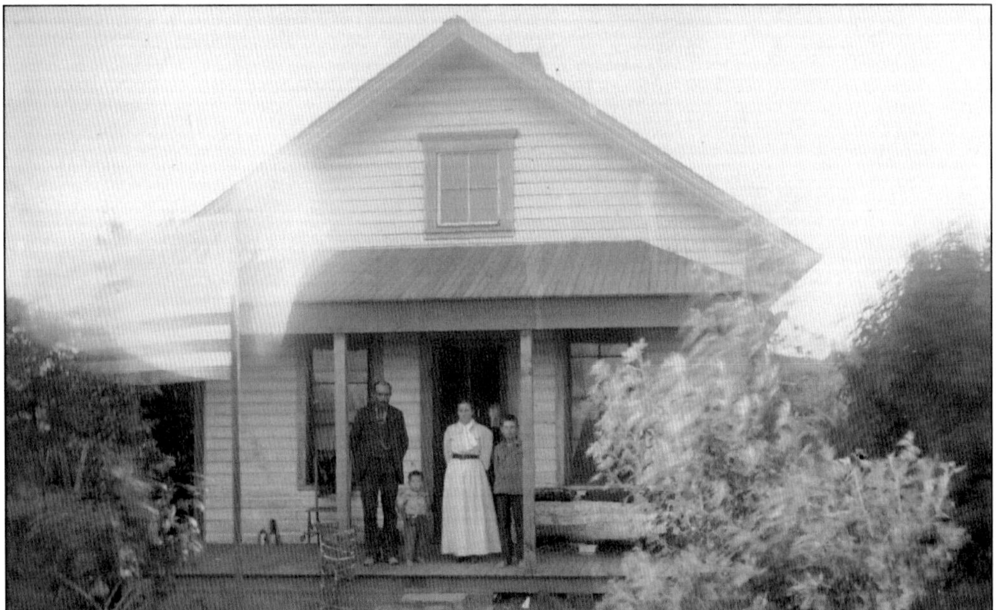

Fred Harris arrived in Pasco as a boy in 1889 with his mother, Gertrude Gordon Harris, and grandfather, Alex Gordon. In 1894, Gertrude married William Storment. This picture, taken in 1900, shows, from left to right, William Storment, Willie Storment, Gertrude Storment, and Fred Harris. Harris married Lura Wallace in 1912 and became a successful diversity farmer along the Columbia River. (Courtesy of FCHS.)

Three

Influential People, Influential Times
1901 to 1910

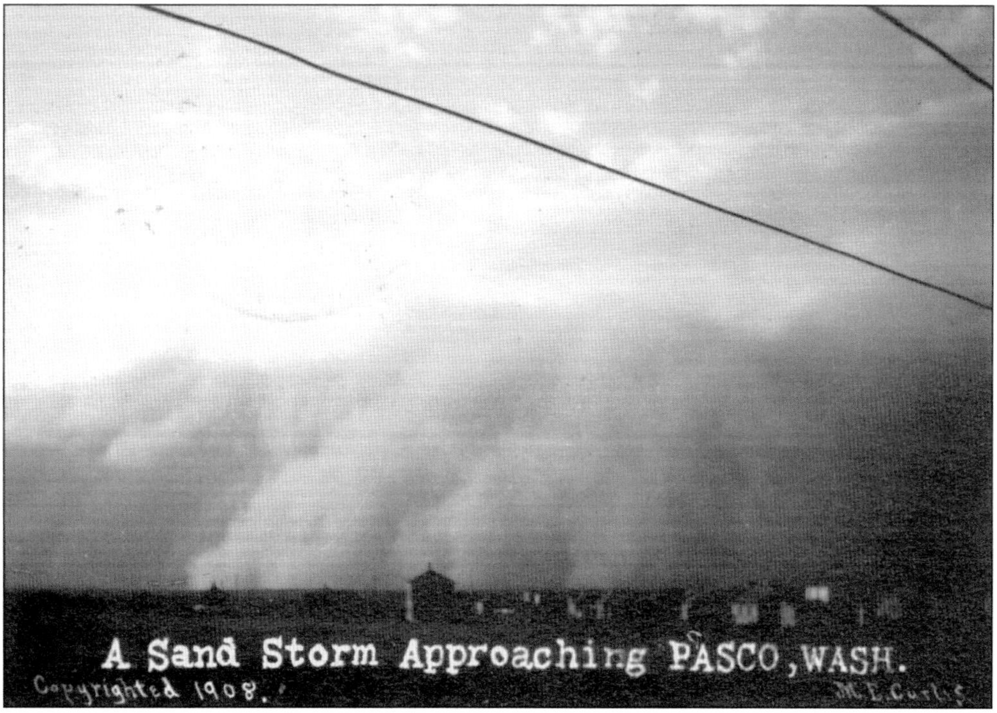

Pasco was known for its light winters, blistering summers, and severe sandstorms. Some Pasco residents referred to storms like the one pictured here as "black storms." In the early 1900s, there were very few trees or buildings to create a windbreak. During black storms, it was necessary to take cover to ward against the bite of the blowing sand. (Courtesy of Dan Stafford.)

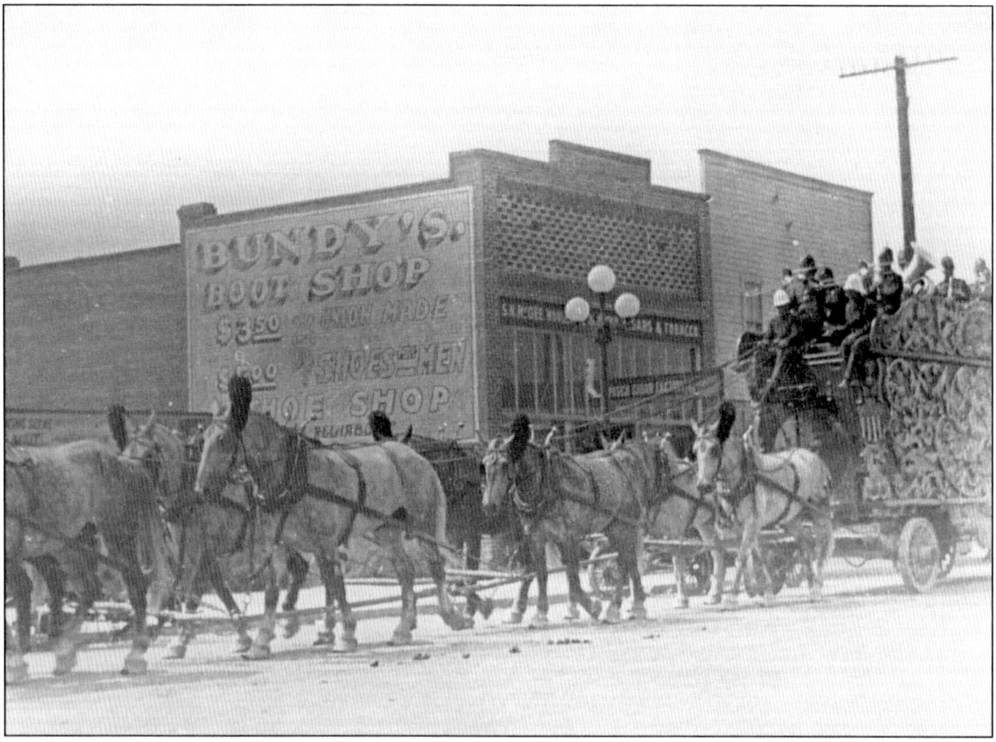

Circuses were popular entertainment for the citizens of Pasco in the early 1900s. The circus would travel by train and arrive in the middle of the night. The next day began with a large parade and ended with the second of two shows. Tents were taken down, and the rail cars were loaded the same night. The circus not only entertained the community, but many individuals in town were sought to help with activities. (Courtesy of FCHS.)

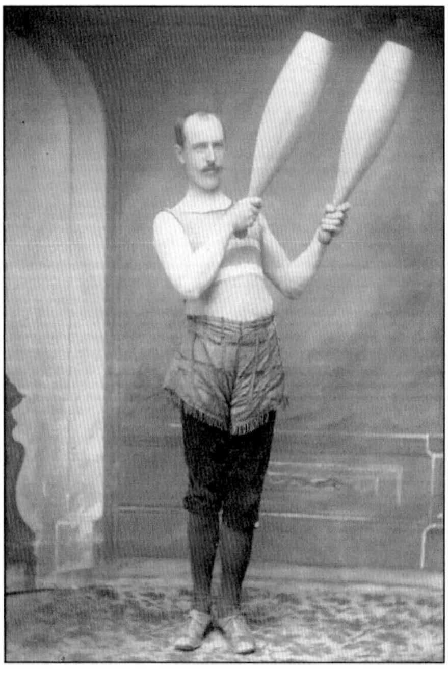

John Buchanan and his wife, Dora, and two sons, Wallie and Alfred, were one of the first families that moved from Ainsworth to Pasco in 1885. John was born in Scotland and worked as a barber. Dora was born in England and managed a restaurant in Pasco in 1900. John was one of many individuals who became enthralled and involved with the traveling circus that came through Pasco. (Courtesy of FCHS.)

Robert Gerry was another lumberman who came to Washington from Maine. He served as Franklin County treasurer in 1891 and 1892. He then served three terms in the legislature representing southeast Washington. He was a prominent Yakima County landowner, but his political and business interests were placed in Pasco, where he lived. (Courtesy of *An Illustrated History of the Big Bend Country, Embracing Lincoln, Douglas, Adams, and Franklin Counties, State of Washington*, 1904.)

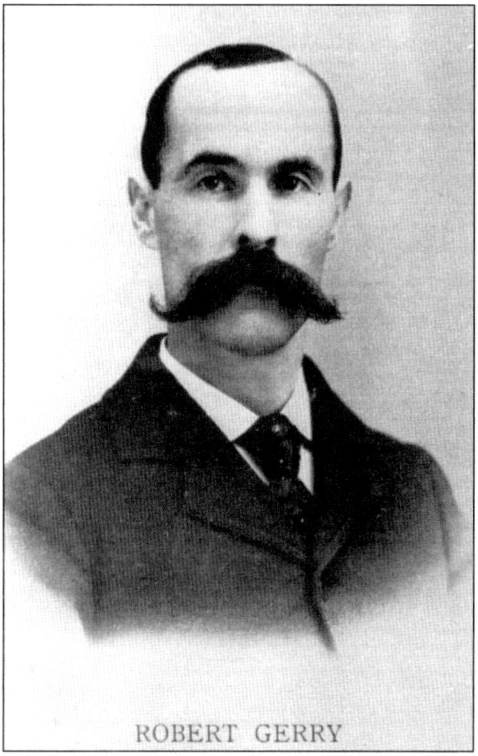

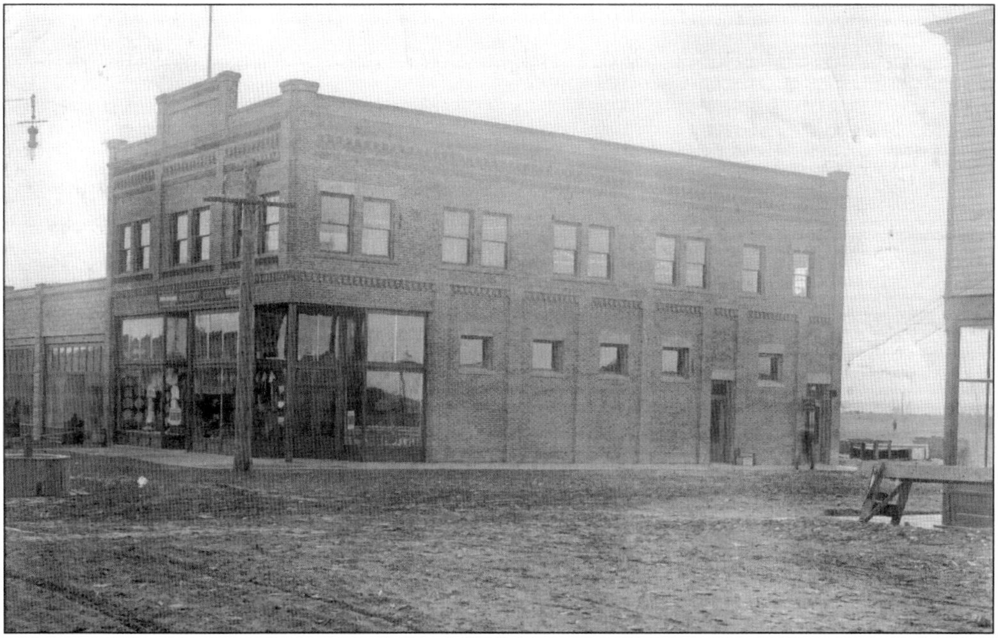

Robert Gerry opened a mercantile store in Ainsworth and then moved it to Pasco. Gerry created a cash register system using rubber slingshots and wires to transfer money from the clerk on the main floor to the cashier, whose office was in the balcony. He refused to barter and only dealt in cash. His building, called the Robert Gerry Building, also had leased office space on the second floor. (Courtesy of Dan Stafford.)

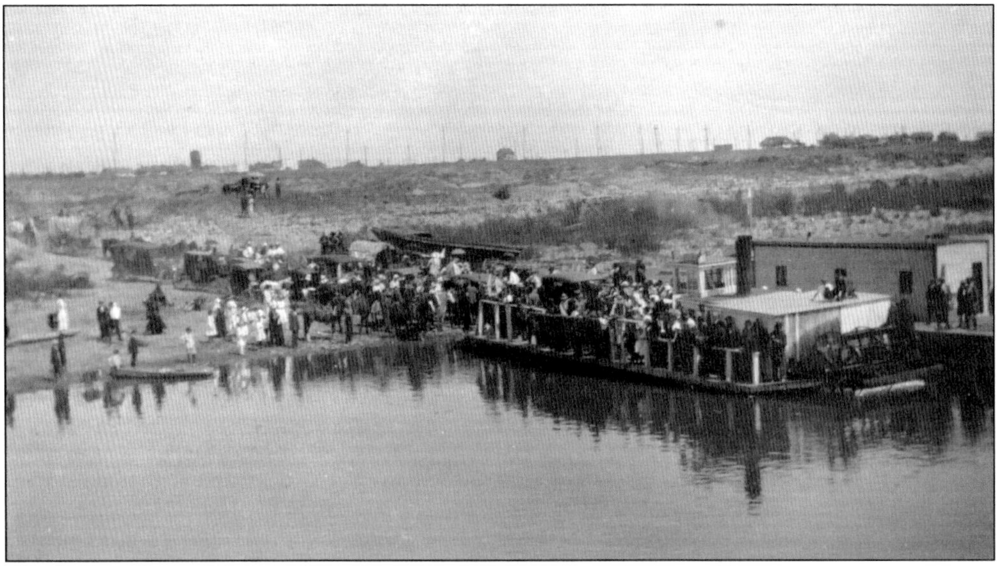

In the early 1900s, the Pasco-Kennewick Ferry was a popular mode of transportation to get from one community to the other. Cars, horses, and people would share limited space for their trip across the Columbia River. A full load would be carried to the dock on the other side of the river and then the ferry would be reloaded to return. (Courtesy of FCHS.)

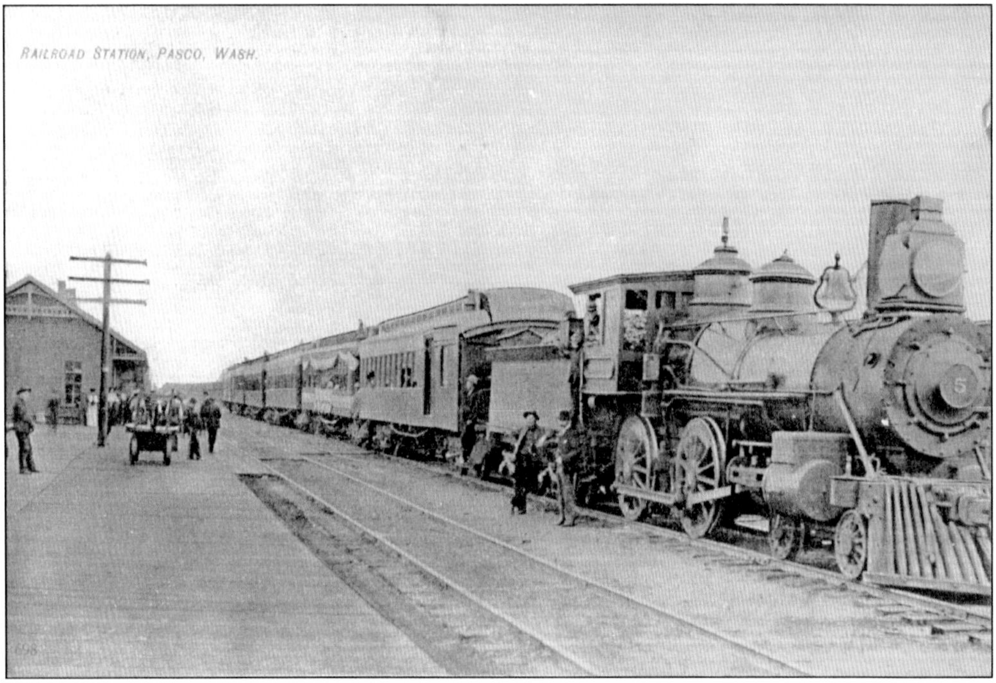

This picture, taken in 1901, shows the first Northern Pacific Railway depot in Pasco, located on Tacoma Street. The wooden sidewalks were a necessity but still posed a tripping hazard to passengers making their way from the train to the depot. With a population of 254 people, Pasco had little to offer. However, the depot was a busy place thanks to promoters selling the idea of living in such a wonderful location. (Courtesy of the Washington State Railroads Historical Society.)

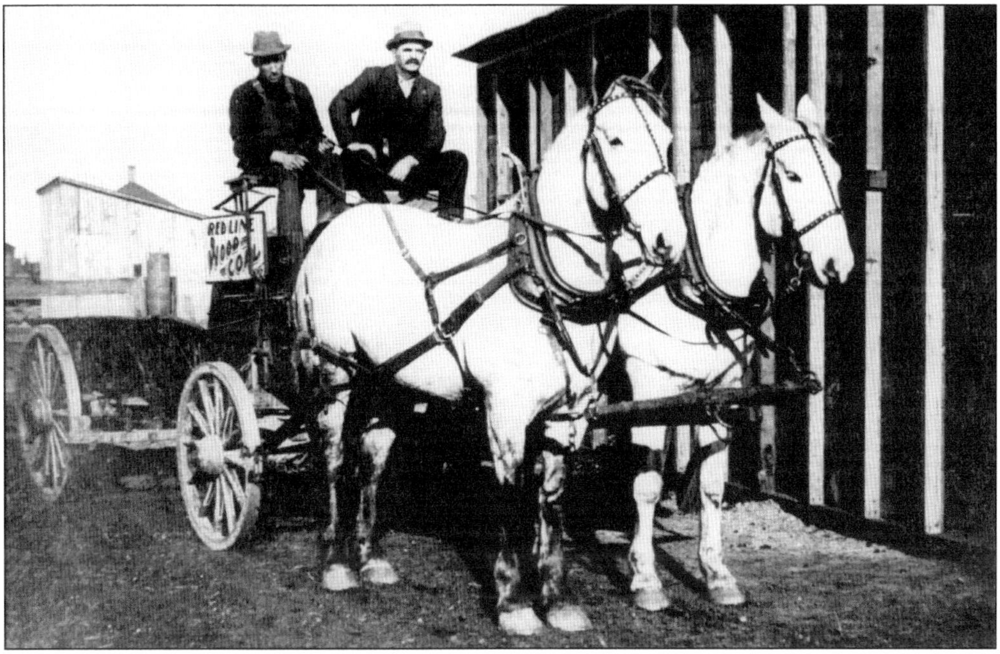

Frank Schuneman was a blacksmith who followed his trade to Ainsworth. His sons—Frank, William, Albert, Henry, Fred, and Adolph—all took jobs representing the community they helped build. Their jobs included farmer, steamboat engineer, locomotive fireman, cattle puncher, horseman, and dray operator. Adolph (Duff) Schuneman is shown here on the right as a drayman for the White River Lumber Company in the early 1900s. Next to him is Edd Jordon. (Courtesy of FCHS.)

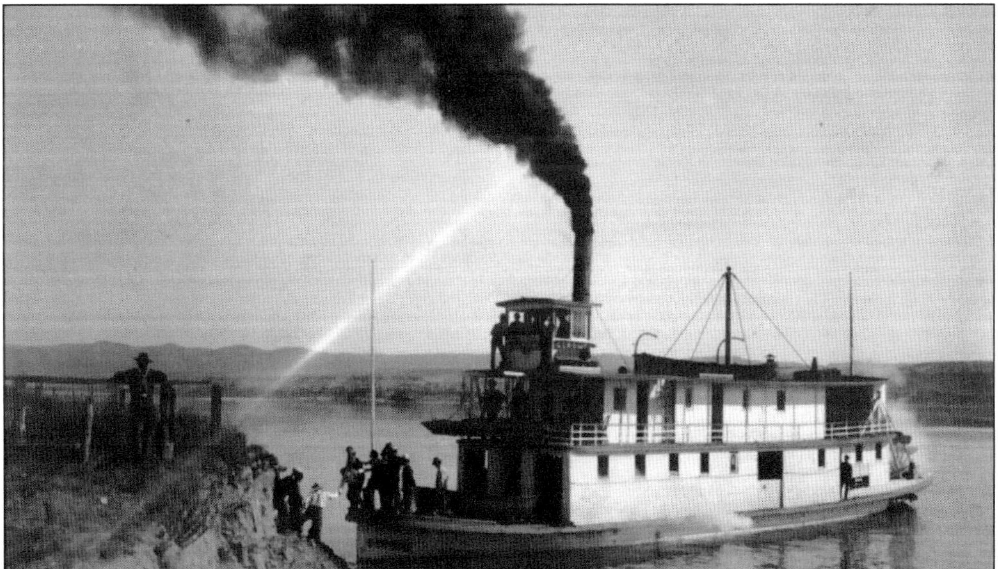

Docks were not always necessary when loading riverboats. Steamboat captains typically knew the river and could navigate to areas that were safe for loading. The *Gerome* was built in 1902 and destroyed in 1905 when she ran into a boulder in the Homly Channel, about 15 miles southeast of Pasco. (Courtesy of the U.S. Department of Energy.)

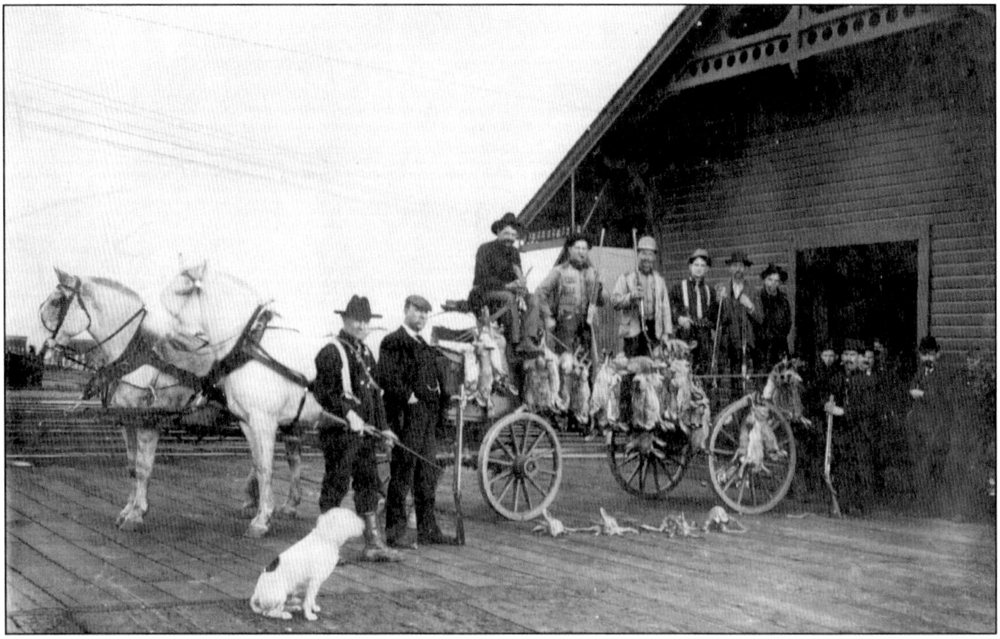

In the early 1900s, jackrabbits caused concern to local farmers. Growing crops was not easy in the desert terrain before irrigation. Rabbits enjoyed feasting on the tender new plant starts, causing even more hardship. This picture of Louis Schuneman (unidentified) and his friends was taken after a successful hunt and posed near the Northern Pacific Railway station. (Courtesy of FCHS.)

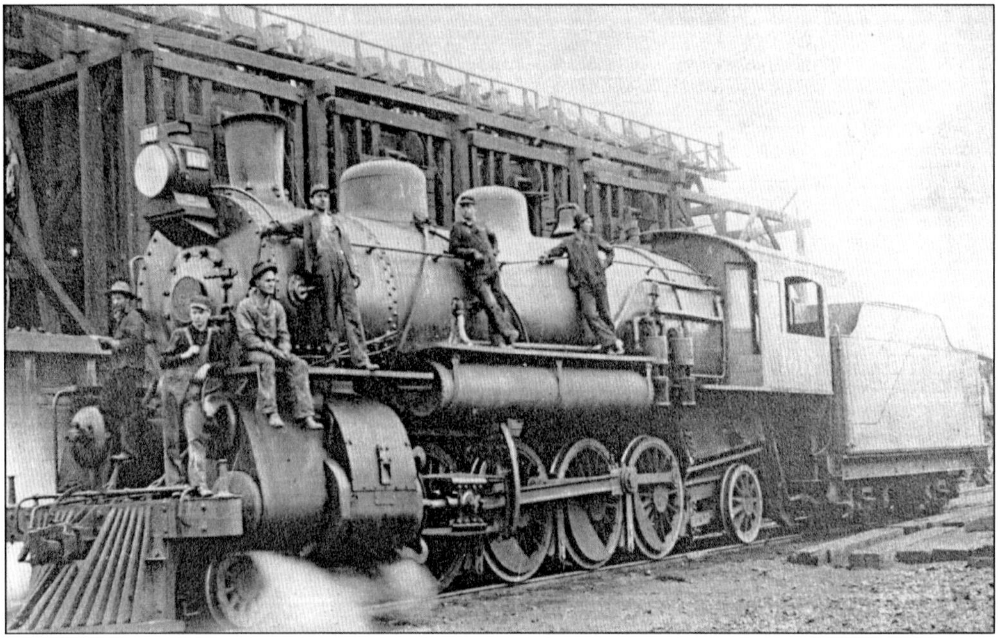

Nearly all locomotives were driven by steam in the early 1900s. The large structure behind this steam engine held the coal that was used by the Northern Pacific Railway and the Spokane, Portland, and Seattle Railway when they refueled in Pasco. Pasco was not adversely impacted by the rivalry between the two railways but rather benefitted from the efforts of both. (Courtesy of Jim Frederickson.)

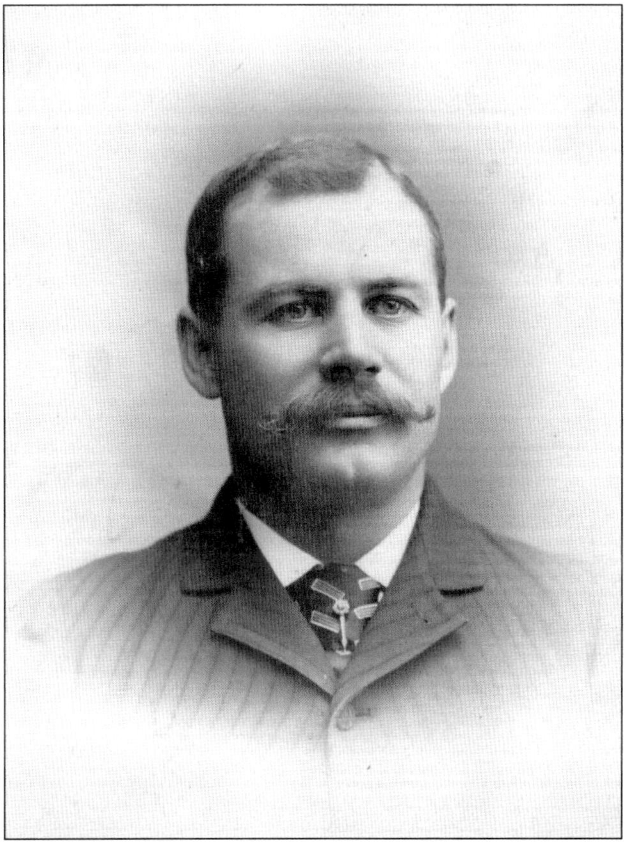

Alvin P. Gray and his brothers Charles, Will, and Lon left Maine and came to Ainsworth around 1882. Their lumberman experience was crucial to the building of Ainsworth and the Snake River Bridge. They were responsible for obtaining lumber from the Cascade Mountains and shipping it to the construction site. Gray became an influential person in the community. Not only did he build many businesses, but he also held the office of postmaster, marshal, and mayor. He married May E. O'Neal in Tacoma and brought her to his area of opportunity. She was not excited and demanded to be taken back to the coast. She eventually made peace with the move and became instrumental in her own right as a Pasco pioneer. Below, she is pictured in front of their well-known People's Store. (Both courtesy of FCHS.)

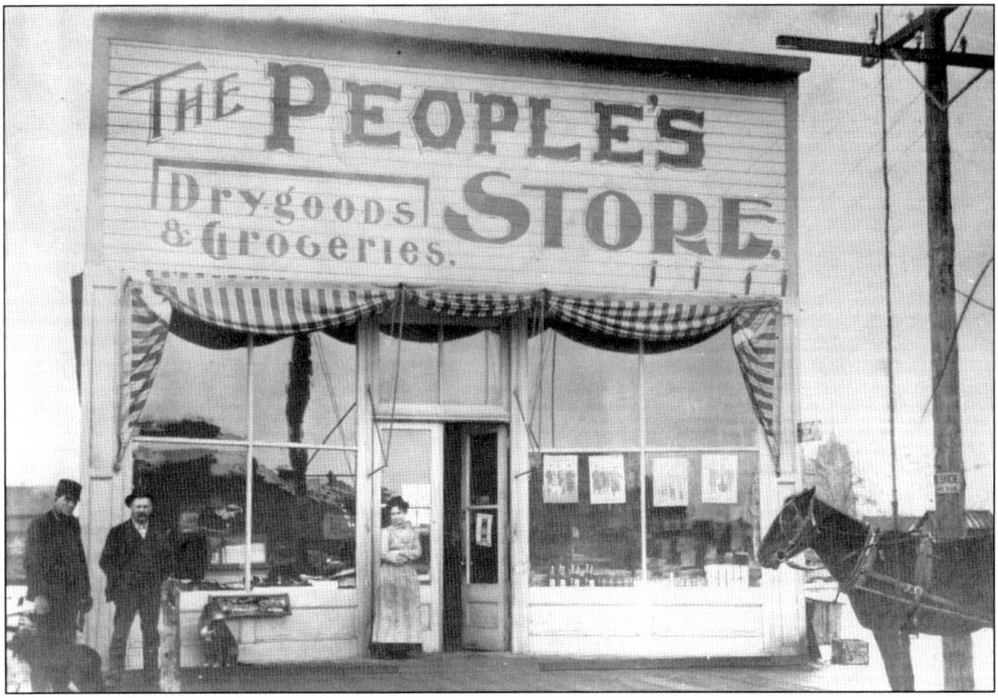

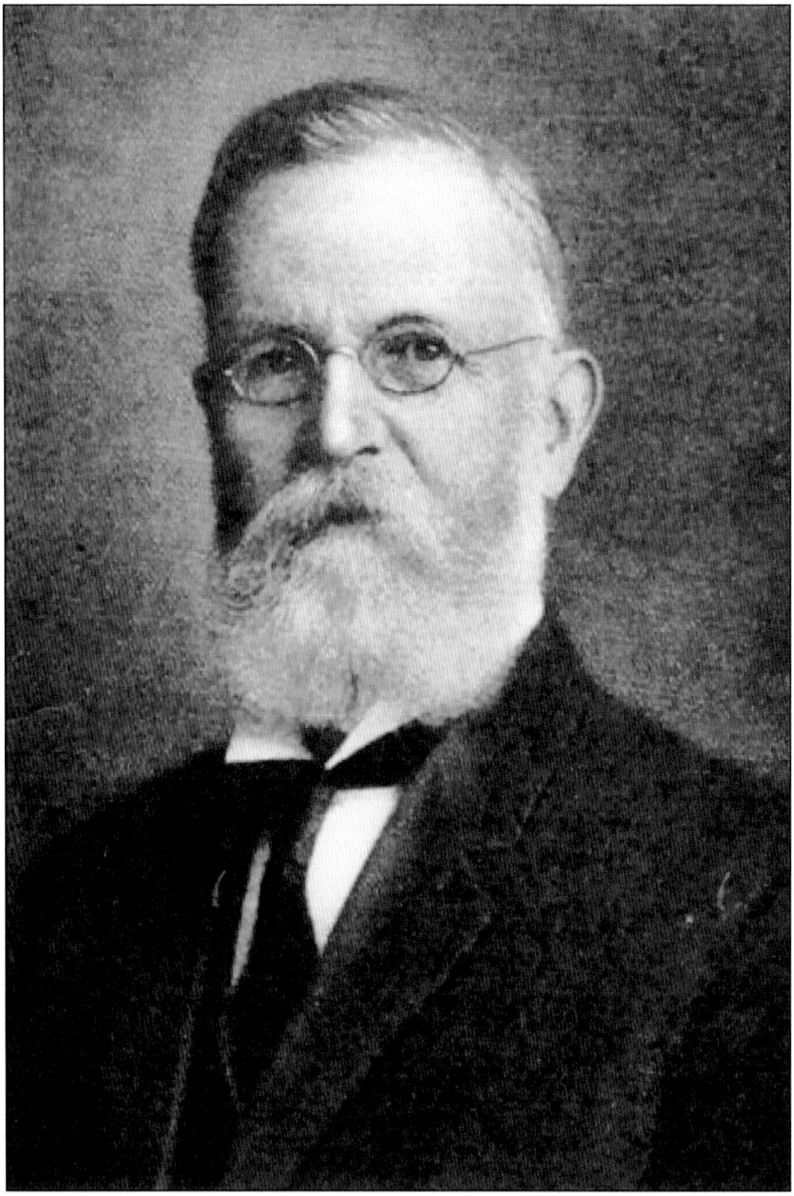

Capt. William Polk Gray wore many hats in the development of Pasco, promoting it everywhere he went with anyone he met. Captain Gray was best known for his prowess as a steamboat captain, with many stories being told of his unbelievable feats. As he traveled the river, he would share products and stories of Pasco with individuals in various towns. He also dabbled in real estate and started the Pasco Land Company. Gray traveled to Washington, D.C., Chicago, Cincinnati, and other large cities to represent Pasco to the rest of the nation. Realizing that Pasco had spiritual and educational needs, he was instrumental in organizing the first church community, the Congregational Church, and the first newspaper, the *Pasco Headlight*. He held the position of county commissioner from 1886 to 1890 and was Pasco's mayor in 1911. In the Open River Celebration of 1915, it was Gray in the sternwheeler *Undine* who transported important guests from Pasco to the celebration at the Dalles-Celilo Canal. (Courtesy of *History of the Columbia River Valley, From the Dalles to the Sea*, S. J. Clarke Publishing Company, 1928.)

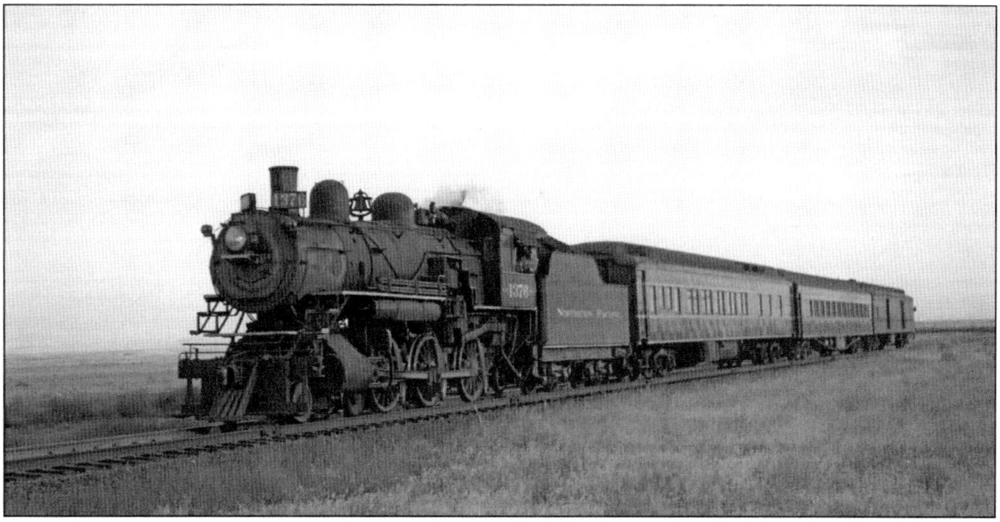

Early in the 1900s, traveling by train became a preferred mode of travel. It proved to be much faster than previous transportation modes and much more comfortable. The Pullman Sleepers were designed to be luxurious hotels on wheels. Many individuals traveling to Pasco, whether relocating or visiting, took advantage of the railroad. (Courtesy of Jim Frederickson.)

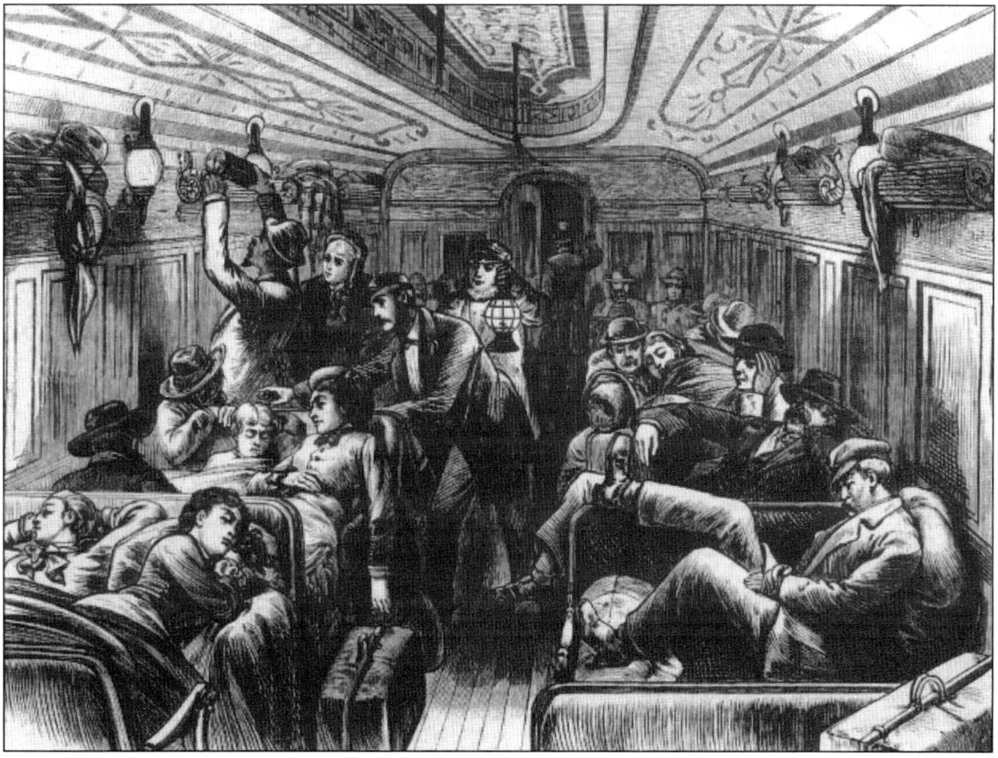

Pasco's railroad depot greeted a variety of travelers. The majority of those traveling from long distances did not travel luxuriously but rather took the most affordable mode of transportation available. Beds in these passenger cars were created from bench seats, and ventilation was available through open windows. Full passenger cars would hold approximately 40 persons. (Courtesy of *Frank Leslie's Illustrated Newspaper*, 1878.)

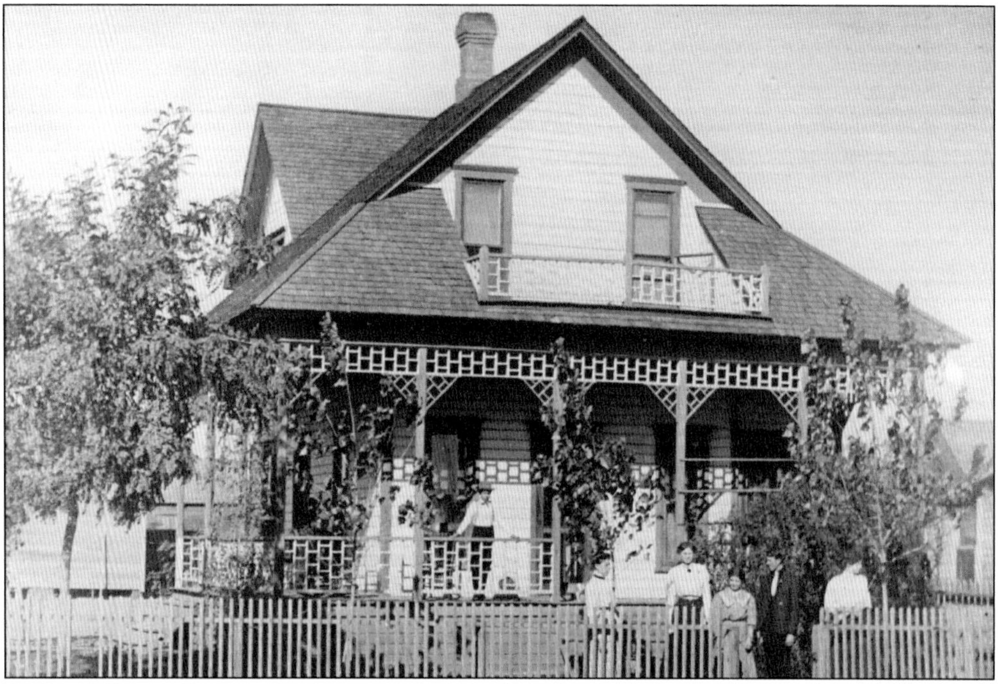

William Hogan was a railroad man who moved his family from Minneapolis to Pasco around 1902. He was killed in a railroad accident shortly after the move, leaving his wife, Leona Hogan, twice widowed. She bought this place on Clark Street for $425 to raise her five children. William is on the veranda. At the gate, from left to right, are Leona, Armosa, Esther, Walter, and Alice. (Courtesy of FCHS.)

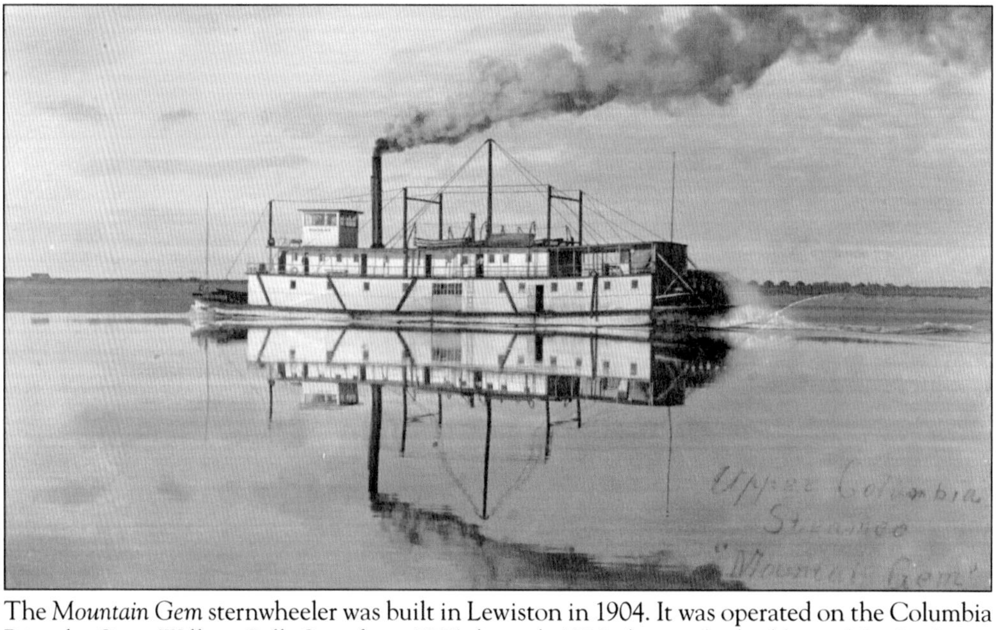

The *Mountain Gem* sternwheeler was built in Lewiston in 1904. It was operated on the Columbia River by Capt. William Polk Gray from 1905 through 1908, during the building of the Spokane, Portland, and Seattle Railway lines. "Red Row," the railroad tenement-housing district, is visible on the horizon. (Courtesy of Dan Stafford.)

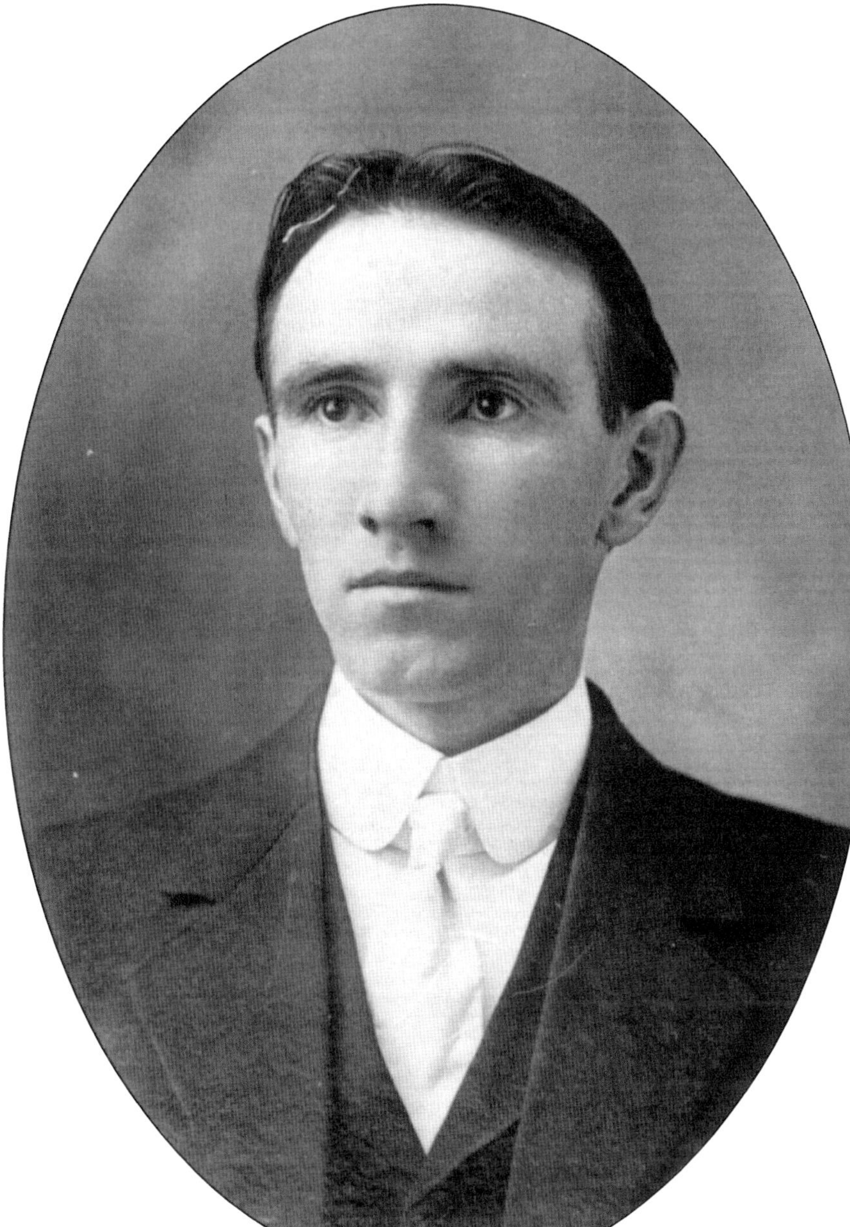

B. B. Horrigan arrived in Pasco as a new attorney in 1904. His first office was a room rented from Wong How on the second floor of How's General Store. The majority of Horrigan's cases involved the financial problems of various local irrigation districts. Irrigation was of utmost importance to the community at the time, and Horrigan's involvement led to his term as Washington state representative from 1911 through 1915. While in office, he encouraged the State of Washington to financially support the Palouse irrigation project survey. He later became involved in gaining financial support for the first Our Lady of Lourdes Hospital in Pasco. His other interests included the Blue Mountain Council of the Boy Scouts and the "Three Flags Highway," which became U.S. Highway 395 in 1926. (Courtesy of FCHS.)

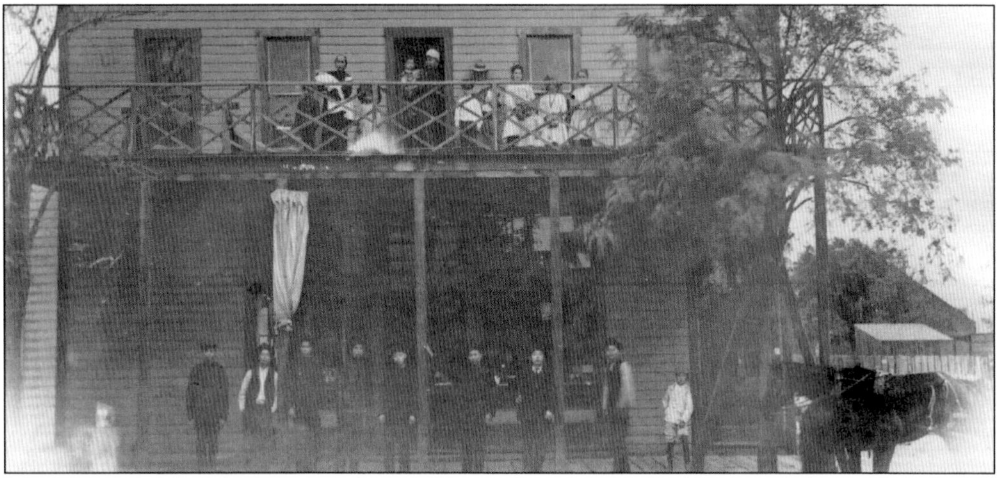

Frank Schuneman imported 200 Chinese laborers and a "Boss Chinee," Wong How, to Ainsworth about 1884. Wong How supervised the Chinese laborers, first in panning for gold and later in constructing the railroad bridge. By 1891, How prospered and built one of Pasco's first general stores, which also had rooms for business and law offices on its upper floor. He made several trips back to his homeland and in 1904 brought his family to Pasco. During this time, the United States was making Chinese immigration laws more restrictive. Wong How, however, was well liked and accepted in Pasco. He is shown below in a 1907 picture with his family: Jimmie with the bicycle, Frank on Wong How's lap, Chester on Ane Shea's lap, and Howard and Mary in the background. (Both courtesy of FCHS.)

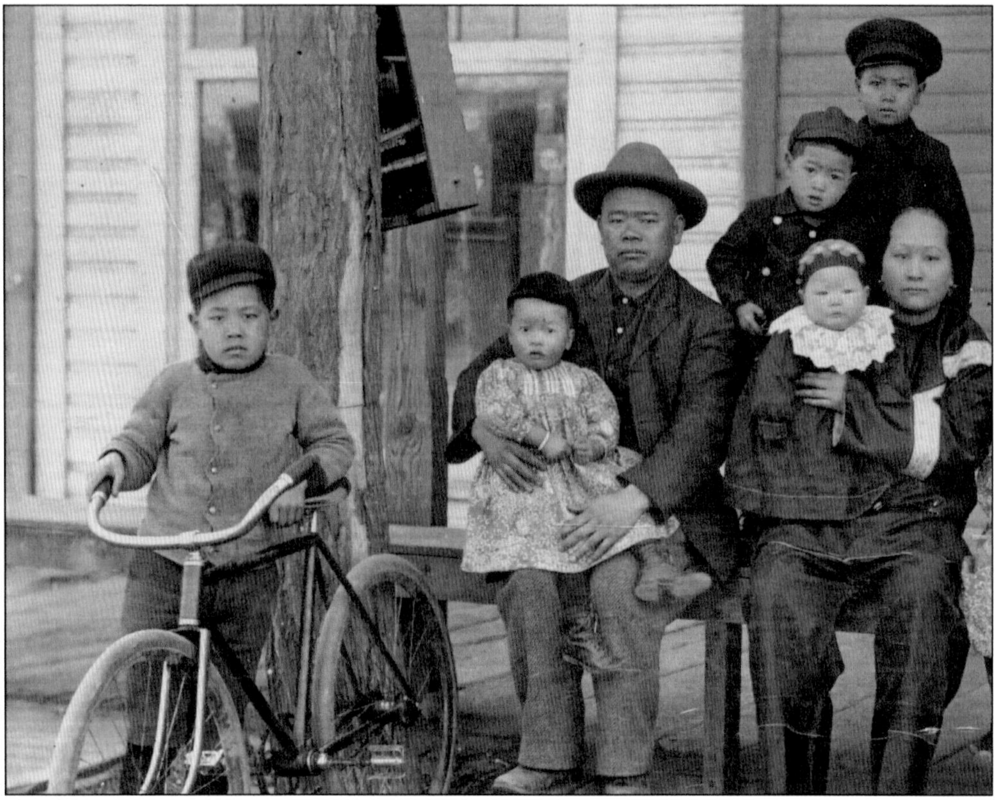

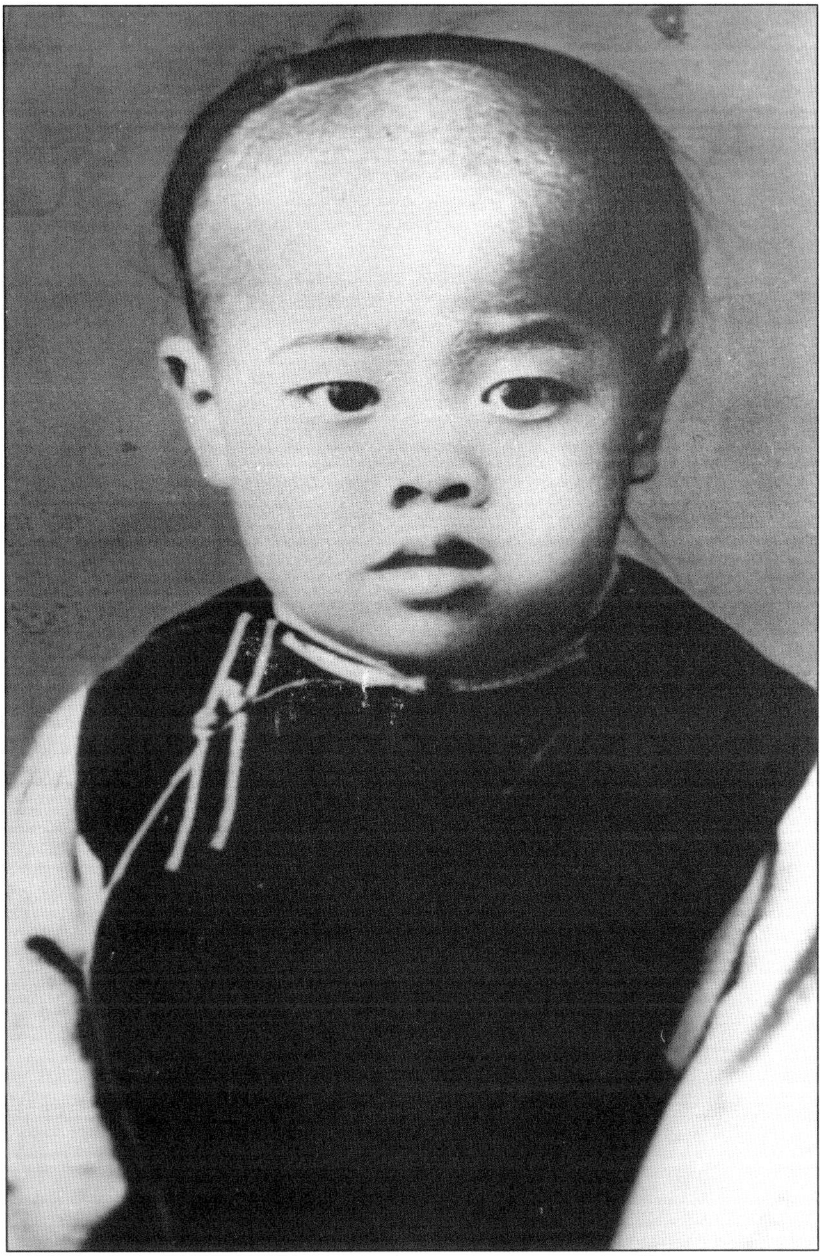

Wong Tung Jim was born in China in 1899. His father, Wong How, legally immigrated the same year and became a successful Pasco merchant. In 1904, Wong How returned to China and brought his family to Pasco. Wong Tung Jim experienced racial bigotry but won many of his schoolmates' friendship by giving them candy obtained from his father's store. He soon anglicized his Chinese name to James Wong Howe. When James was 12 years old, he obtained his first Kodak Brownie camera as payment for odd jobs he did for a Mr. Sullivan who owned a drugstore. The Brownie camera was not equipped with a viewfinder, and many of his first pictures did not include the heads of his subjects, much to his father's dismay. James continued his hobby and eventually became a master cinematographer. His Hollywood career was a success, which earned him many nominations and awards, including two Oscars. (Courtesy of FCHS.)

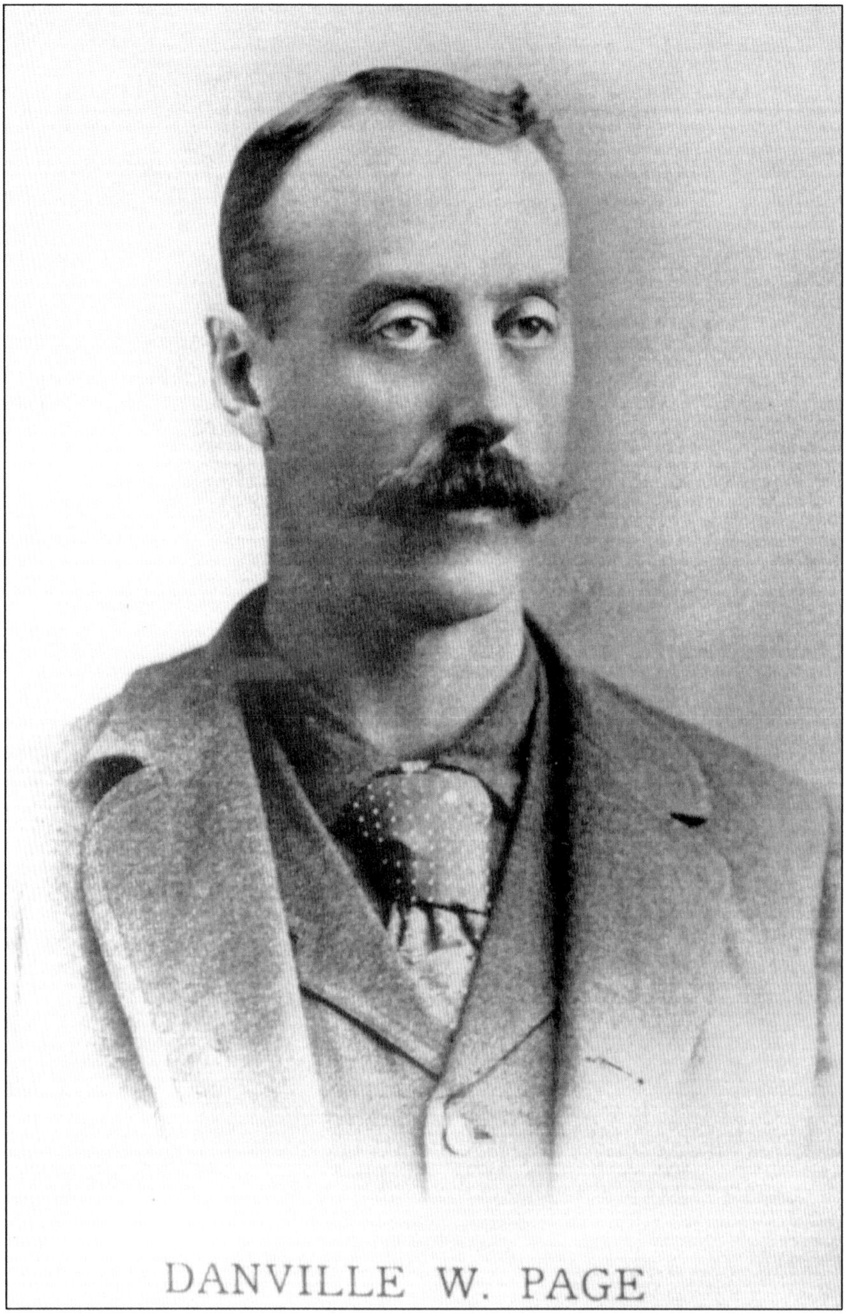

Danville Page served as county commissioner in 1889, 1890, and 1893 and was Pasco's mayor in 1904. He came to Washington in 1880 from Maine, and in 1892, he homesteaded northeast of Ainsworth. On May 22, 1894, he married the 17-year-old Bohemian Maggie Sentel in Walla Walla. Page became well known as a horseman with over 1,000 horses and several hundred head of cattle. He fought land promoters to keep Franklin County debt free by speaking out against bond issues. One of the bond issues Page is credited with fighting was the desire for a $40,000 courthouse before 1904. (Courtesy of *An Illustrated History of the Big Bend Country, Embracing Lincoln, Douglas, Adams, and Franklin Counties, State of Washington*, 1904.)

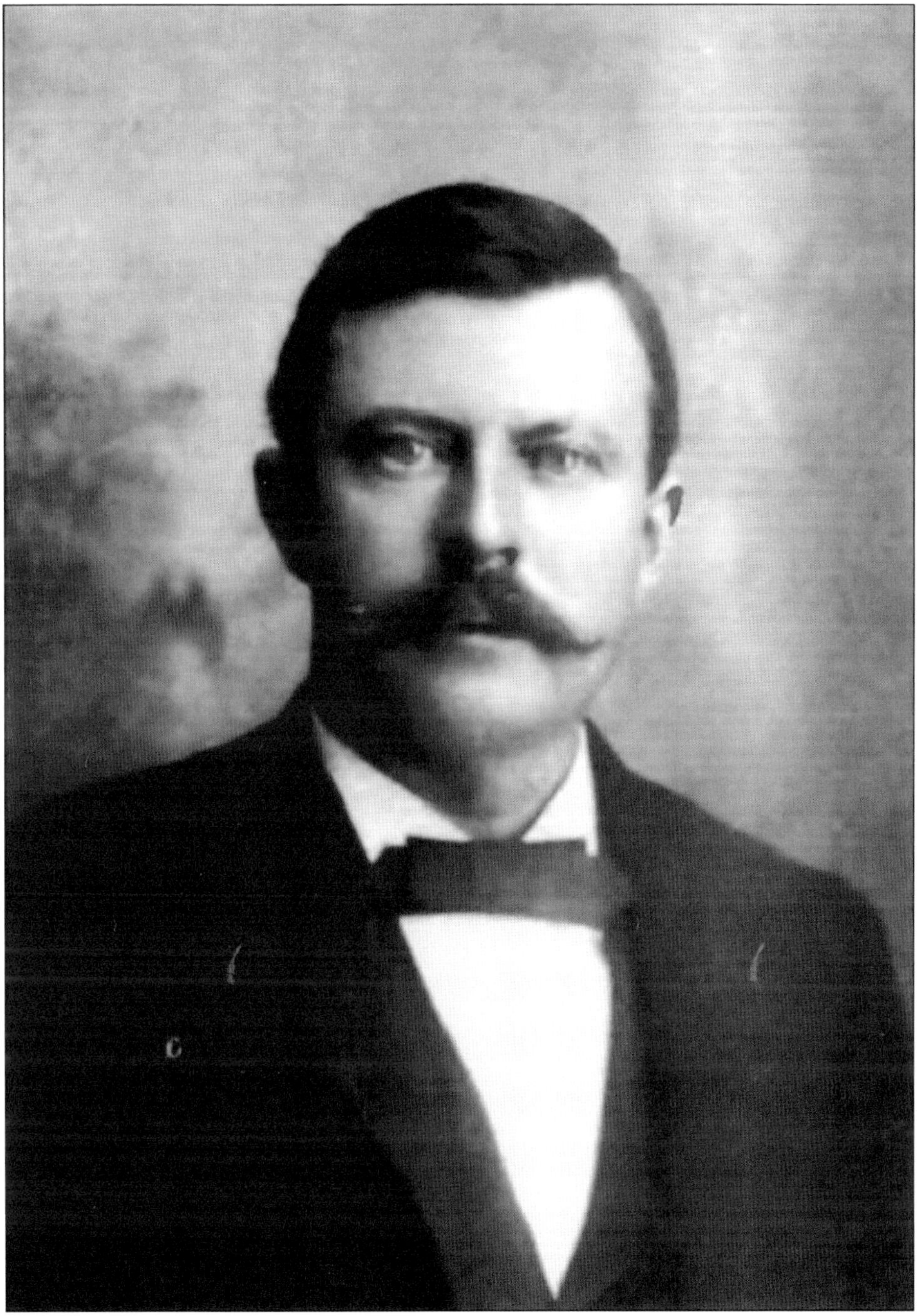

Cornelius S. O'Brien came to Pasco in 1894 and dedicated himself to serving the community. He was Franklin County auditor from 1897 to 1900, as well as Franklin County clerk from 1898 to 1901. He was then elected as a state representative. From 1902 to 1903, he was Franklin County's prosecuting attorney. His longest held office was that of Franklin County treasurer, in which he served from 1902 to 1907. His shortest held office was that of mayor of Pasco, which he held for four months in 1908. (Courtesy of *An Illustrated History of the Big Bend Country, Embracing Lincoln, Douglas, Adams, and Franklin Counties, State of Washington*, 1904.)

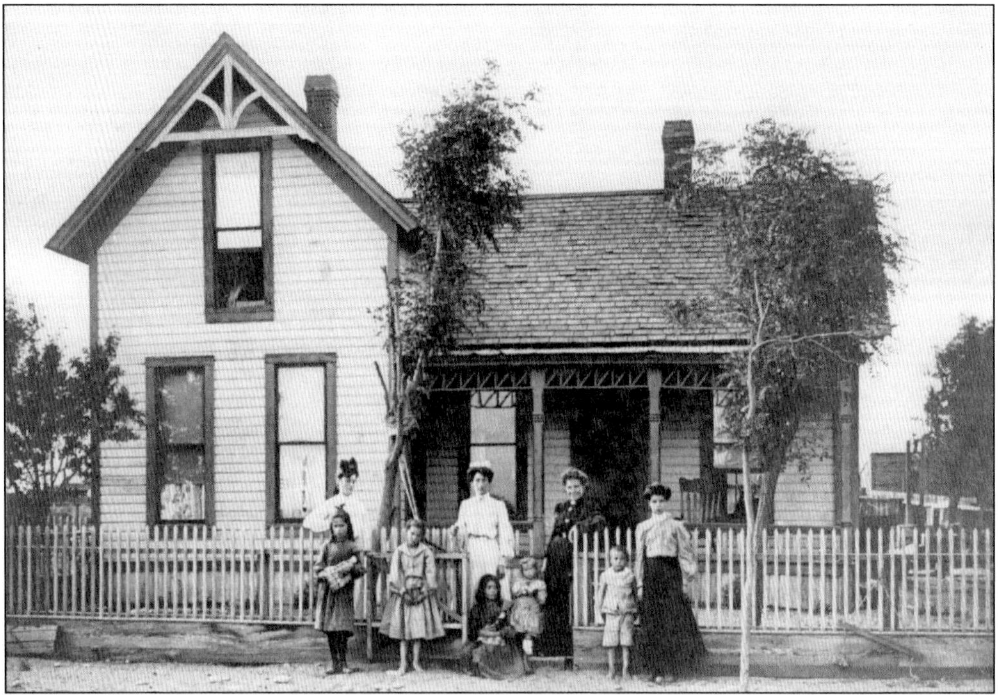

Lineous Koontz, the son of an Ohioan preacher, moved to Washington in the 1870s. He married Sarah Martin in 1887. Both the Koontzes served Franklin County in the early 1900s, Lineous as county clerk and auditor and Sarah as deputy clerk. Their children are shown in front of their home in 1905. From left to right are Edna, Delta, Francis, Jessie, Grace, Pearle, Sarah, William, and Ada. (Courtesy of FCHS.)

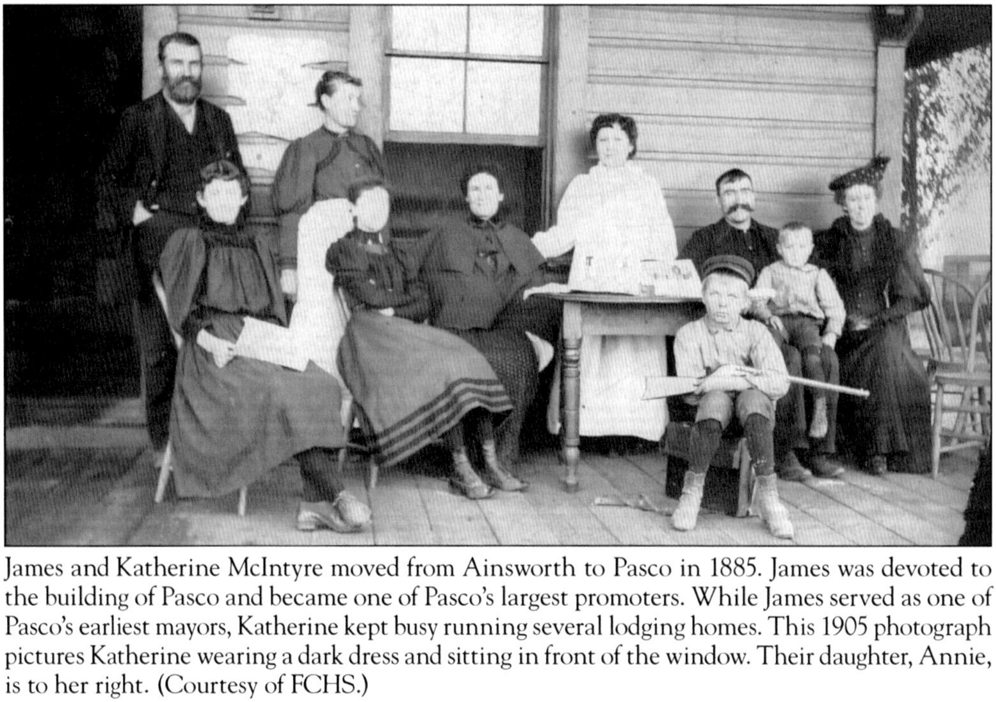

James and Katherine McIntyre moved from Ainsworth to Pasco in 1885. James was devoted to the building of Pasco and became one of Pasco's largest promoters. While James served as one of Pasco's earliest mayors, Katherine kept busy running several lodging homes. This 1905 photograph pictures Katherine wearing a dark dress and sitting in front of the window. Their daughter, Annie, is to her right. (Courtesy of FCHS.)

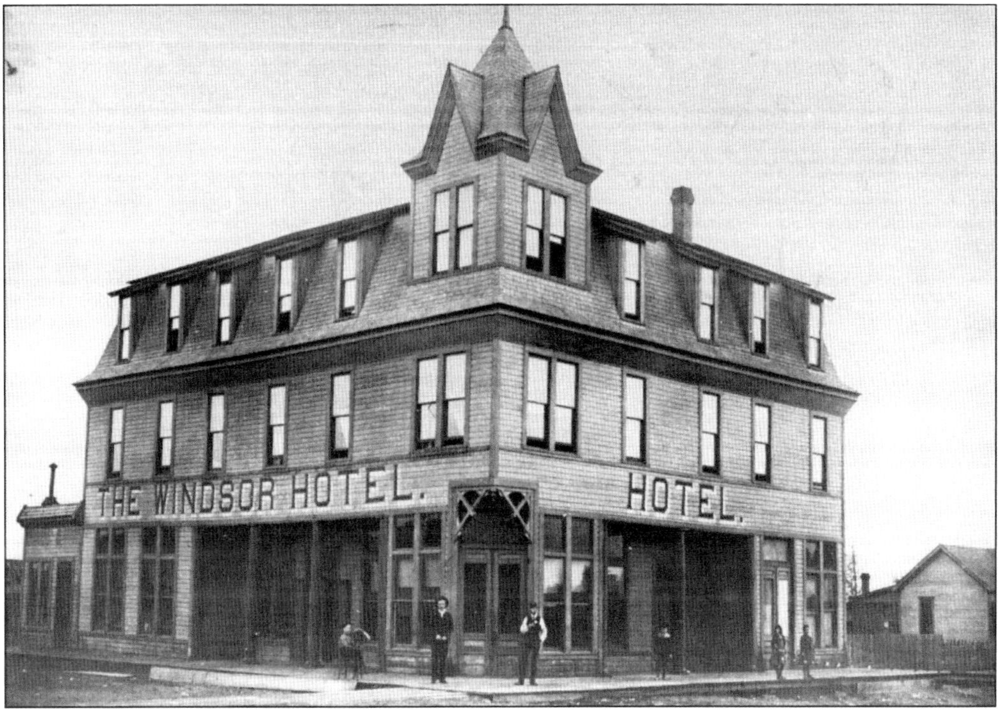

The Windsor Hotel was built in 1893 at the corner of Clark and First Streets and was one of Pasco's first elegant establishments. This picture was taken about 1905, when board rate was set at $4.50 a week. One story states that a traveling man traded two weeks' board for two town lots, and there was a debate as to whether the land was worth an even trade. One of the lots was sold two years later for $250. (Courtesy of FCHS.)

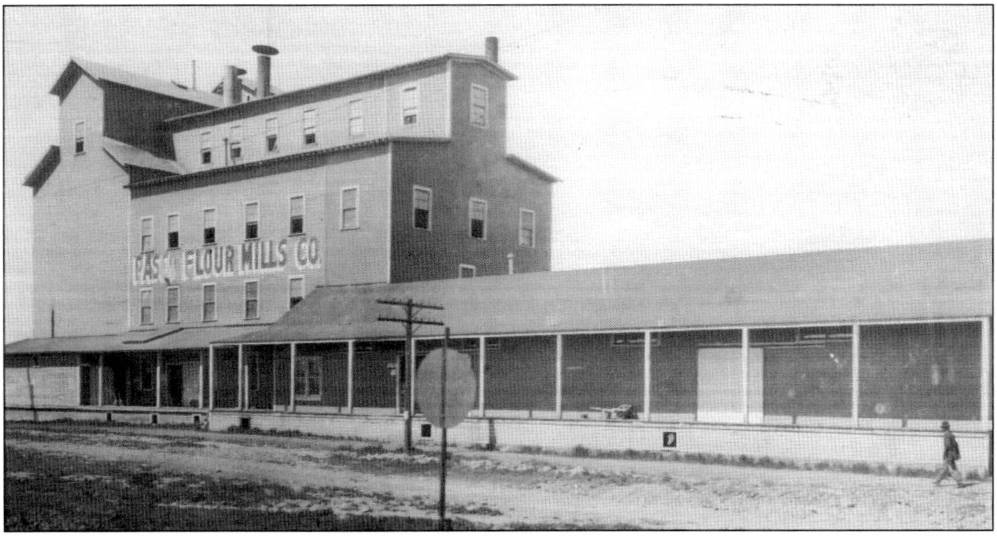

Pasco was surrounded by agricultural communities like Connell, Kahlotus, and Page. Due to the large influence the railroad played in Pasco, it was necessary to have a local flourmill. Farmers would bring their harvested grain to the flour mill, which was located near the railroad roundhouse, to have the grain converted to flour. The flour would then be shipped via the railroad to markets. (Courtesy of FCHS.)

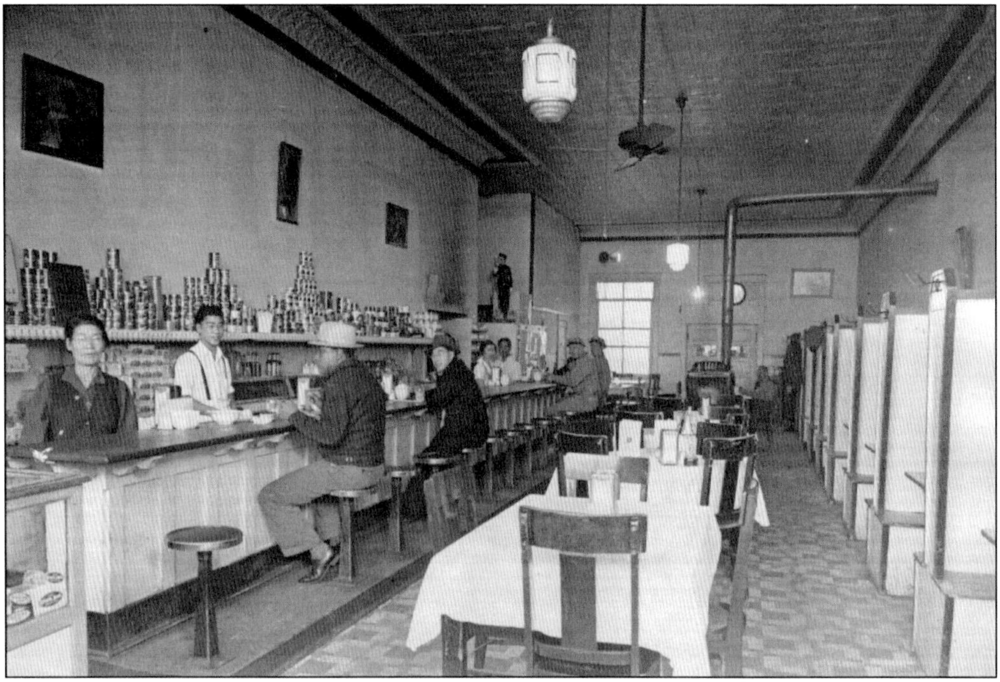

The M&M Café was owned and operated by the Yamauchi family. Asiachno, or Harry, and his wife, Chika, were born in Japan. They immigrated to the United States in 1905. By 1906, they were in Washington and soon became Pasco entrepreneurs. The M&M Café was a popular breakfast spot, appreciated by hunters as they left for the day. (Courtesy of FCHS.)

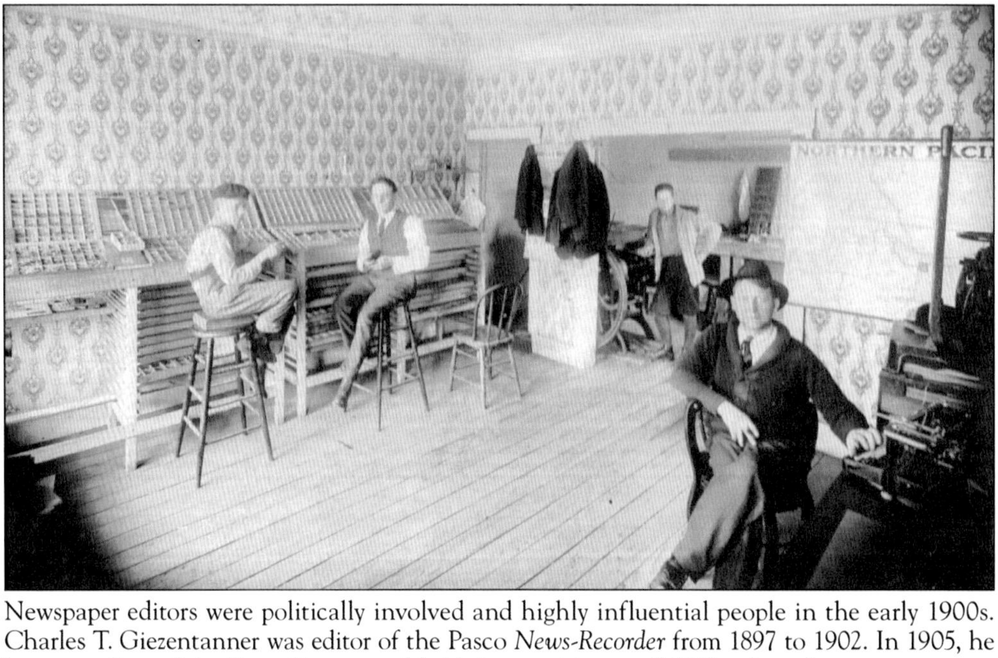

Newspaper editors were politically involved and highly influential people in the early 1900s. Charles T. Giezentanner was editor of the Pasco *News-Recorder* from 1897 to 1902. In 1905, he became editor of the *Pasco Express* and held that position until 1918, when the newspaper was sold. Jacob Giezentanner, his father, is identified in the lower right-hand corner of the picture above. (Courtesy of FCHS.)

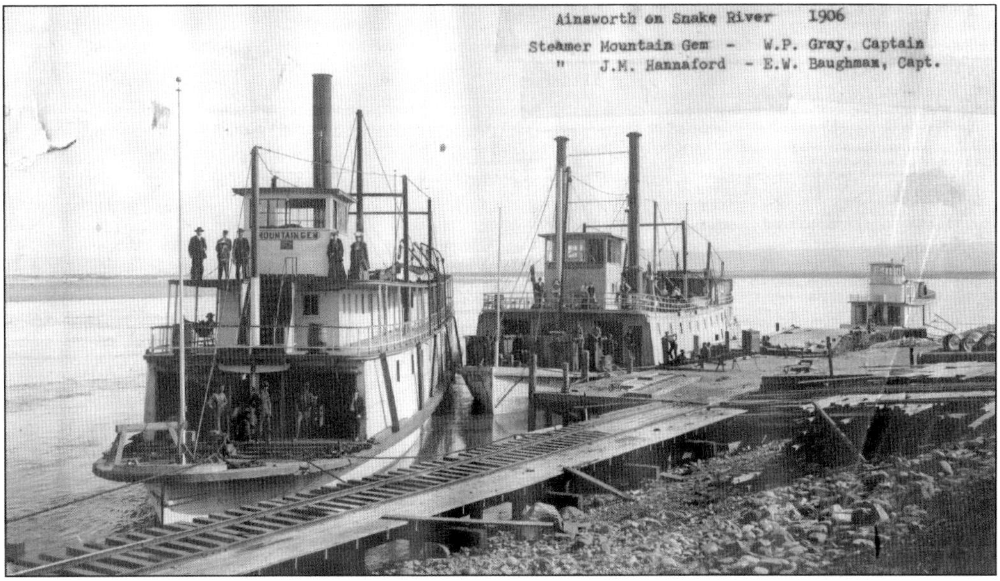

Ainsworth was officially vacated in 1898, but the dock was still used long after the town disappeared. In the early 1910s, it was used as a shipbuilding site. This 1906 photograph shows the *Mountain Gem* and the *J. M. Hannaford*. The sternwheeler in the back is the *Gerome*, awaiting repairs. Looking at the attire of those in this picture, repairs were not the order of this day. (Courtesy of FCHS.)

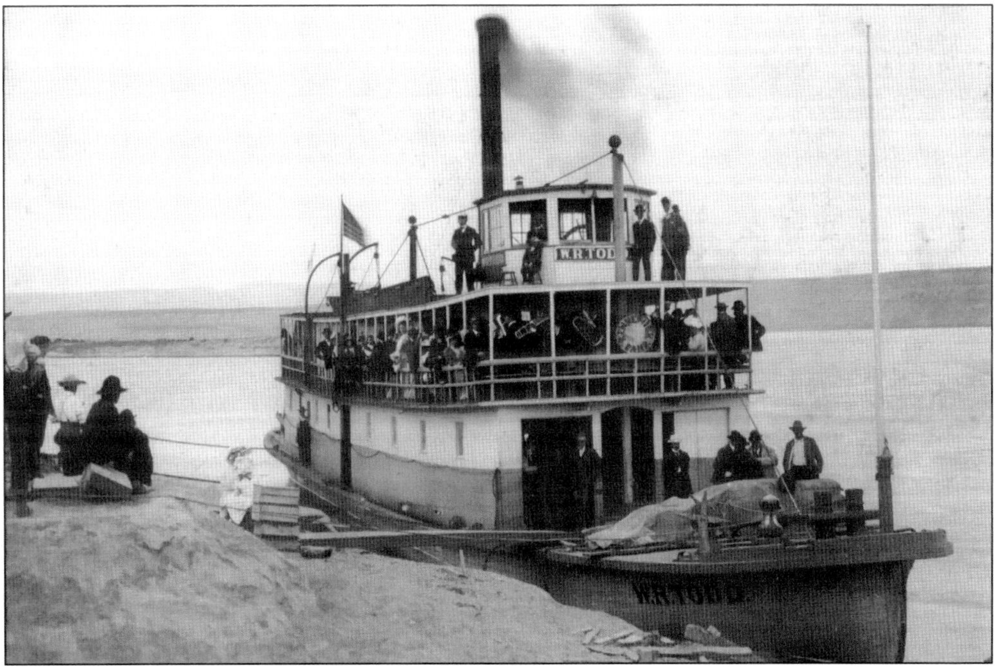

The *W. R. Todd* was built in Ainsworth in 1906. Three riverboats, the *W. R. Todd*, the *Mountain Gem*, and the *Queen City Flyer*, made runs between Hanford and Pasco to deliver mail and transport crops to outside markets. In 1912, the *W. R. Todd*'s steering gear malfunctioned, and the riverboat hit the Northern Pacific Railway bridge and sank. (Courtesy of the U.S. Department of Energy.)

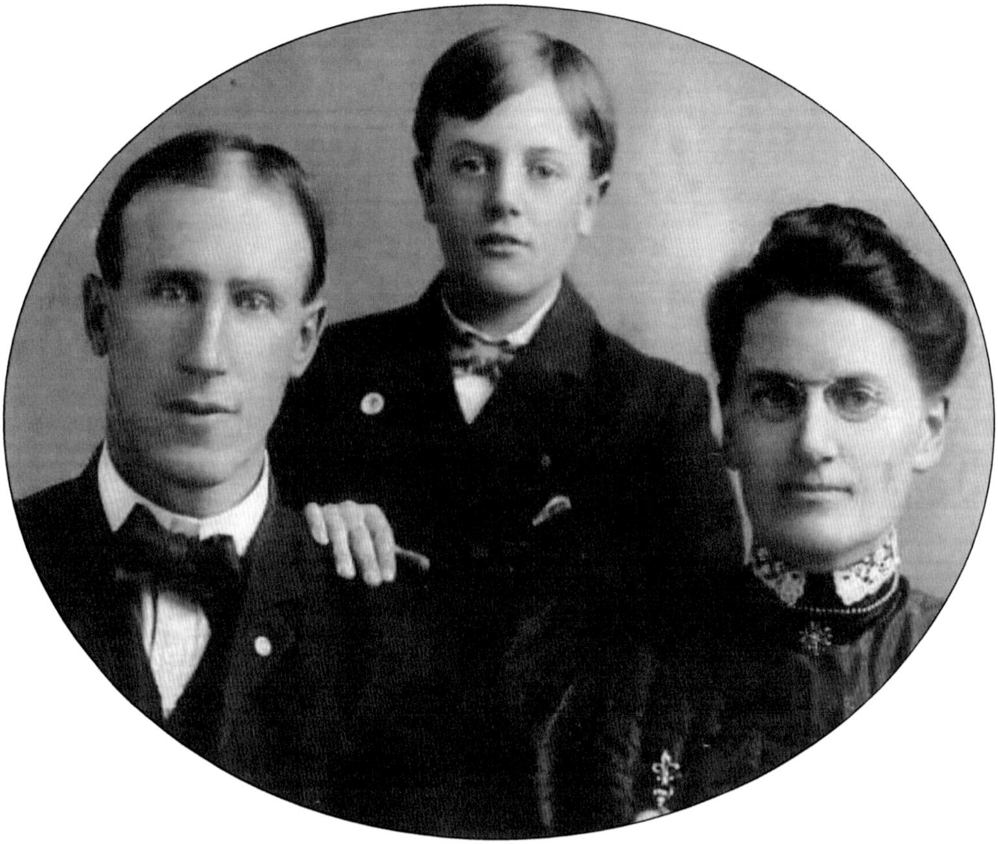

Gustaves and Myrtle Bertholet and their only child, Frank, moved to Pasco from Minnesota in the early 1900s. Myrtle helped organize the American Red Cross and the Pasco Women's Club. Frank graduated from Pasco High School in 1913 and began his military career at West Point in 1917. Col. Frank Bertholet served his country in World War I, World War II, and in the Korean War. (Courtesy of Tina Herbst.)

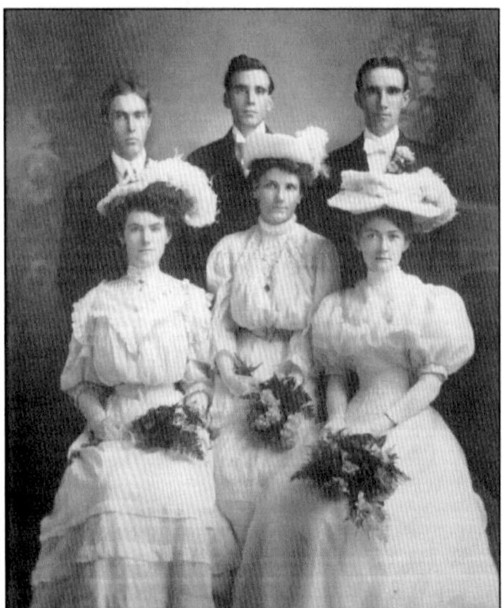

B. B. Horrigan and his bride, Bernice Crotty, are shown on the far right in their 1907 wedding picture. Like many young couples, they celebrated their wedding in Spokane yet made their home in Pasco. B. B. Horrigan was a lawyer involved in irrigation litigation, while Bernice left her teaching career to build a home and to help build the Our Lady of Lourdes Hospital. (Courtesy of FCHS.)

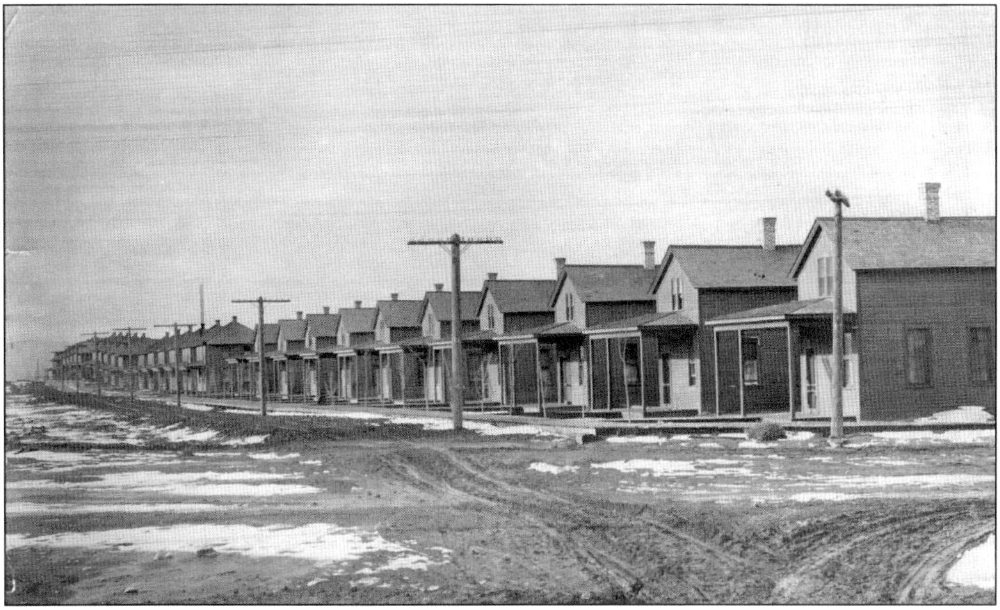

The first five houses in "Red Row" were built by the Northwestern Improvement Company for the Northern Pacific Railway in 1884 as tenements for railroad employees. The need for housing increased, and by 1907, sixteen more houses were added. The railroad houses on A Street were painted the official Northern Pacific Railway colors of Indian Red with Bottle Green trim, thus naming these houses "Red Row." (Courtesy of Dan Stafford.)

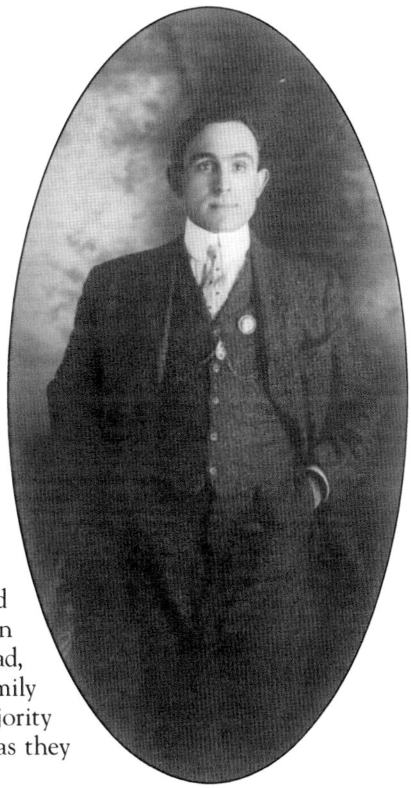

Jesse Keyser was born in 1875 in Pennsylvania. He served his country in the Philippine Insurrection in 1899 as an artificer, or craftsman. After the war, he followed the railroad, which brought him to Pasco. By 1910, he had moved his family to Lind, Washington. Jesse Keyser represents a large majority of hardworking Americans who passed through Pasco as they left their mark on the world. (Courtesy of FCHS.)

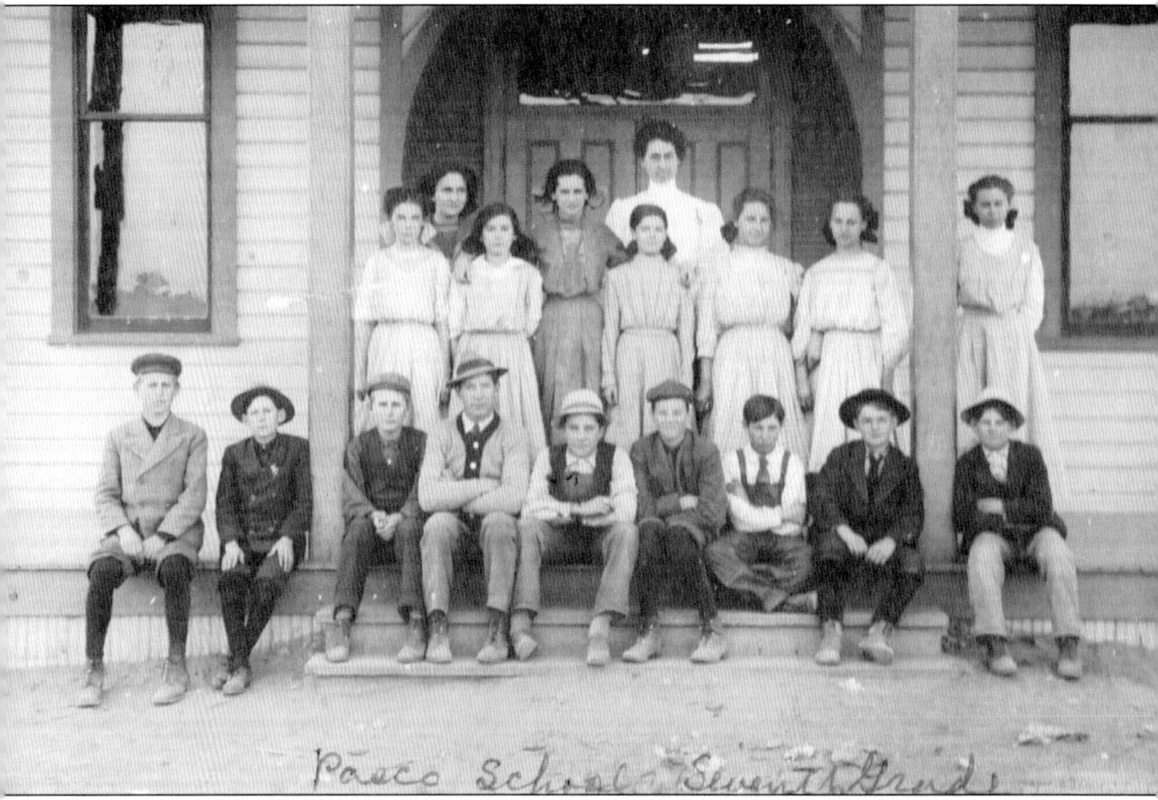

The 1907 seventh-grade class of Pasco School consisted of 17 students from 12 different states. It was obvious that land promoters and railroad land agents were successful in promoting the advantages of living in Pasco. Families moved to Pasco from various areas to take advantage of the promises of inexpensive land and upcoming irrigation. From left to right are (first row) Waldo Klein (California), James Blanton (Colorado), Bernard Sandman (New York), Bill Hays (Washington), Karl Robinson (Oregon), Francis Cole (Montana), Bill Savage (Washington), Paul Browers (birth location unknown), and Fenton Fales (California); (second row) Edna Poindeville (California), Matilda Schrader (Michigan), Blanche Ross (Missouri), Zella Jewell (Idaho), Esther Hogan (Wisconsin), teacher Minnie Small (Iowa), Clara Page (Washington), Eileen Becker (Kansas), and Frankie Wallace (Washington). (Courtesy of FCHS.)

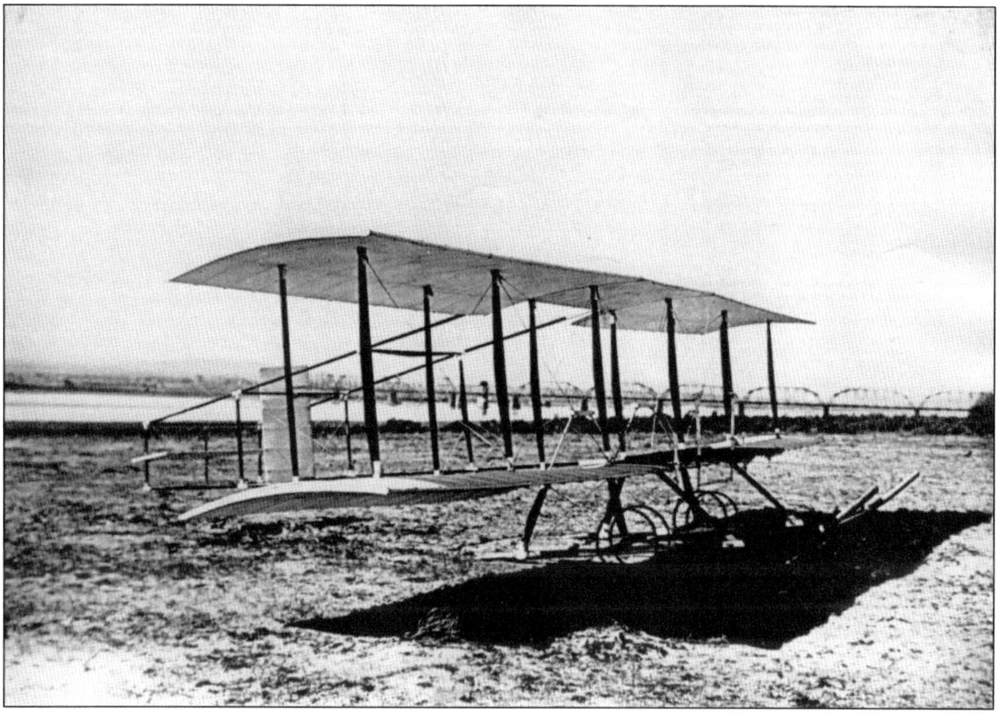

Charles Zornes had an airplane factory, airstrip, and flying school along the Pasco banks of the Columbia River in 1908. When his family moved from St. Louis to Richland, he brought his aviation education with him. He used his skills to build airplanes and teach others the art of flying. The Zornes airport was thought to be the first airport west of the Mississippi River. (Courtesy of FCHS.)

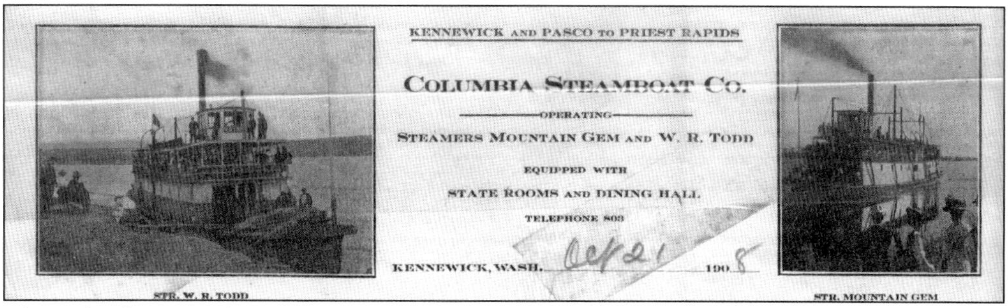

KENNEWICK AND PASCO TO PRIEST RAPIDS

COLUMBIA STEAMBOAT CO.

OPERATING

STEAMERS MOUNTAIN GEM AND W. R. TODD

EQUIPPED WITH

STATE ROOMS AND DINING HALL.

TELEPHONE 803

KENNEWICK, WASH. Oct 21 1908

STR. W. R. TODD

STR. MOUNTAIN GEM

The Columbia Steamboat Company operated the *Mountain Gem* and the *W. R. Todd* in the early 1900s. Their letterhead advertised routes from Kennewick and Pasco, which were across the river from each other, to Priest Rapids, which was almost 100 miles away. Staterooms and a dining hall were advertised as being available to passengers. (Courtesy of Dan Stafford.)

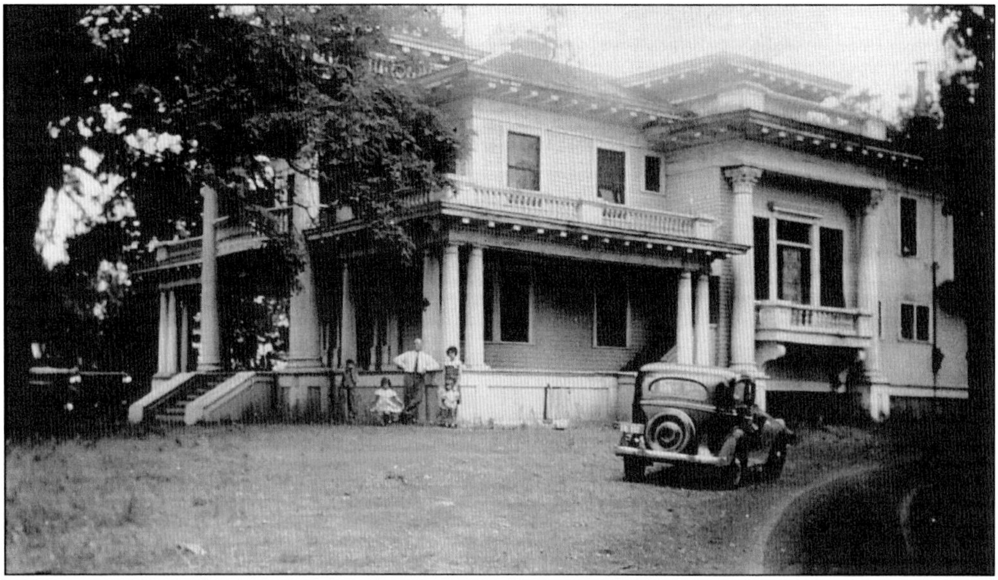

The Moore Mansion was built in 1908 by James A. Moore of Seattle. Moore's wife suffered from tuberculosis. The dry climate of Pasco promised to be a cure. Moore built the beautiful home on the Columbia River with thoughts of moving his family to Pasco. Mrs. Moore died months before the home was completed. In 1911, it was sold to Thomas Carstens. (Courtesy of Brad and Debra Peck.)

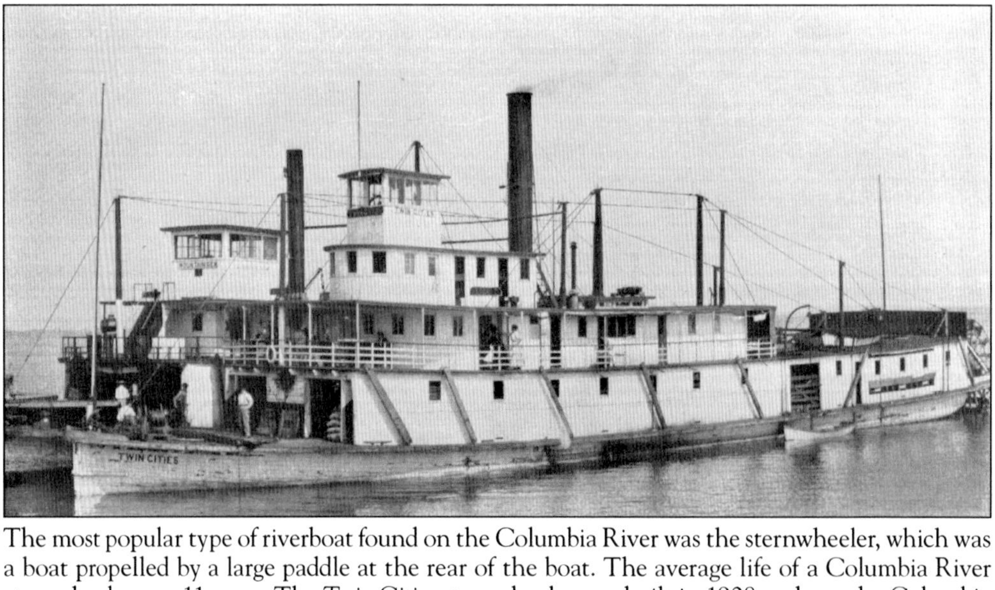

The most popular type of riverboat found on the Columbia River was the sternwheeler, which was a boat propelled by a large paddle at the rear of the boat. The average life of a Columbia River sternwheeler was 11 years. The *Twin Cities* sternwheeler was built in 1908 and ran the Columbia River until 1931, which was twice as long as most of the Columbia River sternwheelers. (Courtesy of the Franklin County Irrigation District.)

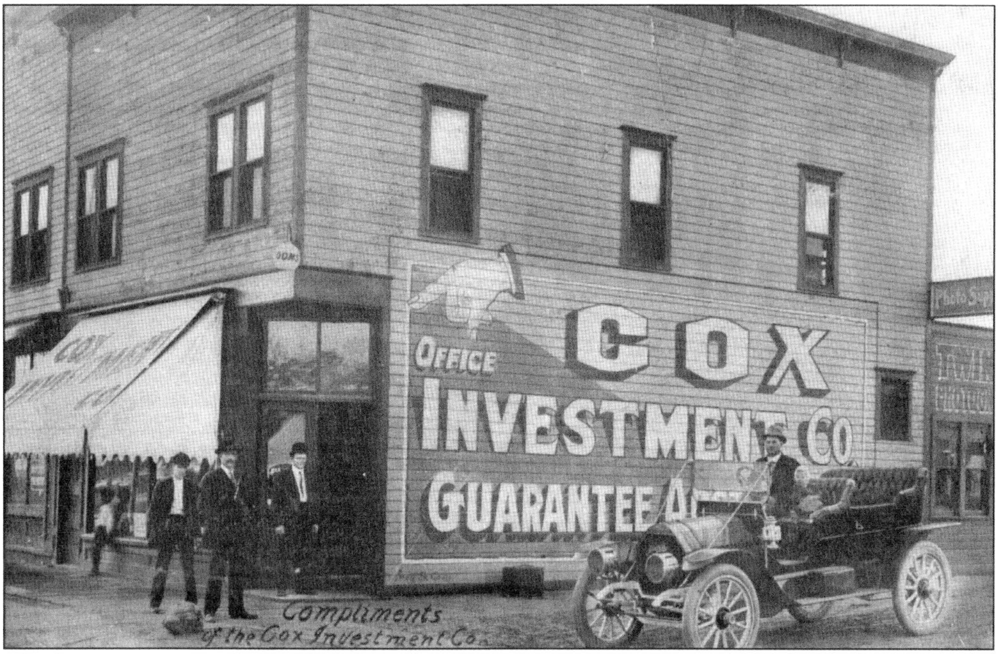

Cox Investment Company was situated on the corner of Fourth and Lewis Streets. This 1909 photograph shows the dirt roads and wooden sidewalks common to Pasco during that time. Volney B. Cox, owner of the company, is shown seated in the touring car next to his son Howard. Herman Warden, clerk, is standing in the doorway. (Courtesy of Dan Stafford.)

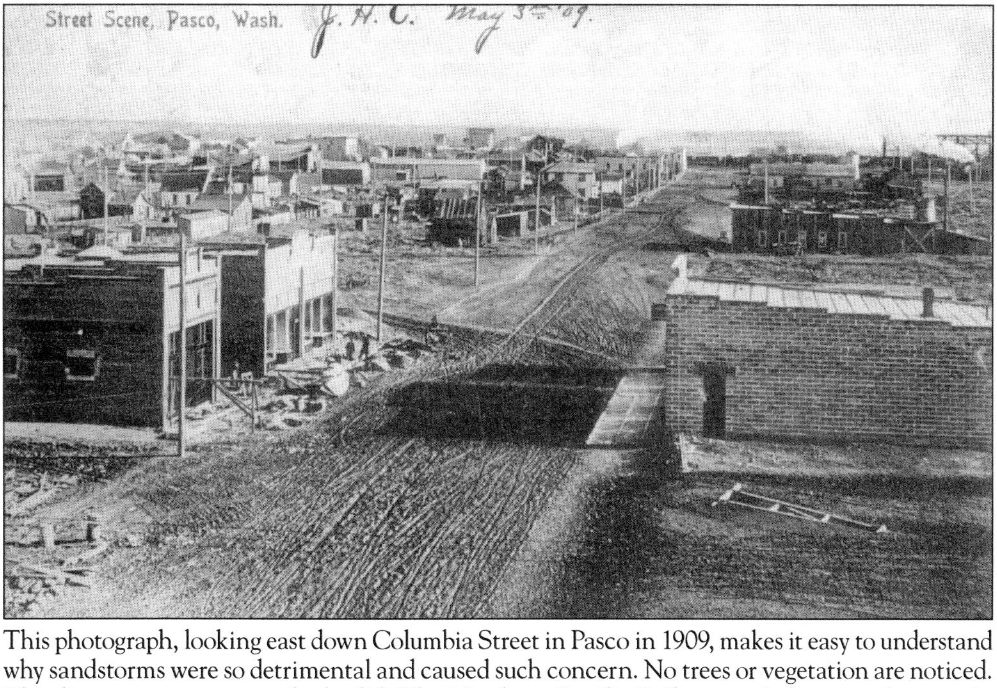

This photograph, looking east down Columbia Street in Pasco in 1909, makes it easy to understand why sandstorms were so detrimental and caused such concern. No trees or vegetation are noticed. The dirt streets are not packed solid. The Northern Pacific Railway coal chute can be seen in the distance at the right. At the very end of Columbia Street, the first Knights of Pythias hall can also be seen. (Courtesy of Dan Stafford.)

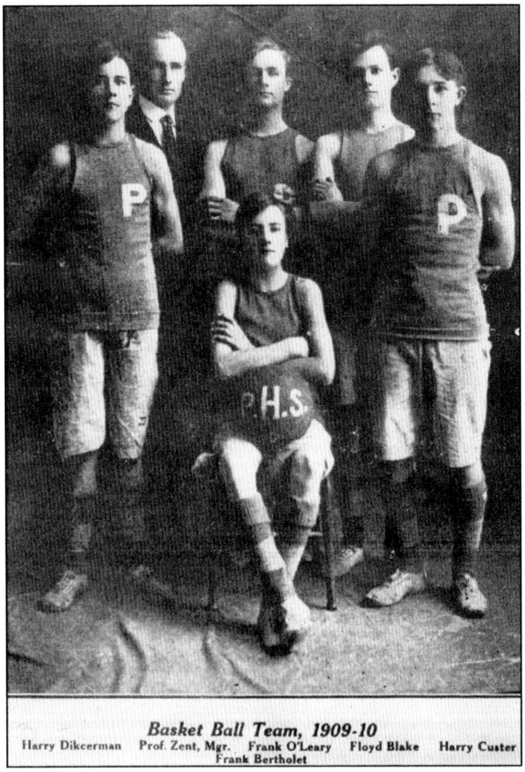

Pasco High School's first athletic team was the basketball team of 1909–1910. The high school's annual reported, "The visiting teams were always ready to smile at the end of the first half, and to grin at the end of the game." The team members pictured from left to right are (first row center) Frank Bertholet; (second row) Harry Dickerman, Prof. George W. Zent, Frank O'Leary, Floyd Blake, and Harry Custer. (Courtesy of FCHS.)

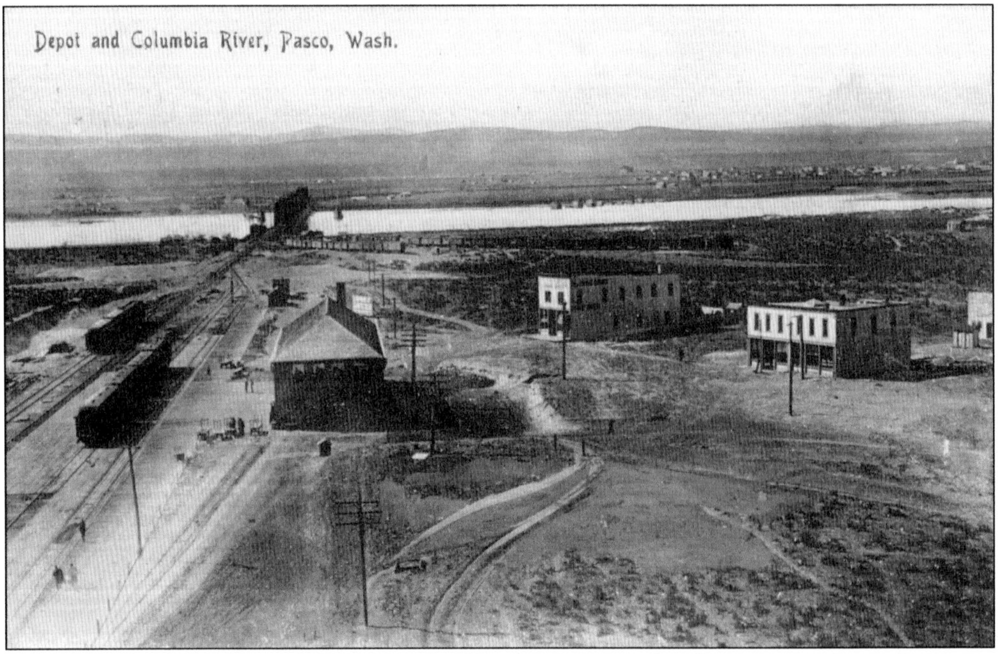

Pasco was well known for its sand and sagebrush. This picture, taken before 1910, shows the barren land that Pasco pioneers made home. The Columbia River looms in the background between the towns of Kennewick and Pasco. Businesses were built near the railway depot yet far enough away that walking through the dirt streets was necessary. (Courtesy of Dan Stafford.)

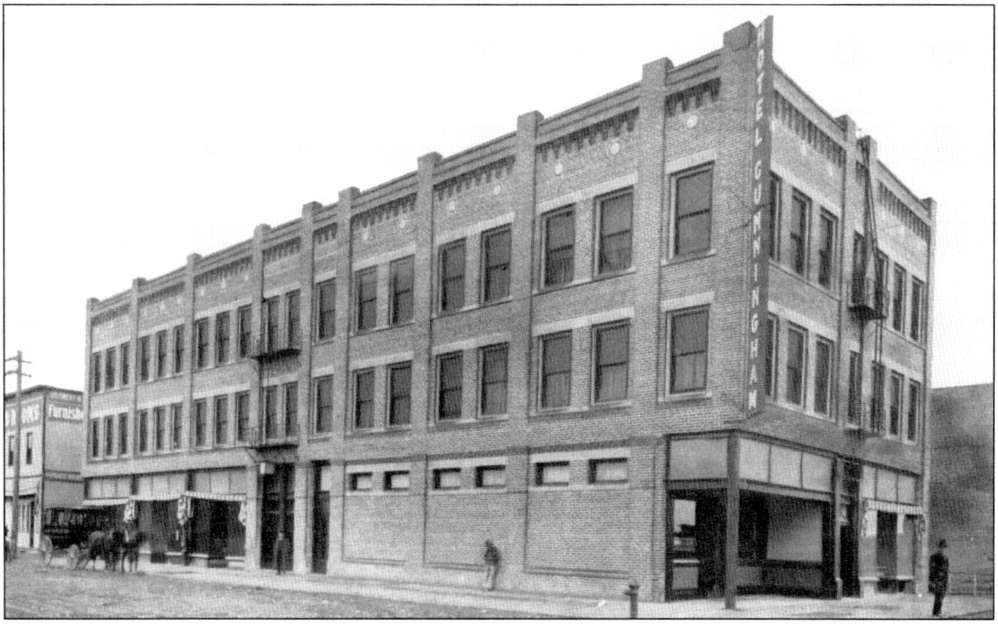

The Hotel Cunningham was built in 1909 by wealthy sheep king Charles Cunningham. The hotel was well built and ornately furnished, including steel ceilings. Construction costs were approximately $100,000. Many of Pasco's hotels were demolished by fire in the early 1910s, but the Hotel Cunningham stood the test of those times. (Courtesy of the Franklin County Irrigation District.)

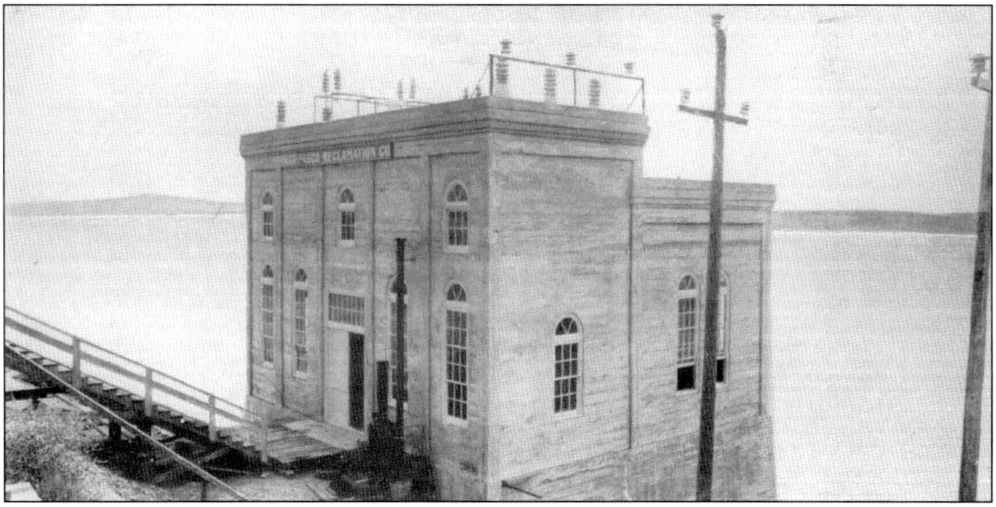

The Pasco Reclamation Company built the Snake River pumping plant in 1909 about 3 miles north of the old town site of Ainsworth. The footings were built on the rock bed of the river, which reached 22 feet below ground. This pumping plant was considered innovative for that time as a result of the installation of multiple pumps and transformers used to minimize outages. (Courtesy of the Franklin County Irrigation District.)

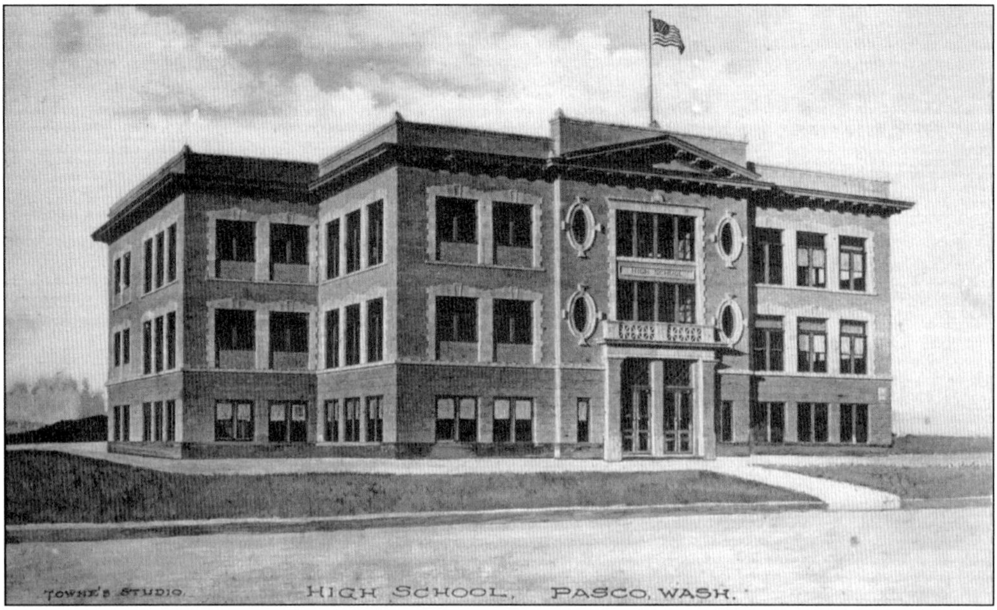

The West Side School, later named the Longfellow School after Henry Wadsworth Longfellow, was built in 1909 for $9,000 by William Oliver. Land adjoining the school was sold to the public in an auction held in May 1910. This school was used as a combination grade and high school until 1921, when a new high school was built on North Third Street. (Courtesy of Dan Stafford.)

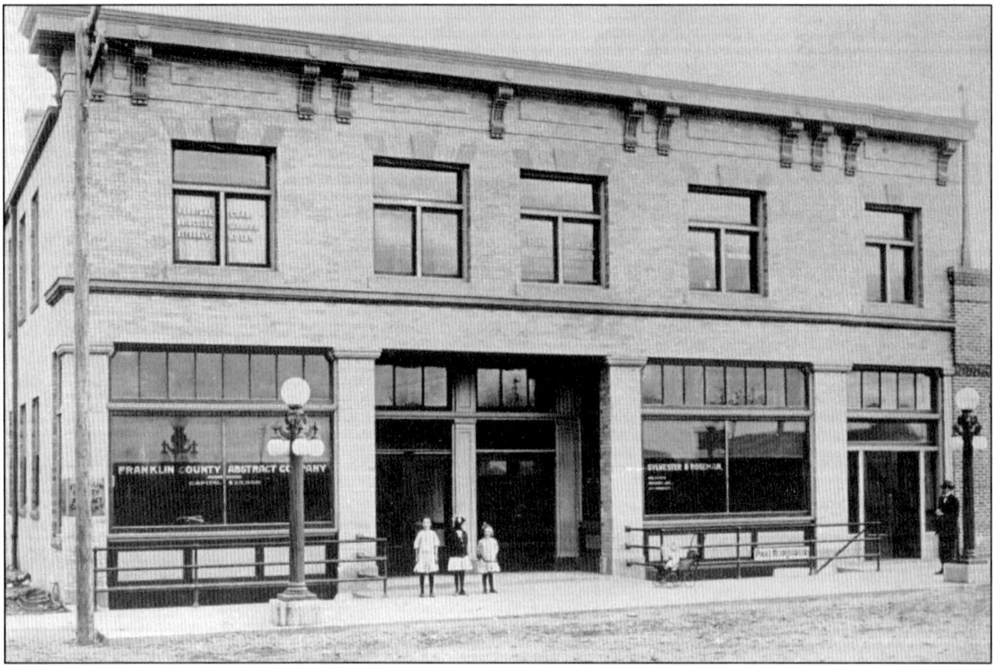

Many offices conveniently shared space in the Title and Trust Building on the 400 block of West Lewis Street in 1910, when this picture was taken. Sylvester and Roseman, Real Estate Agents, shared the first floor with the Franklin County Abstract Company. On the second floor, attorneys Horrigan and Driscoll shared space with a surveyor and doctor. The basement was reserved for the Pasco police headquarters. (Courtesy of FCHS.)

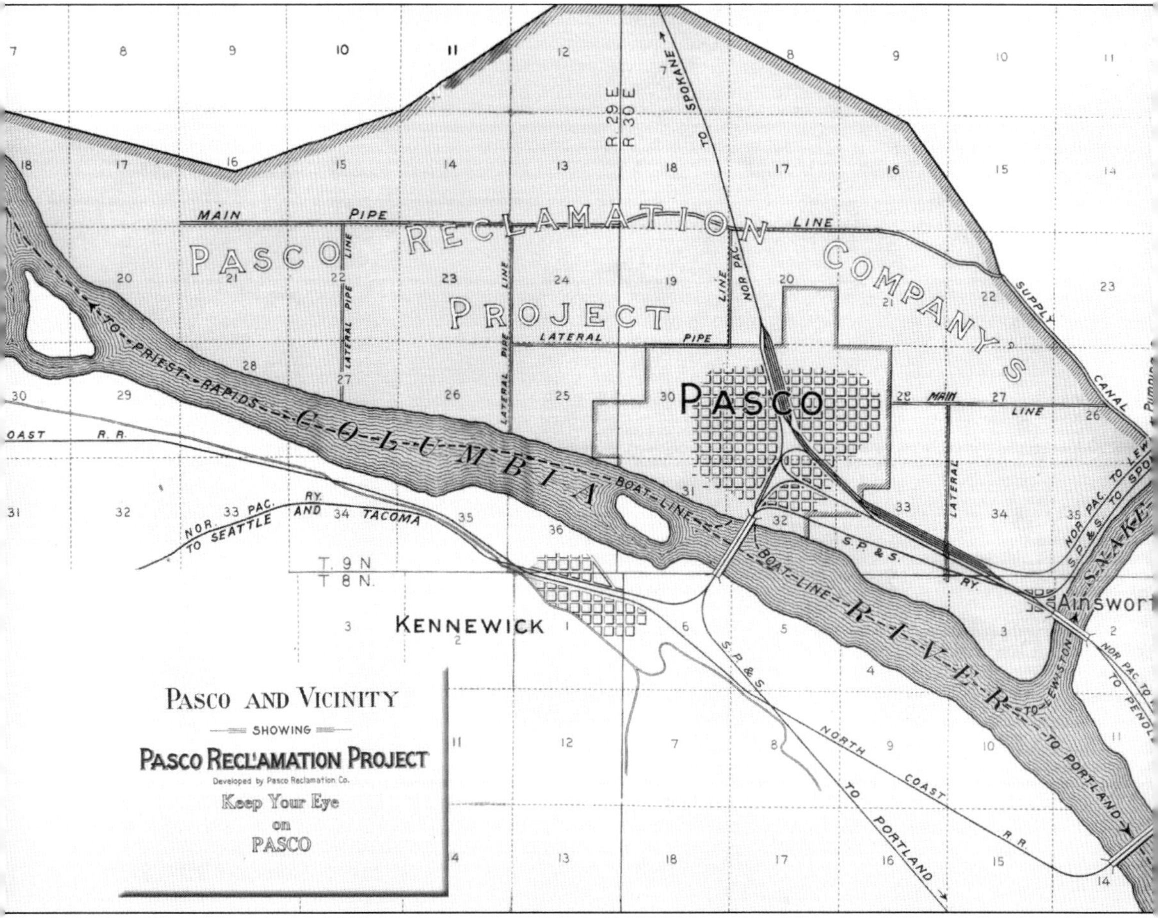

Pasco's rich soil brought many farmers to the area in the late 1890s. Dry-land farming was attempted and found difficult because of the approximately 8 inches of annual precipitation accumulated in the arid climate. Water was plentiful in the rivers surrounding the community, but bringing the water from the river for irrigation was arduous. Several individuals and small groups attempted various methods to obtain the river water, yet all failed. The Pasco Reclamation Company, incorporated in 1909, was one of the first successful irrigation ventures. Above is a map showing the Snake River pumping station on the far right and various water lines used to feed irrigation water through the community. Due to continuous problems of water leakage, the Pasco Reclamation Company went into receivership in 1917. The Franklin County Irrigation District was formed in 1918 to purchase the Pasco Reclamation Company. (Courtesy of the Franklin County Irrigation District.)

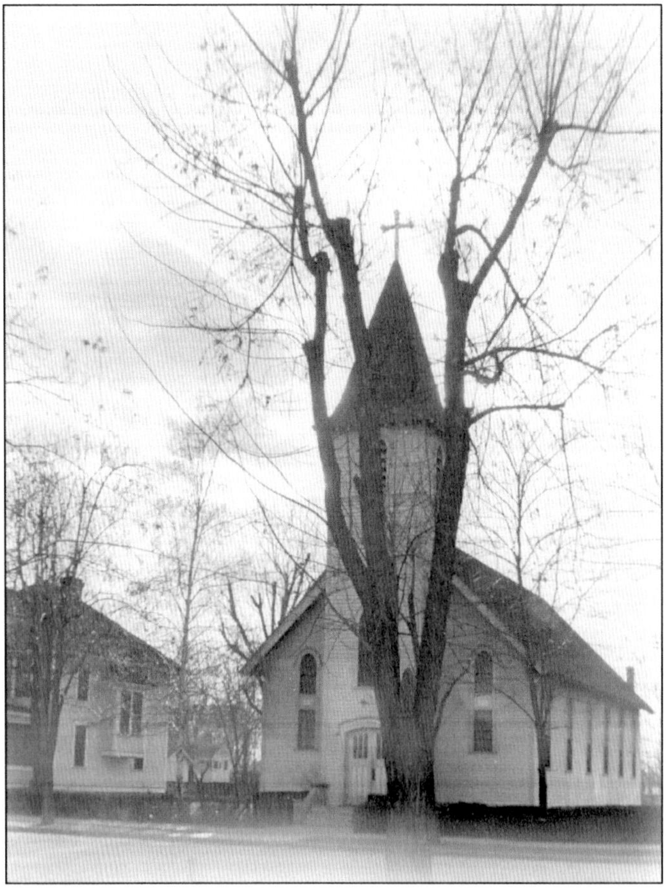

The first official religious leader in Pasco was Fr. E. Frederick in 1908. His ministry covered Sunnyside to Connell and Wallula to Priest Rapids. With the congregation from the Pasco area, he built the first Catholic church in the area, St. Patrick's Church, which was located at Fourth and Sylvester Streets. St. Patrick's Church held its first service in the fall of 1910. (Courtesy of FCHS.)

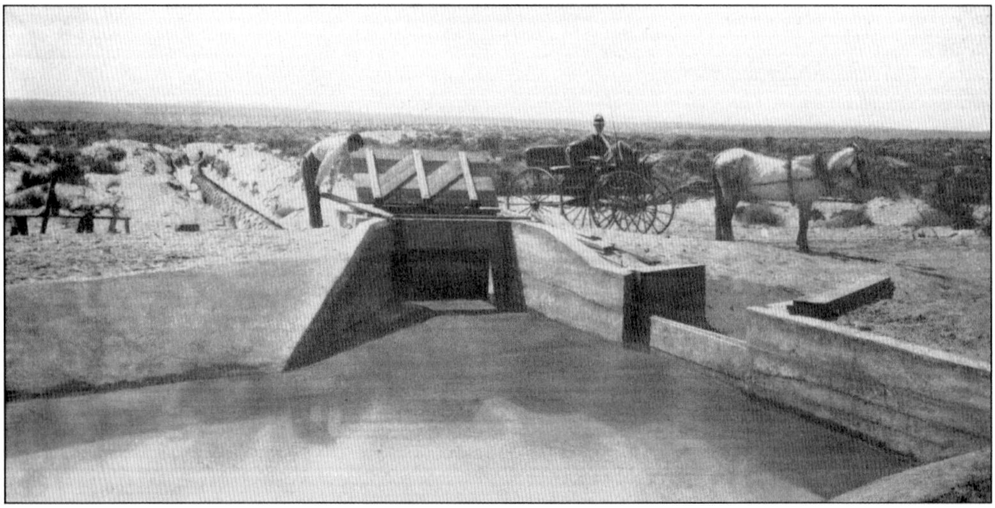

A reservoir was built in 1910 to hold water obtained from the Snake River pumping plant. This reservoir was 2.5 miles long and was northwest of the pump house. It held enough water to supply the area it served for 12 hours should the pump house fail. This photograph shows the main artery that supplied the majority of the water leaving the reservoir. (Courtesy of the Franklin County Irrigation District.)

Four

Early Pasco Boom Years
1911 to 1920

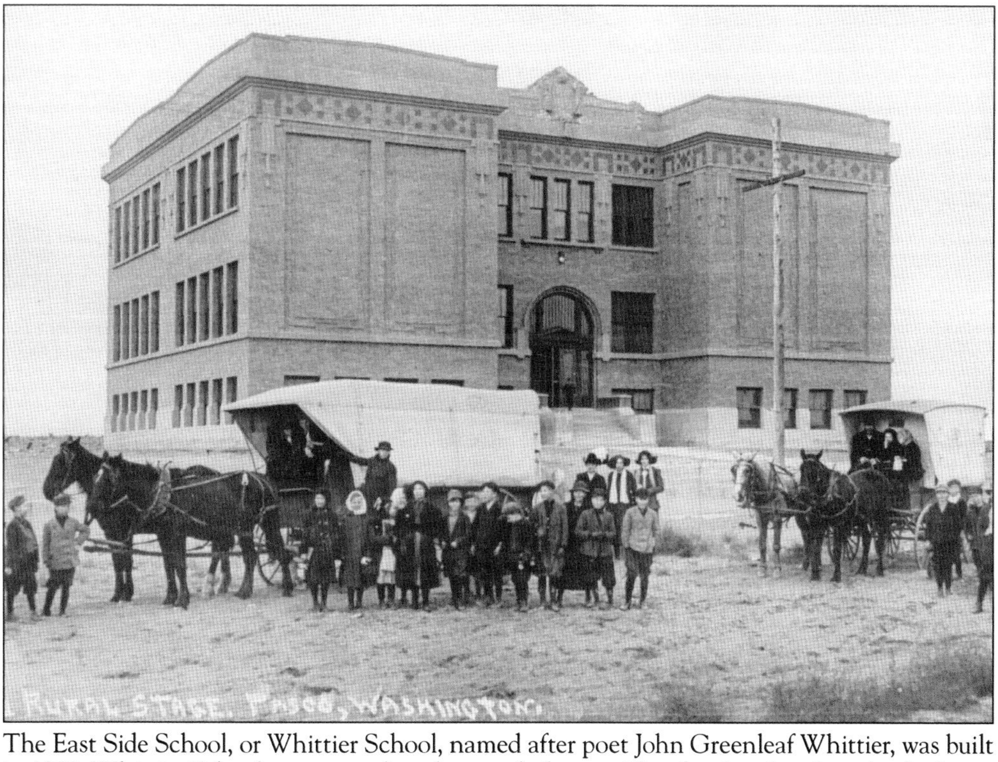

The East Side School, or Whittier School, named after poet John Greenleaf Whittier, was built in 1912. Whittier School was remembered not only for providing hot lunches, but also for being the first school in the state of Washington to provide transportation. Here H. A. Smull is shown with his school buses. He was paid $75 a month to transport children to and from Whittier School. (Courtesy of Dan Stafford.)

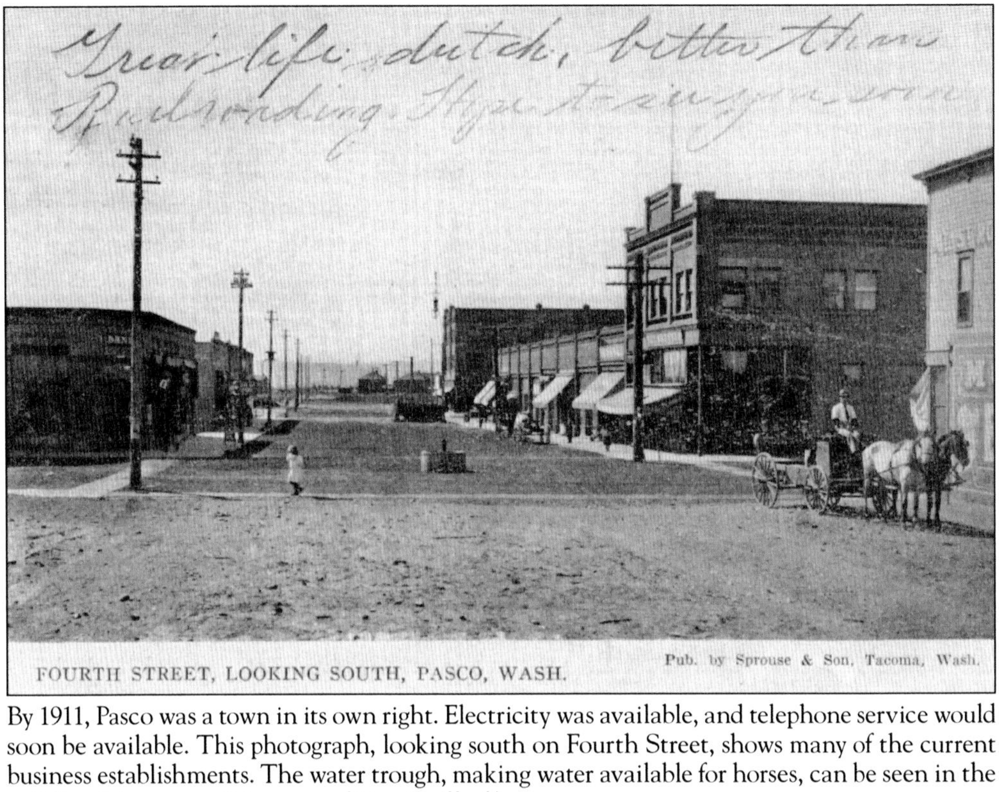

By 1911, Pasco was a town in its own right. Electricity was available, and telephone service would soon be available. This photograph, looking south on Fourth Street, shows many of the current business establishments. The water trough, making water available for horses, can be seen in the middle of the street. (Courtesy of Dan Stafford.)

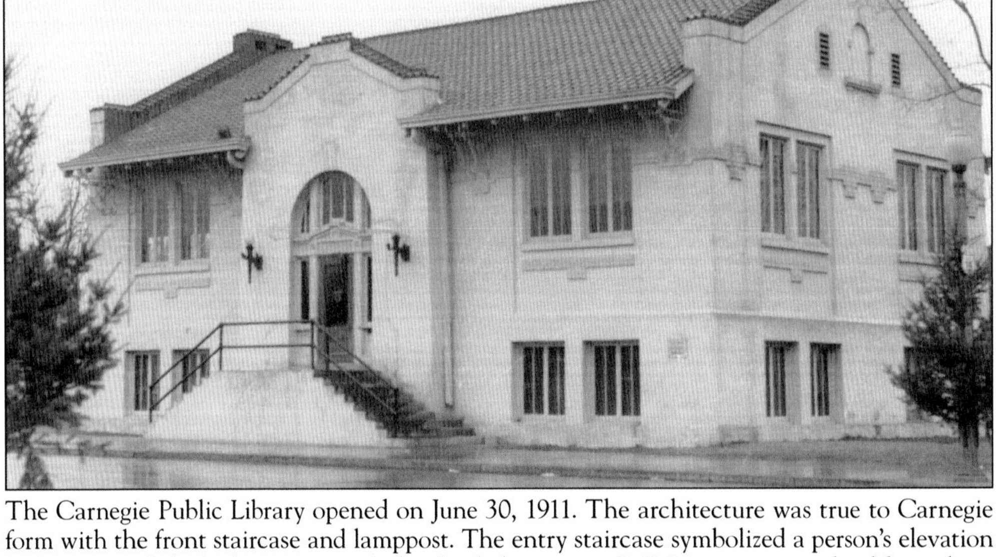

The Carnegie Public Library opened on June 30, 1911. The architecture was true to Carnegie form with the front staircase and lamppost. The entry staircase symbolized a person's elevation by learning, while the lamppost symbolized enlightenment. B. B. Horrigan is credited for making the first contact with Andrew Carnegie. The first board members were Maggie Page, Alice D. Jahnke, Bernice Horrigan, Walter T. Ricks, and Patrick Lenard. (Courtesy of FCHS.)

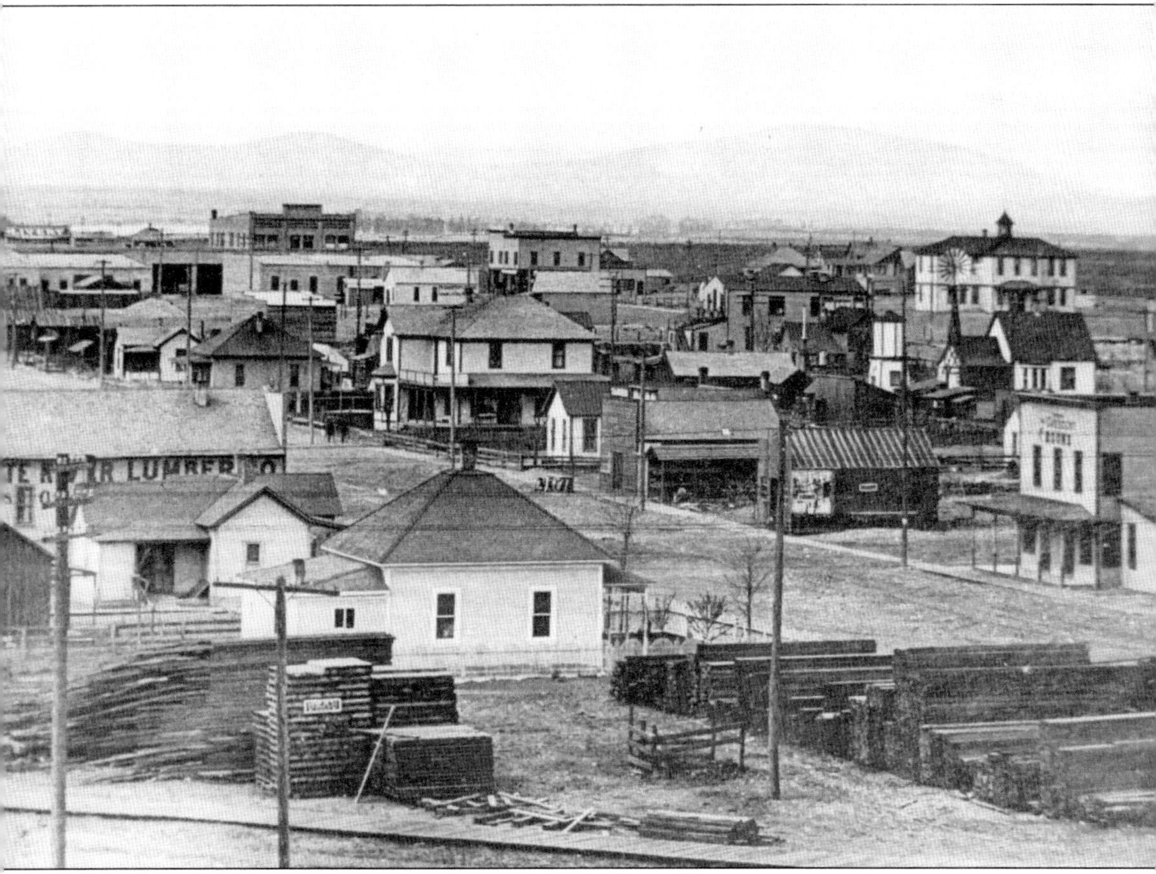

As homes and businesses relocated from Ainsworth to Pasco, debates started over the location of the new town in relation to the Northern Pacific Railway track. Many believed Pasco should be on the west side of the tracks, while others promoted the east side. Areas of Pasco were referred to as the East Side, West Side, and even the South Side. This picture of early Pasco shows the west side. (Courtesy of FCHS.)

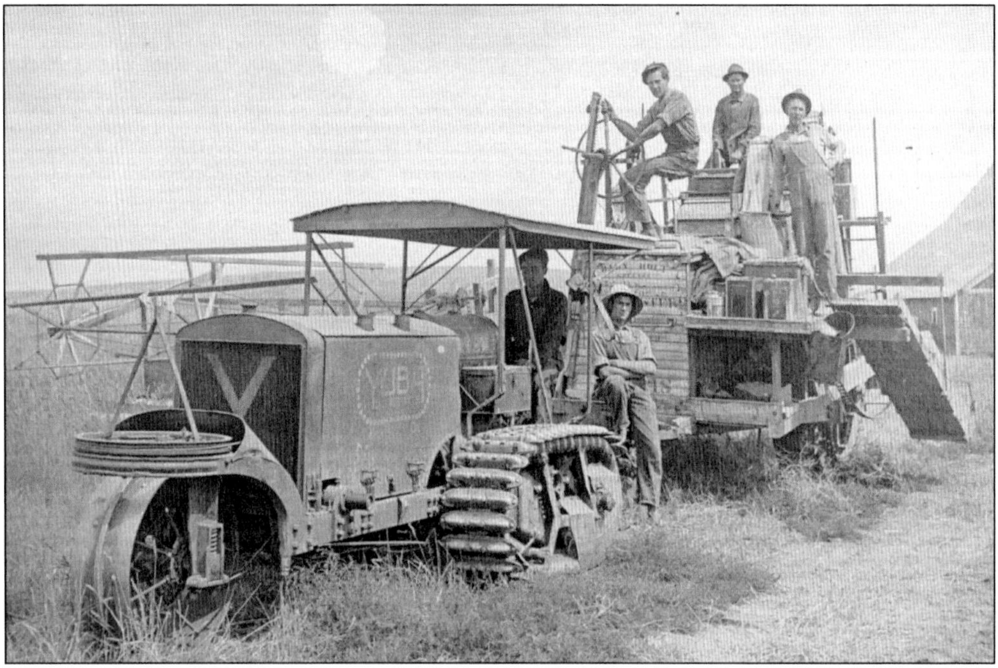

This Yuba tractor had a ball-bearing track system that pulled a Holt combine. Combines were used to cut, thresh, clean, and sack grain. Earlier models were drawn by as many as 40 horses. Mechanical engineering brought farming into a new era in Pasco in the early 1910s. By 1925, Holt Manufacturing merged with C. L. Best Tractor Company to form Caterpillar Tractor Company. (Courtesy of FCHS.)

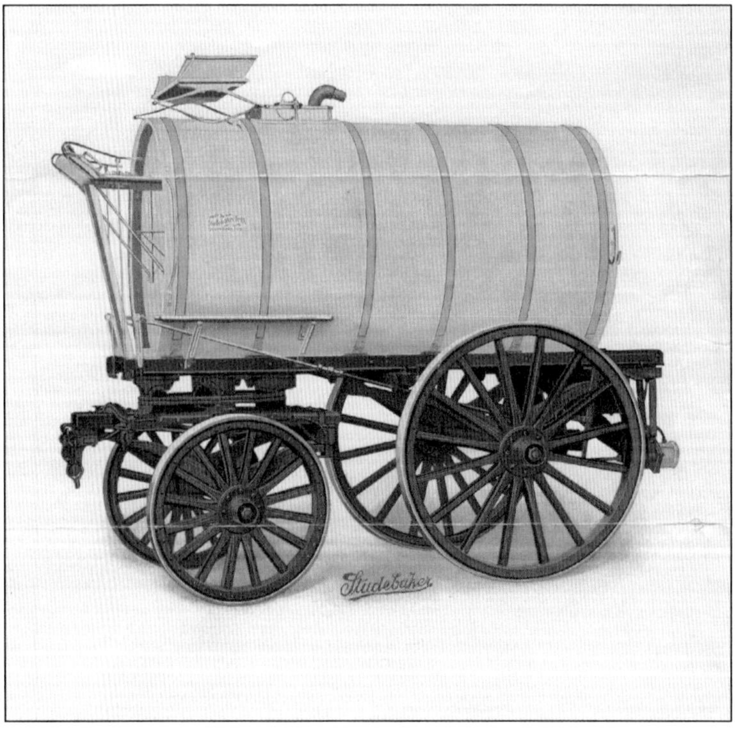

The city of Pasco resolved to install grading, streets, and sidewalks in 1912. In anticipation of this action, two Studebaker sprinklers, model 252, were purchased from Kerfoot Hardware Company for a total of $725 in May 1911. Mayor William Polk Gray signed the Kerfoot contract, which was attested by City Clerk L. H. Koontz. (Courtesy of Washington State Archives, Central Regional Branch.)

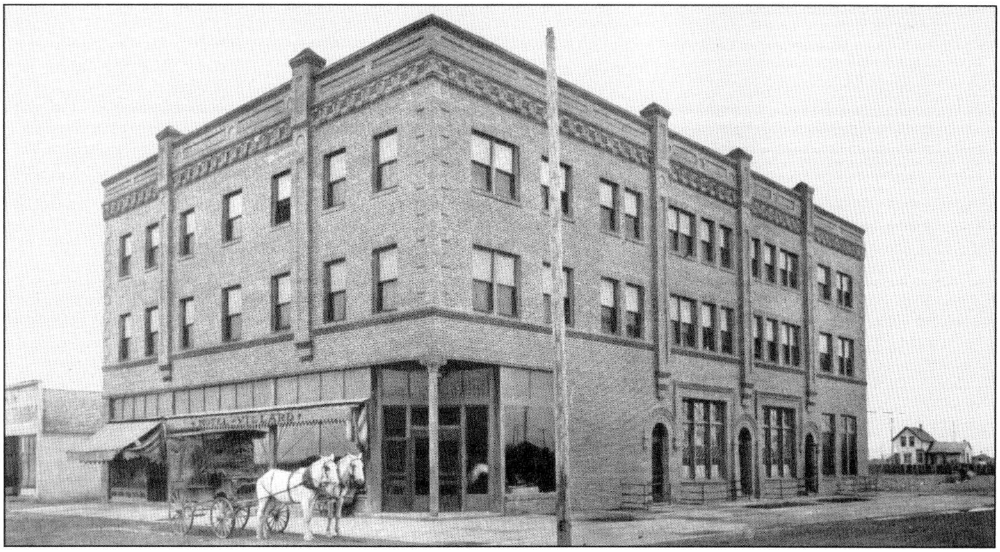

One of most prestigious hotels in Pasco at the turn of the century was the Hotel Villard, named for Northern Pacific Railway's president, Henry Villard. It was an impressive three-story brick building with white tablecloths adorning the tables of the Grill Room. Patrons were met at the railroad depot by a white two-horse team. These luxuries came standard for a nightly rate of $1 in 1911. (Courtesy of the Franklin County Irrigation District.)

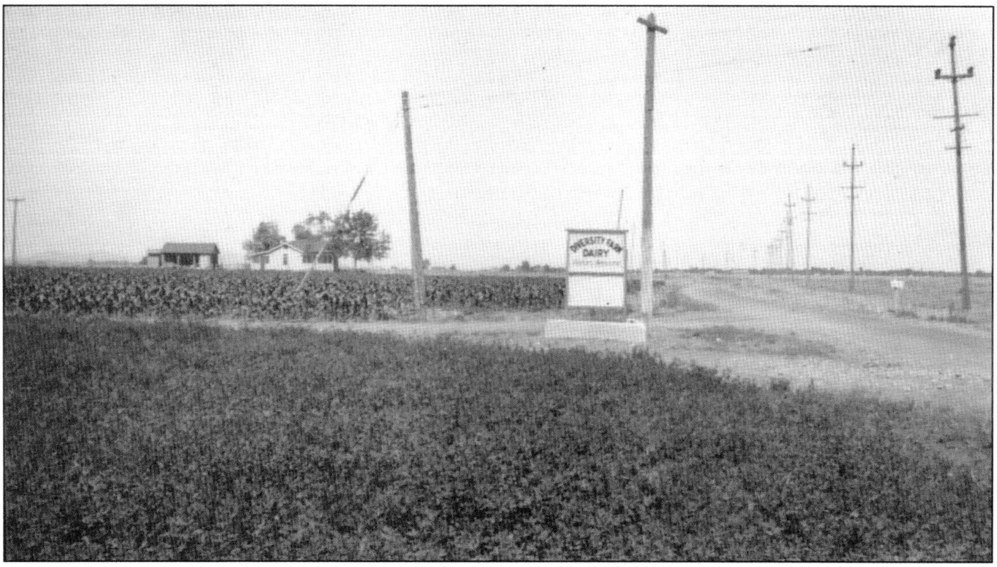

The Diversity Farm was built and run by Fred and Lura Harris, who were married in 1912 and spent the next 30 years creating a showcase of agricultural prosperity. From the Diversity Farm, their family ran a milk route that delivered not only dairy products but also various poultry items, fresh orange juice, cuts of meat, and seasonal vegetables to their customers' doors. (Courtesy of the Harris family.)

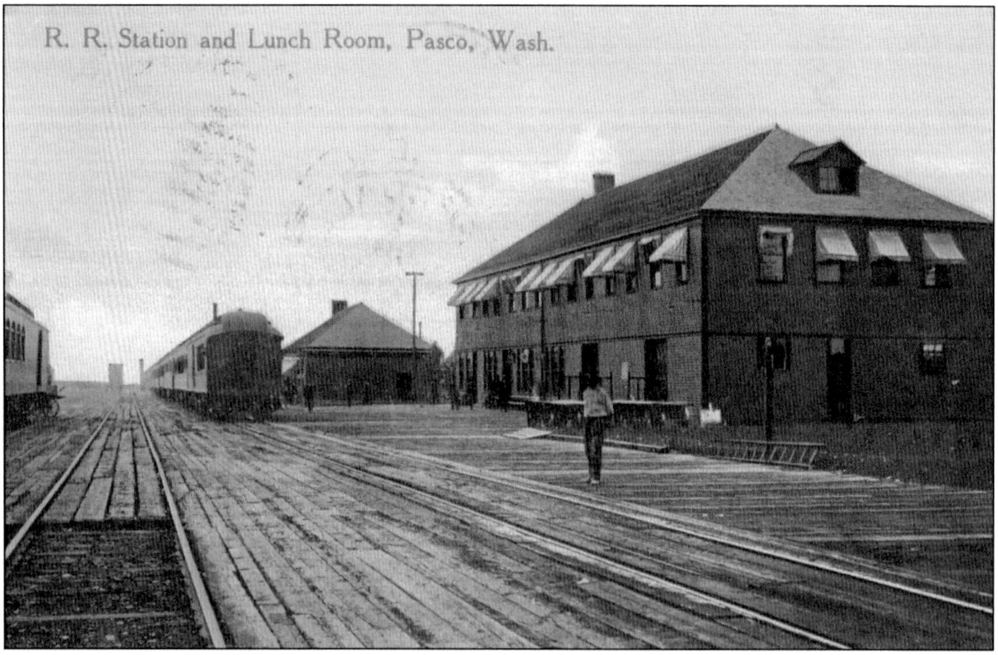

The second Pasco depot, built in 1912, was an impressive two-story building. It was not built on the same site as the first depot, but rather around the corner on Fourth Street. Shortly after building this depot, the Northern Pacific Railway built the Clubhouse, which was used for railroad employees to rest between shifts. (Courtesy of Dan Stafford.)

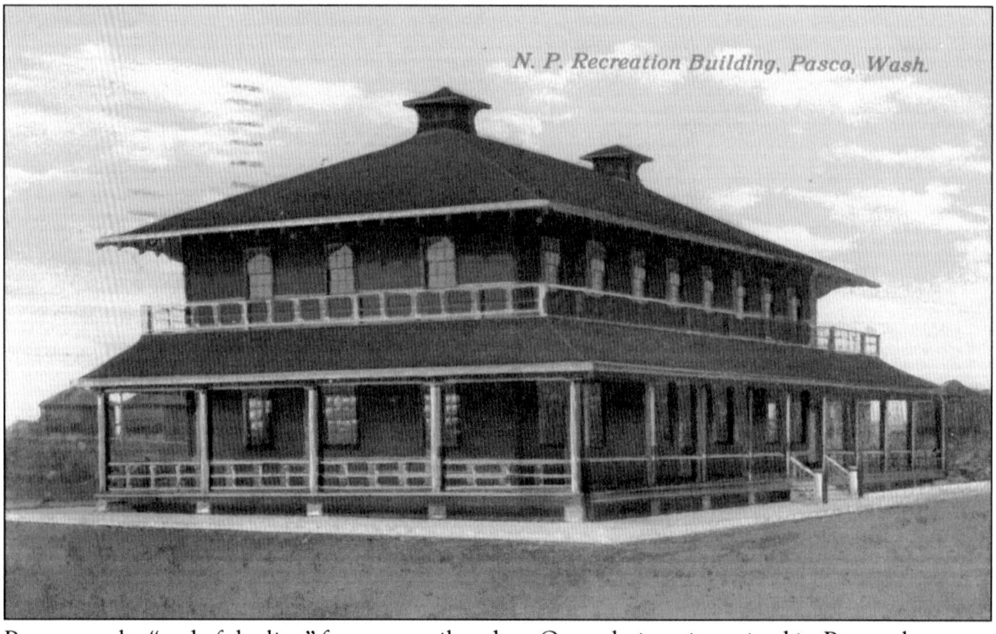

Pasco was the "end of the line" for many railroaders. Once their train arrived in Pasco, they were required to rest before their next shift. The Northern Pacific Railway provided this hotel and recreation center for railroaders to sleep and socialize during their layovers. It was located on South Fourth Street across from the Northern Pacific Railway depot. (Courtesy of Dan Stafford.)

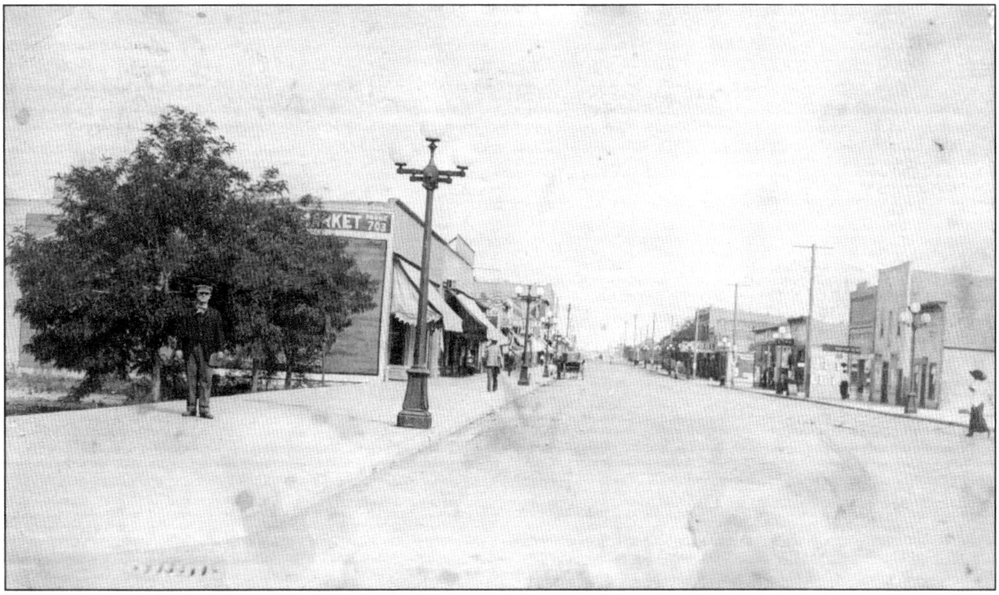

By 1912, Pasco's city streets were starting to look more civilized and finished. This image proudly displays electric streetlights and telephone poles along the sidewalk-lined street. Landscaping was also a consideration. Unlike many photographs of Pasco at this time, a tree graces the left side of this photograph. (Courtesy of Dan Stafford.)

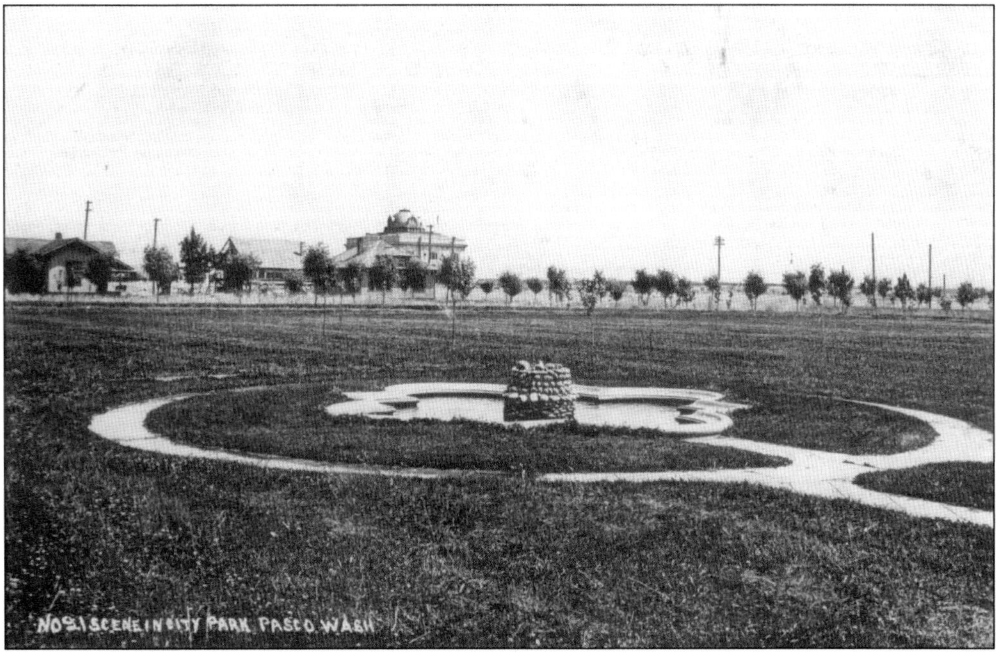

In 1889, Dieu Donne Sylvester homesteaded 160 acres. In 1912, he purchased adjoining land from the Northern Pacific Railway. Large amounts of this combined land were given to the city of Pasco for public use. This photograph is of Sylvester Park, which was developed as a playground for the children of Pasco. (Courtesy of Dan Stafford.)

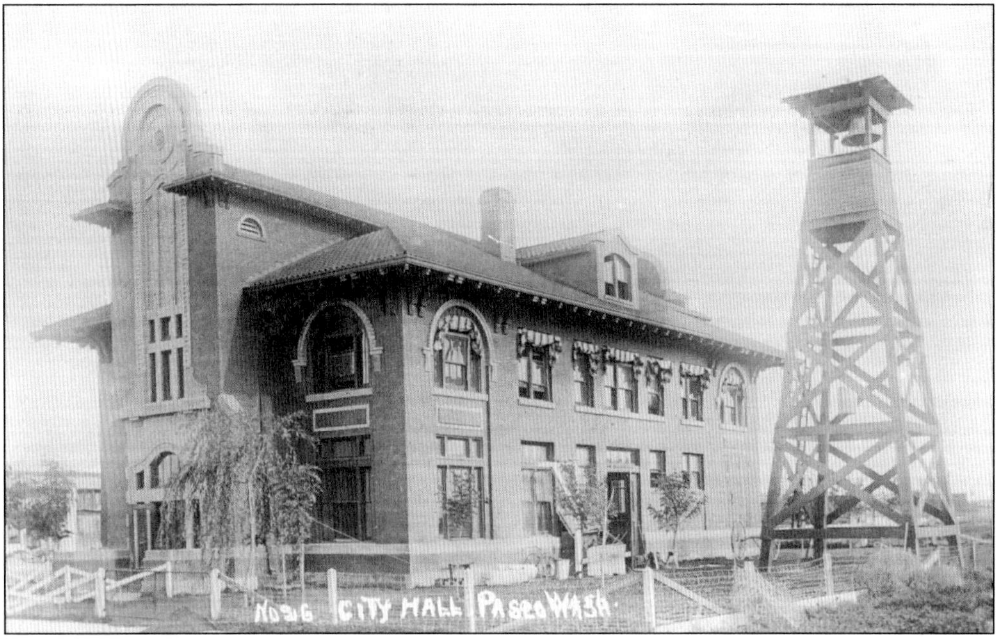

The year 1912 was one of building and growth in Pasco. Population had increased dramatically in a short period of time. Improvements were necessary, but there was concern about the financial obligations that a community of 2,500 could bear. One of the community improvements built in 1912 was the city hall and fire bell tower, which cost $30,000. (Courtesy of Dan Stafford.)

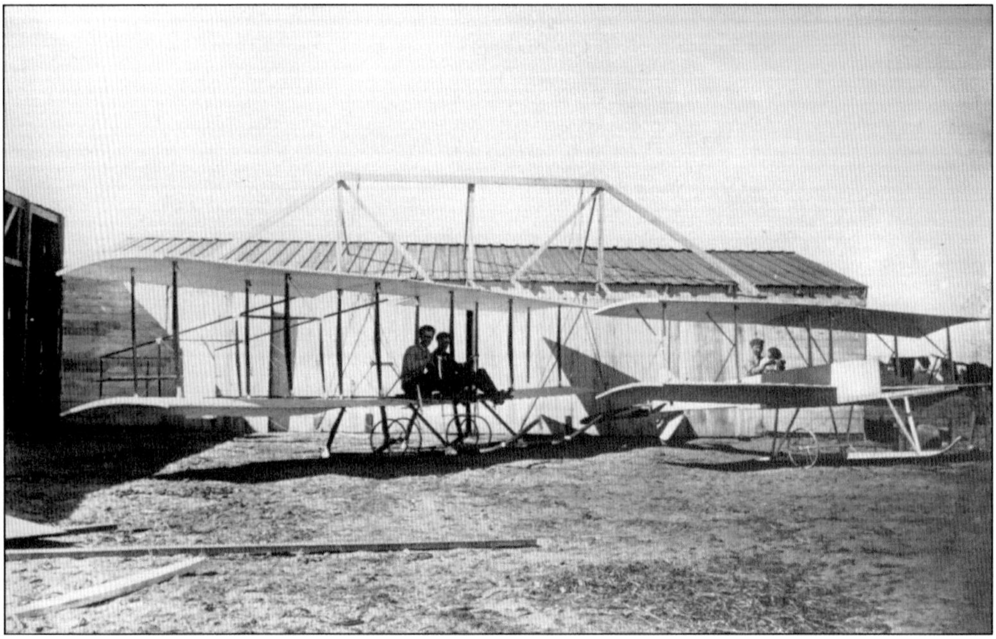

Zornes Aviation Company was incorporated by Charles Zornes, Johnny Ludwig, J.E. Steffins, Dr. E. F. White, and R. C. Schriever with articles of incorporation sent to the Secretary of State in March 1912. The company was formed to manufacture airplanes, which included necessary practice flights. These two-passenger biplanes were used for instruction. Charles and his wife, Bessie, were both aviators. Their son Aero was born in 1909. (Courtesy of FCHS.)

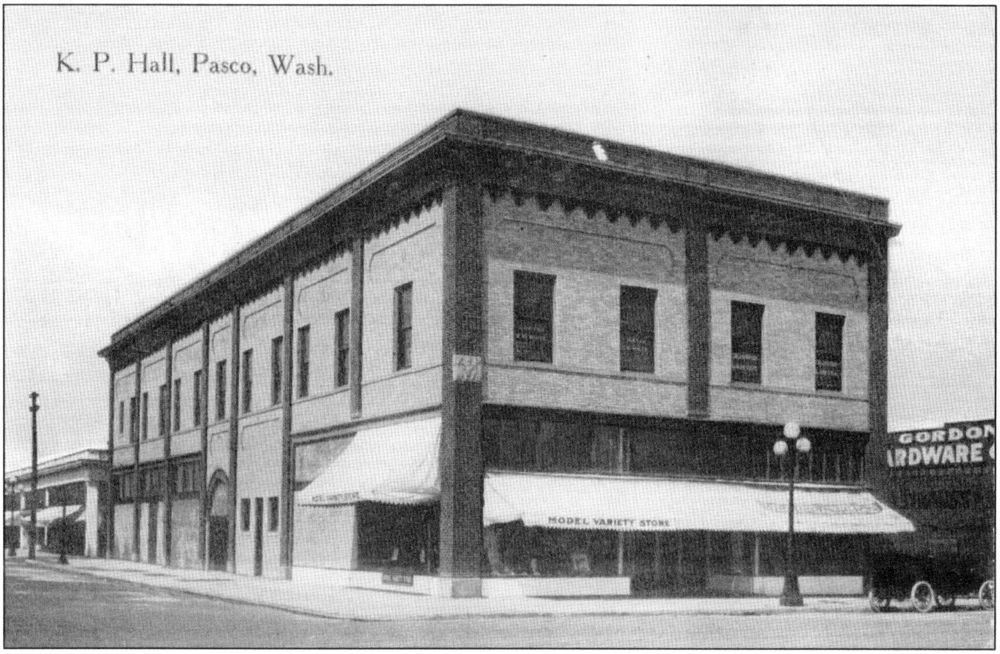

The Knights of Pythias started their second lodge, the Castle Hall Association of Pasco, around 1912. This lodge built their hall on the west side of the Northern Pacific Railway tracks at Third and Lewis Streets. The Franklin Lodge Number 60 deeded land for this building to the Castle Hall Association for "one dollar and other good and valuable consideration." (Courtesy of Dan Stafford.)

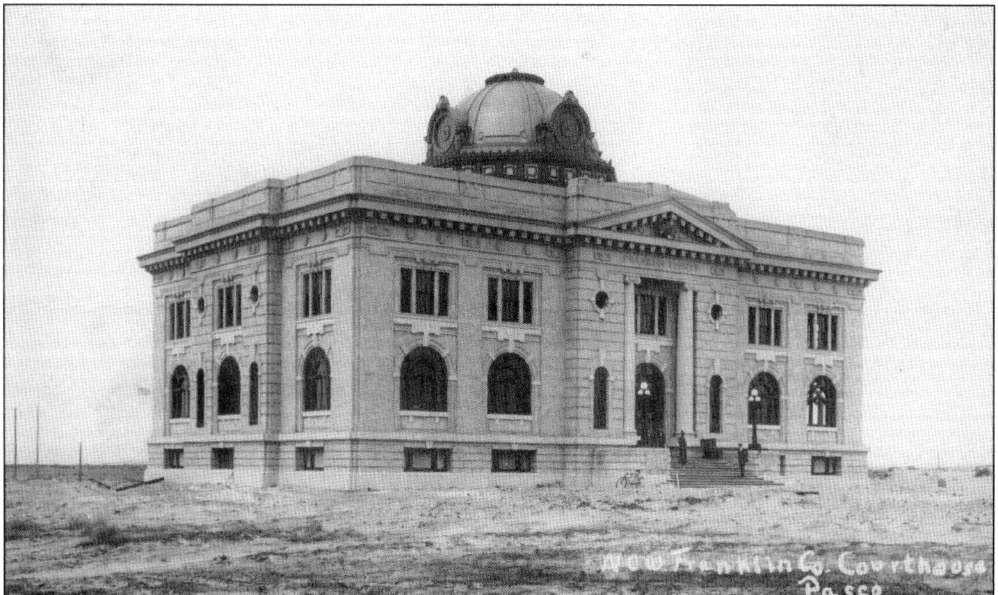

Franklin County's third courthouse was built in Pasco in 1913 on land donated by the Sylvester family. The balances of funds needed for construction were raised by bond issues. The first courthouse was built in the town of Ainsworth in 1883 and moved to Pasco in 1887, making it both the first and second county courthouse. (Courtesy of Dan Stafford.)

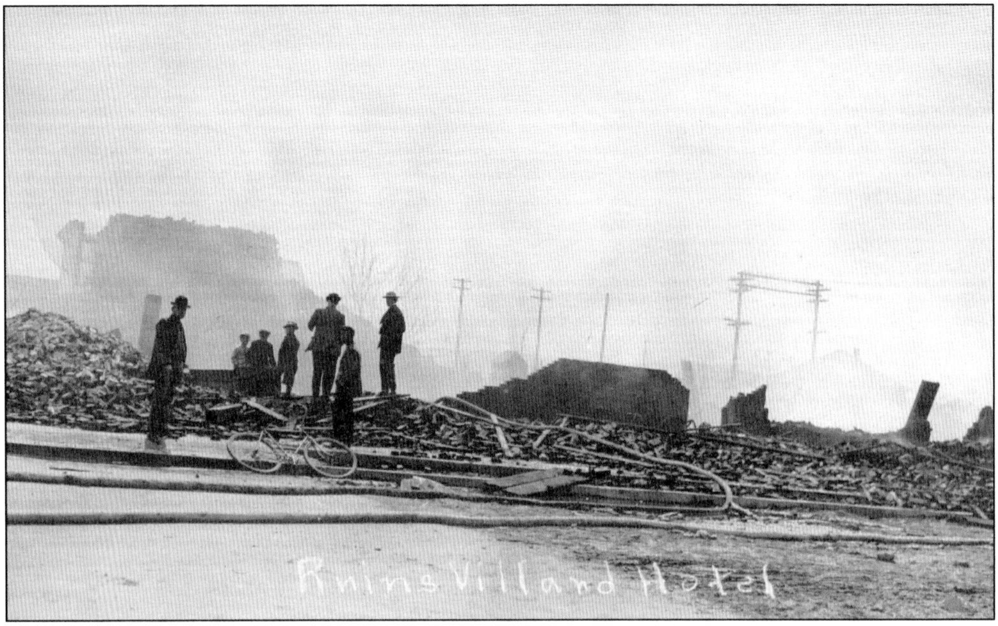

The Hotel Villard was located at Fourth and Columbia Streets. It burned the morning of April 13, 1913, which was the day the Franklin County Courthouse was dedicated. Even though the courthouse dedication banquet had to be relocated at the last minute due to the fire, the dedication festivities went on as planned and overshadowed this catastrophic event. (Courtesy of Dan Stafford.)

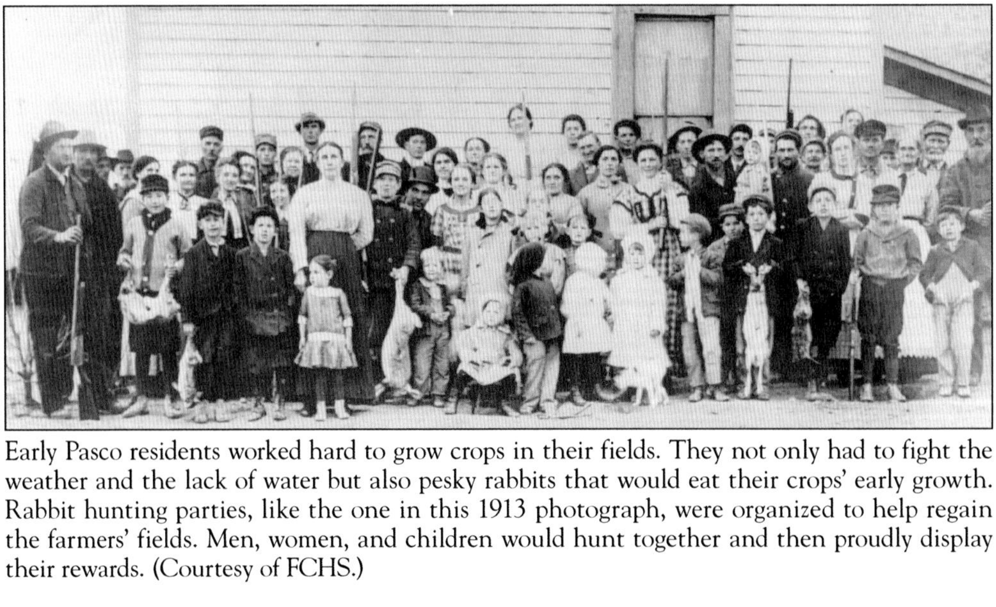

Early Pasco residents worked hard to grow crops in their fields. They not only had to fight the weather and the lack of water but also pesky rabbits that would eat their crops' early growth. Rabbit hunting parties, like the one in this 1913 photograph, were organized to help regain the farmers' fields. Men, women, and children would hunt together and then proudly display their rewards. (Courtesy of FCHS.)

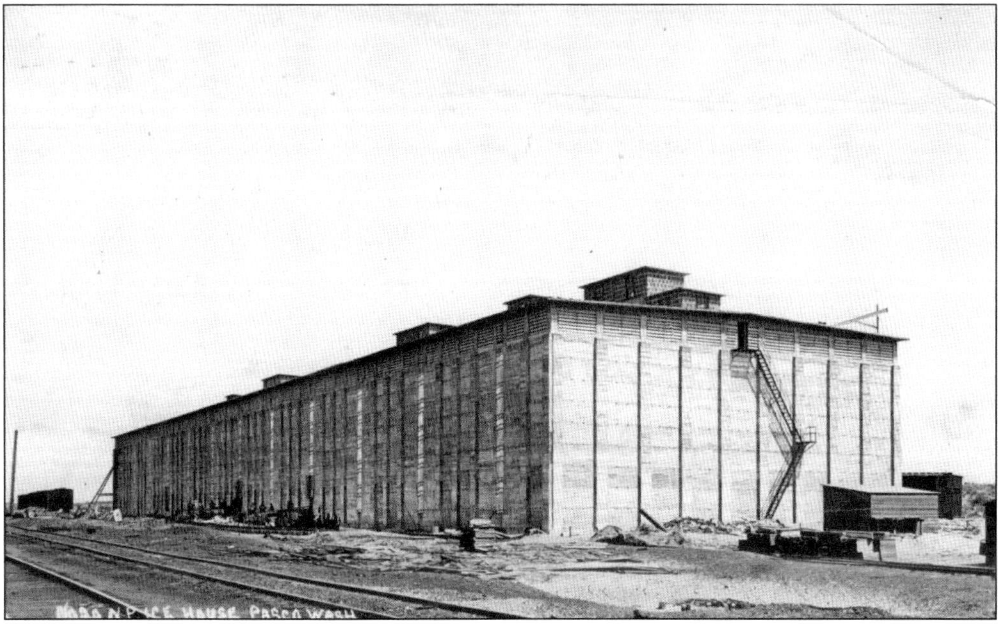

The Northern Pacific Railway icehouse was built in 1913, after a fire in the previous year destroyed the existing icehouse. The new icehouse could store 40,000 tons of ice. Ice was manufactured at a rate of 125 tons daily to supplement tons of ice brought in from Cocolalla Lake in northern Idaho. Individual railroad cars transporting perishables required as much as thirty 400-pound blocks of ice as they passed through Pasco. (Courtesy of Dan Stafford.)

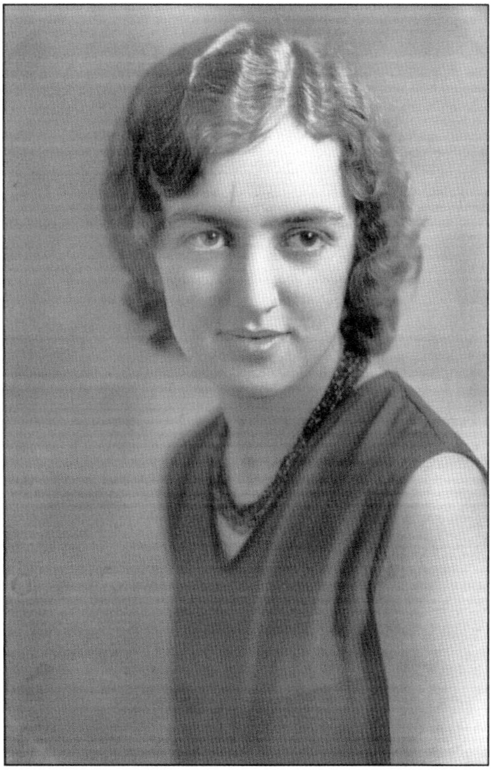

The *Woman's Home Companion* magazine cosponsored Better Babies Contests to address the high infant mortality rate. Contestants were measured for physical and intellectual development against a healthy predetermined standard. In 1914, eight of the 101 winners were from Pasco. At right is one of Pasco's winners, Catherine Landt, shown as a young adult. Other winners were Frances Avery, Grace Avery, Gertrude Austin, Lois Hawkins, Earl Munger, Clair Prescott, and William Sylvester. (Courtesy of FCHS.)

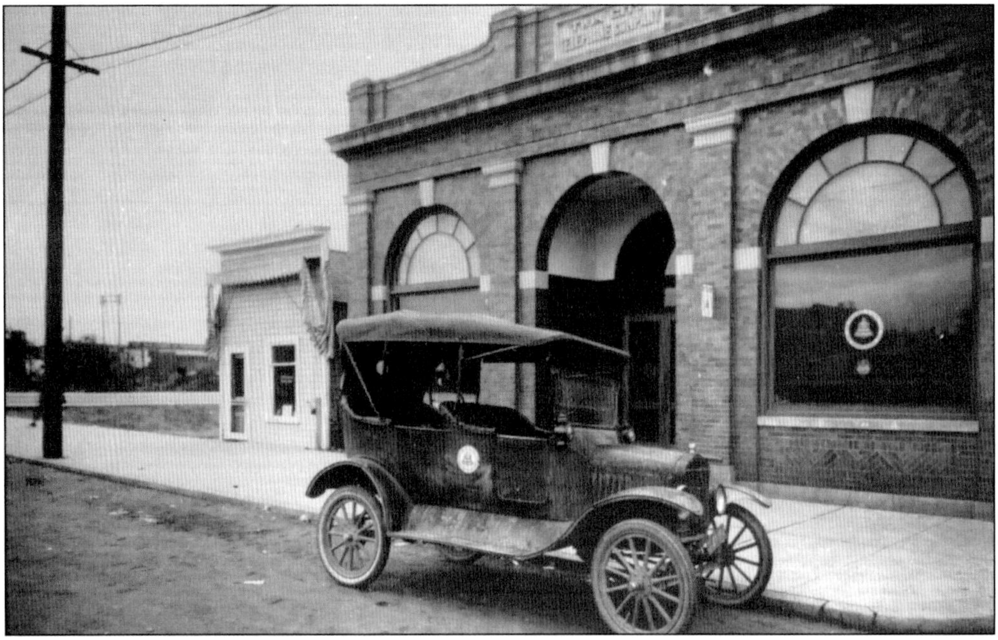

The Twin City Telephone Company, which serviced Pasco and Kennewick, was started by R. A. Klinge in 1903. Bessie Gray was the first telephone operator. Klinge moved his company to this Second Street location in 1905. By 1914, Pasco's population of close to 2,500 individuals demanded more service, and Klinge built the brick addition to his first building. (Courtesy of FCHS.)

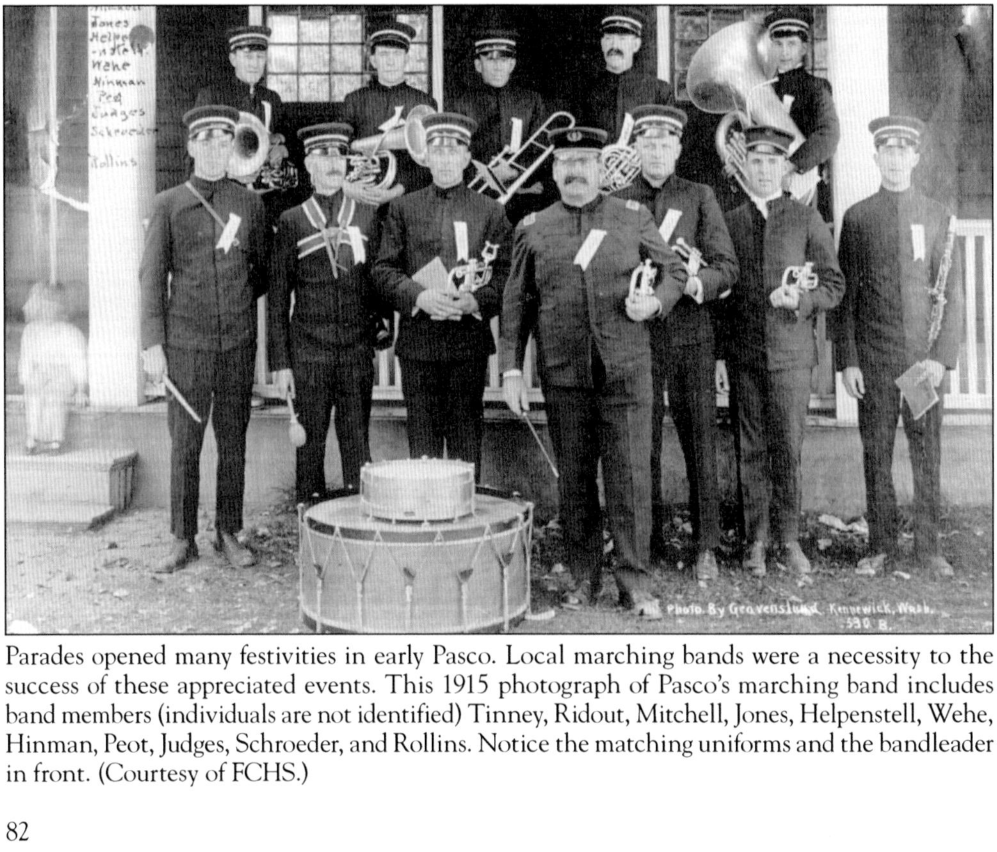

Parades opened many festivities in early Pasco. Local marching bands were a necessity to the success of these appreciated events. This 1915 photograph of Pasco's marching band includes band members (individuals are not identified) Tinney, Ridout, Mitchell, Jones, Helpenstell, Wehe, Hinman, Peot, Judges, Schroeder, and Rollins. Notice the matching uniforms and the bandleader in front. (Courtesy of FCHS.)

The Snake and Columbia Rivers played many important roles in the Pasco community. They were geographical barriers that needed to be crossed, but they provided crucial transportation and connections to other communities. They offered hope of irrigation for the arid landscape while also providing much-needed recreation. Pictured here enjoying the river in 1915 are, from left to right, (first row) Thelma Liberty and Loretta Matheny; (second row) Fran Douglas, Viola Everett, Grant Ellison, Kittie Ellison, and Martha Liberty. (Courtesy of FCHS.)

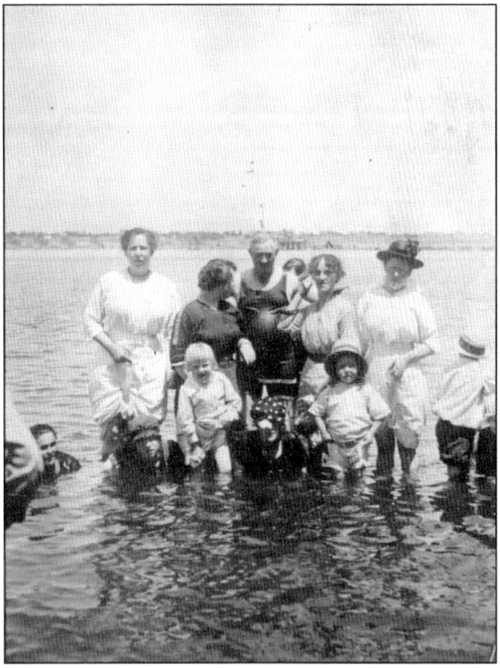

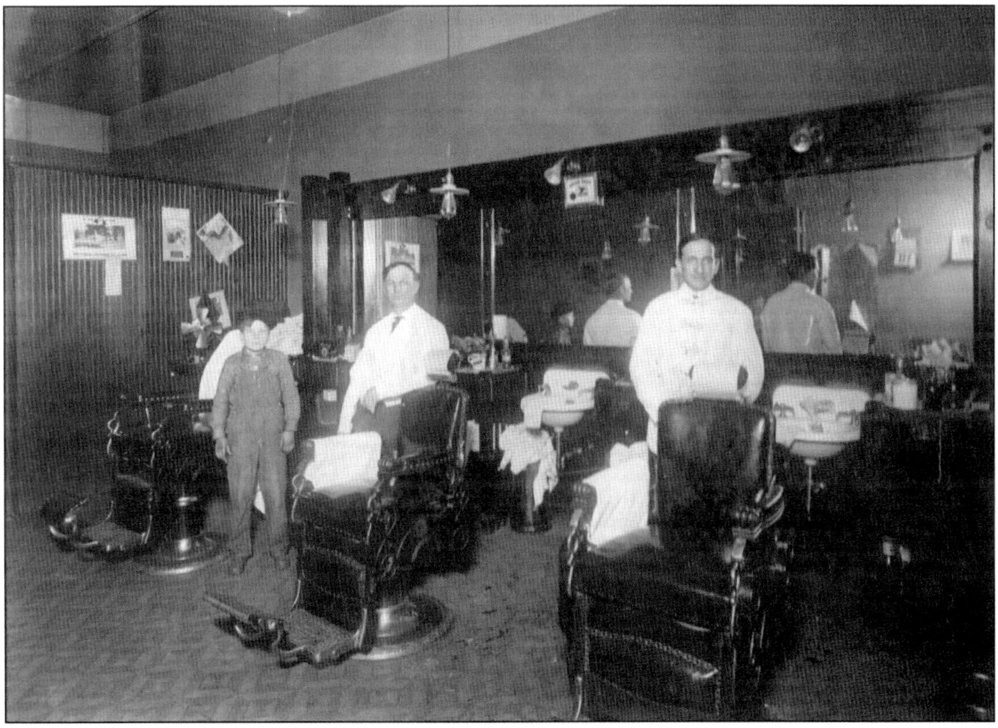

In 1910, Carl Myers was transferring trains from Oregon to Loon Lake, Washington. A couple of local Pasco men noticed his barber bag and asked if he would fill in for the local barber, who was recuperating from a fall. Myers agreed to stay, and his barber business succeeded. This picture, taken about 1915, shows his son, Buzz, to the left and Myers in the middle of the room. (Courtesy of FCHS.)

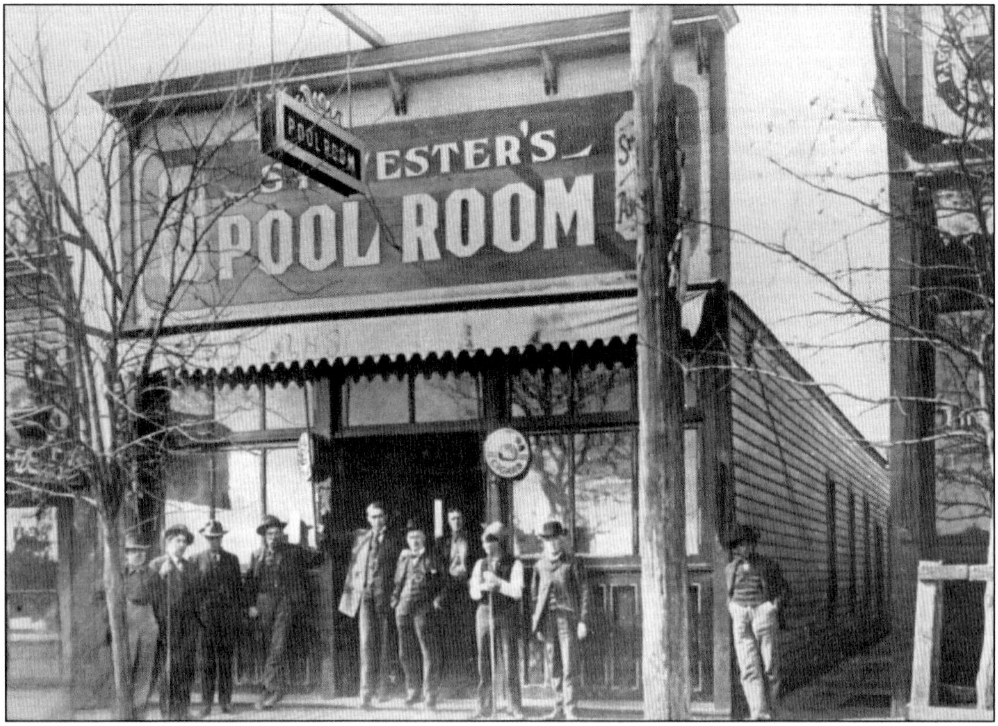

Prohibition began in Washington at midnight on December 15, 1915, which made it one of 18 states to adopt Prohibition before it was congressionally ratified in 1919. During Prohibition, pool halls, like the one pictured here, were allowed to sell soft drinks but no liquor. Many Pasco saloon owners, like brothers John Henry Sylvester and Ainsworth Sylvester, changed their careers from saloon owners to cigar merchants. (Courtesy of FCHS.)

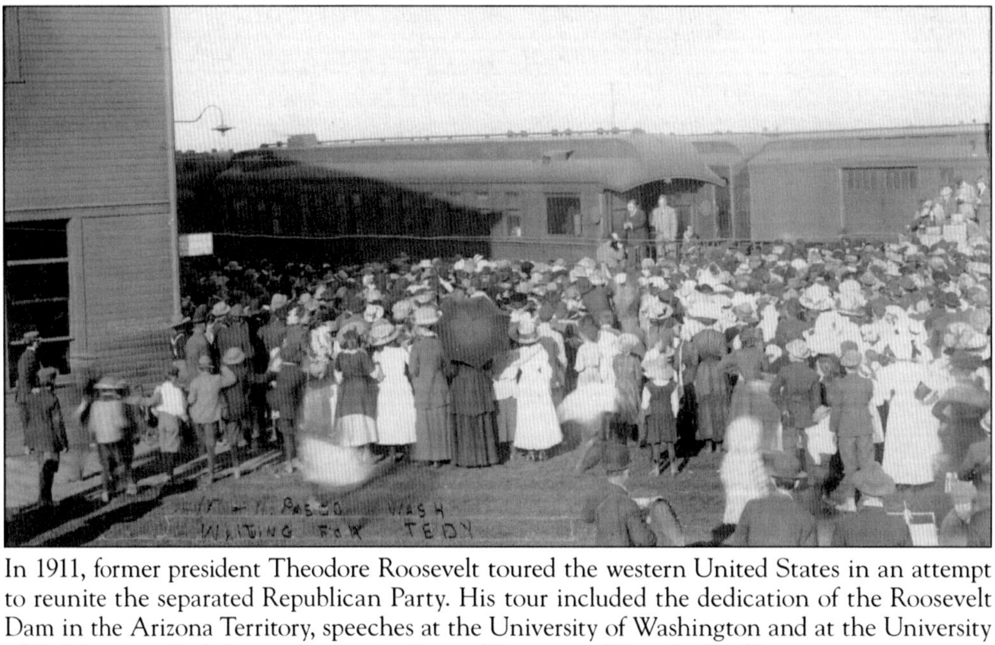

In 1911, former president Theodore Roosevelt toured the western United States in an attempt to reunite the separated Republican Party. His tour included the dedication of the Roosevelt Dam in the Arizona Territory, speeches at the University of Washington and at the University of California at Berkeley, and a stop in Pasco. (Courtesy of Dan Stafford.)

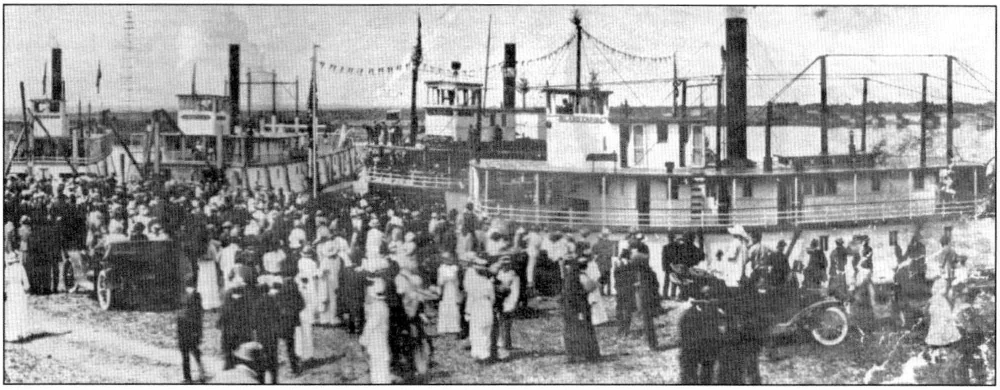

The largest celebration held along the Columbia and Snake Rivers in 1915 was the Open River Celebration. The Dalles-Celilo Canal was completed, which provided continuous river navigation from Lewiston on the Snake River to the Pacific Ocean via the Columbia River. With the new "open river," riverboats would be able to compete with the railroads for agriculture transportation. (Courtesy of Dan Stafford.)

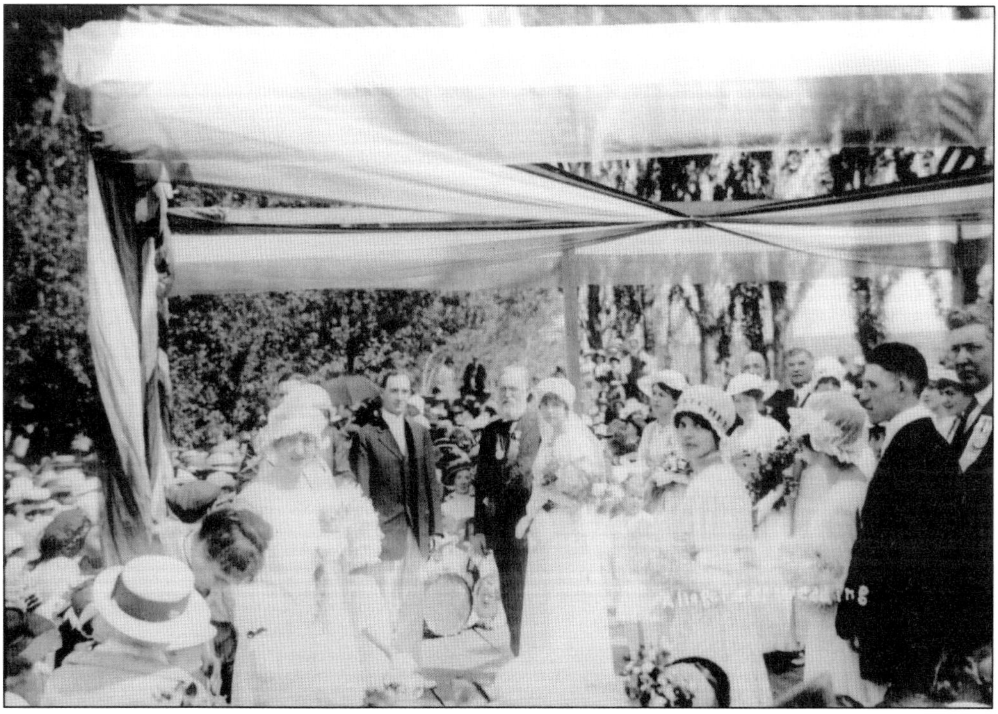

The high point of the Open River Celebration in 1915 was an allegorical wedding held in Kennewick. Miss Columbia, daughter of the State of Washington, wed Mr. Snake of Idaho and Oregon. Citizens of Kennewick, Pasco, and Yakima played parts in the wedding ceremony. Pasco citizens included Frank Jones as Mr. Snake, William Polk Gray as the father of the bride, 18 bridesmaids, and 13 men of honor. (Courtesy of FCHS.)

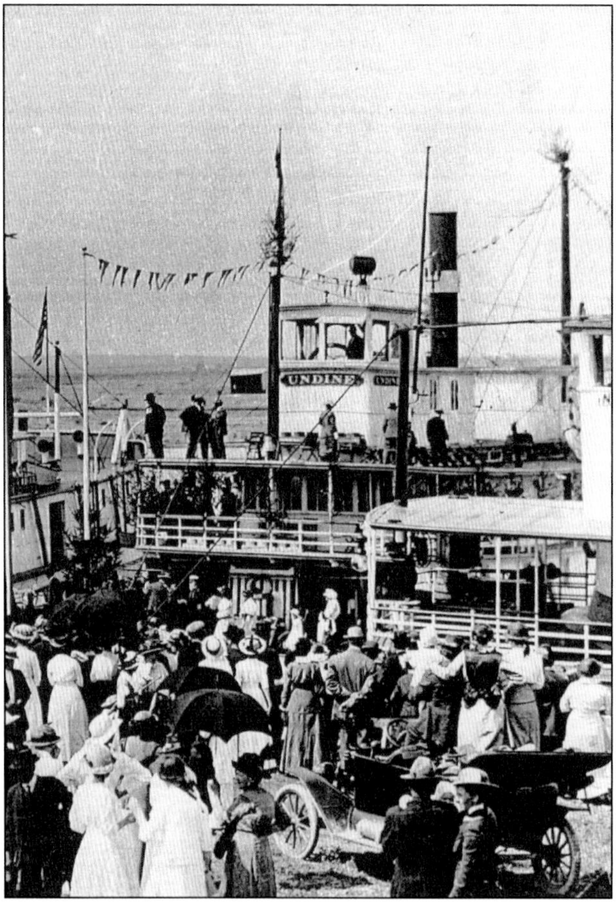

Capt. William Polk Gray, at the helm of the *Undine*, led the way in a parade of riverboats from Pasco to the new Celilo locks during the Open River Celebration. The fleet left at 4:30 a.m. after celebrating in the Twin Cities of Pasco and Kennewick late the night before. (Courtesy of FCHS.)

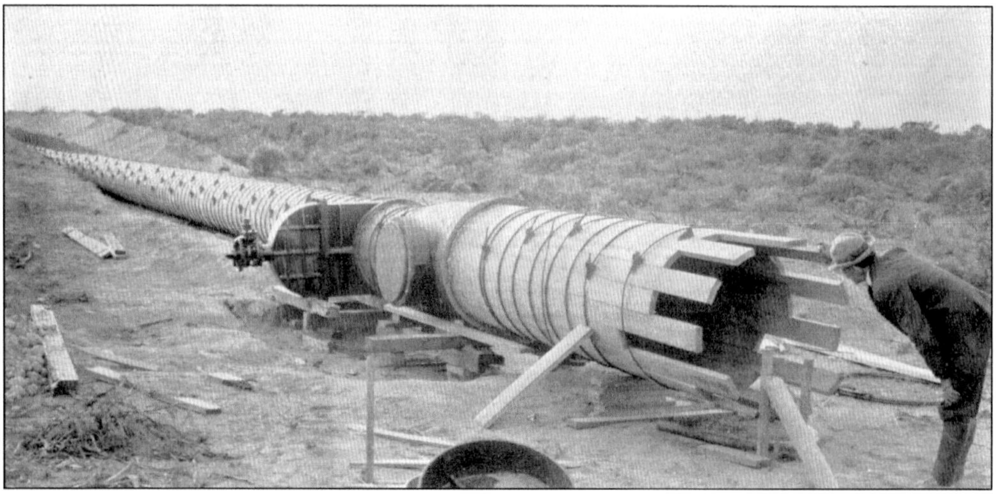

The Pasco Reclamation Company was concerned about water evaporating and percolating from the water supply before it reached intended farms. Their solution, well engineered and thought out, was to bury wooden pipes as conduits. Ironically, these wooden pipes were the demise of the Pasco Reclamation Company, as unforeseen deterioration rotted the pipes and allowed life-giving water to escape. (Courtesy of the Franklin County Irrigation District.)

Anna Crotty owned the Montana Hotel, which was converted into the first Our Lady of Lourdes Hospital in 1916. The hotel was named for the state where Crotty lived before moving to Pasco and was probably built by her husband, John J. Crotty, a carpenter. The family was instrumental in the growth of Our Lady of Lourdes Hospital. (Courtesy of Lourdes Health Network.)

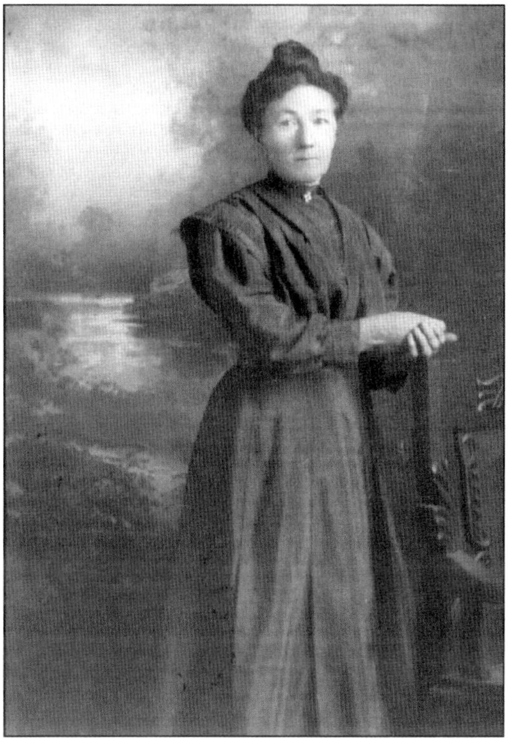

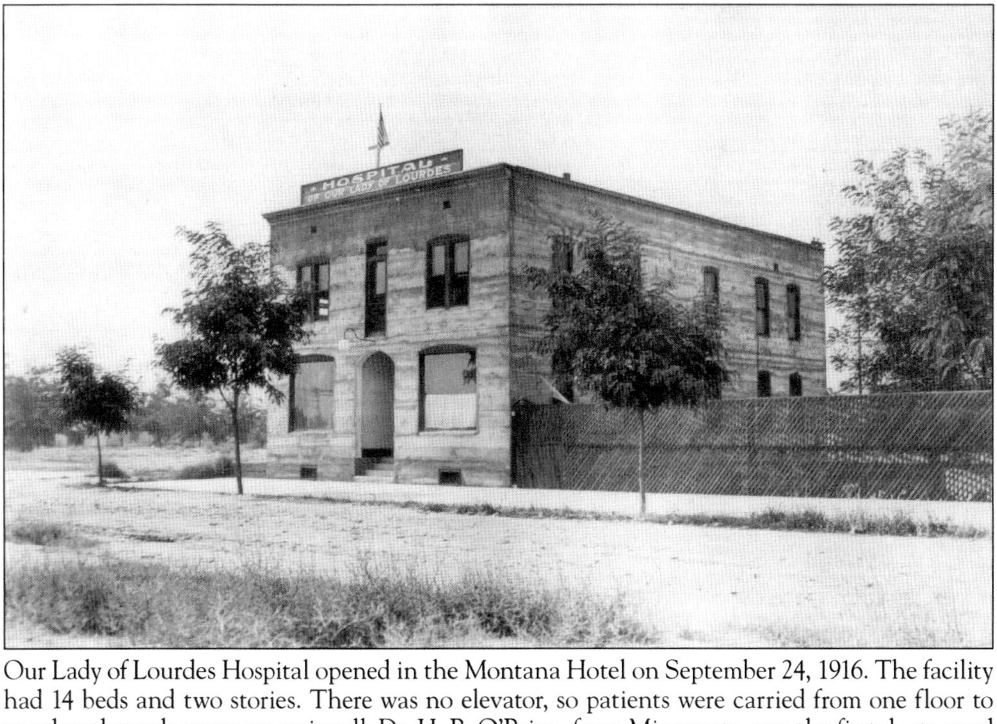

Our Lady of Lourdes Hospital opened in the Montana Hotel on September 24, 1916. The facility had 14 beds and two stories. There was no elevator, so patients were carried from one floor to another through a narrow stairwell. Dr. H. B. O'Brien, from Minnesota, was the first doctor and was well acquainted with the practice of using kitchen tables as operating tables and wash boilers for sterilizers. (Courtesy of Lourdes Health Network.)

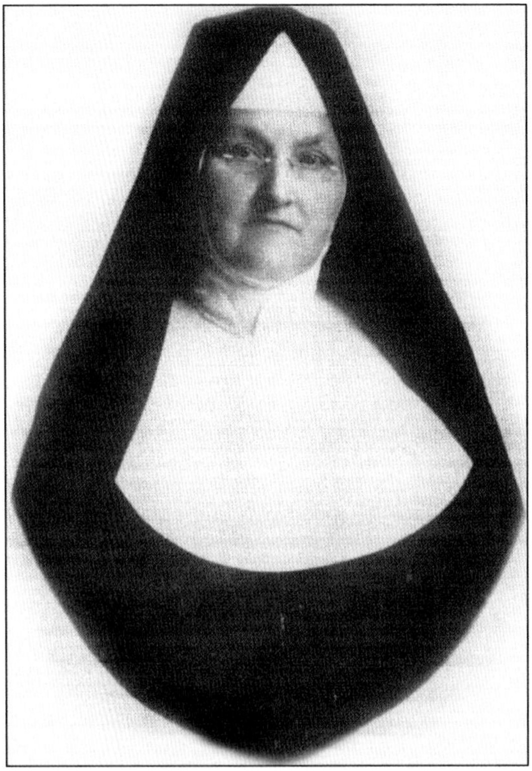

The flu pandemic of 1918 made it obvious that Pasco had outgrown the 14-bed facility at the Montana Hotel. Dr. E. G. Hamley and Mother Borgia Tourscher worked with a hospital board to find another suitable location. An entire city block adjacent to St. Patrick's Church was purchased from the Northern Pacific Railway for $1 to build the new facility. (Courtesy of Lourdes Health Network.)

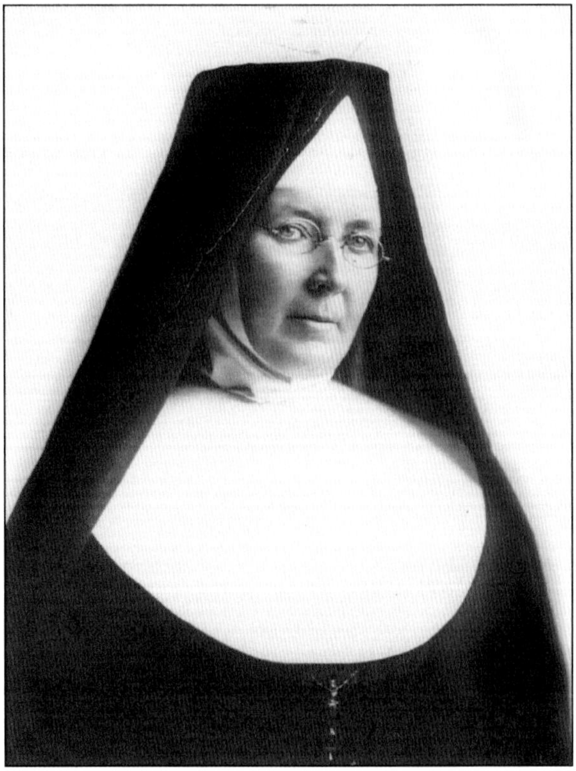

Mother Augustine led a group consisting of the Sisters of St. Joseph and local housewives in preparing the Montana Hotel to be used as a hospital. She then served as Our Lady of Lourdes's first superior/administrator from 1916 to 1921. Our Lady of Lourdes Hospital admitted 607 patients in its first year. (Courtesy of Lourdes Health Network.)

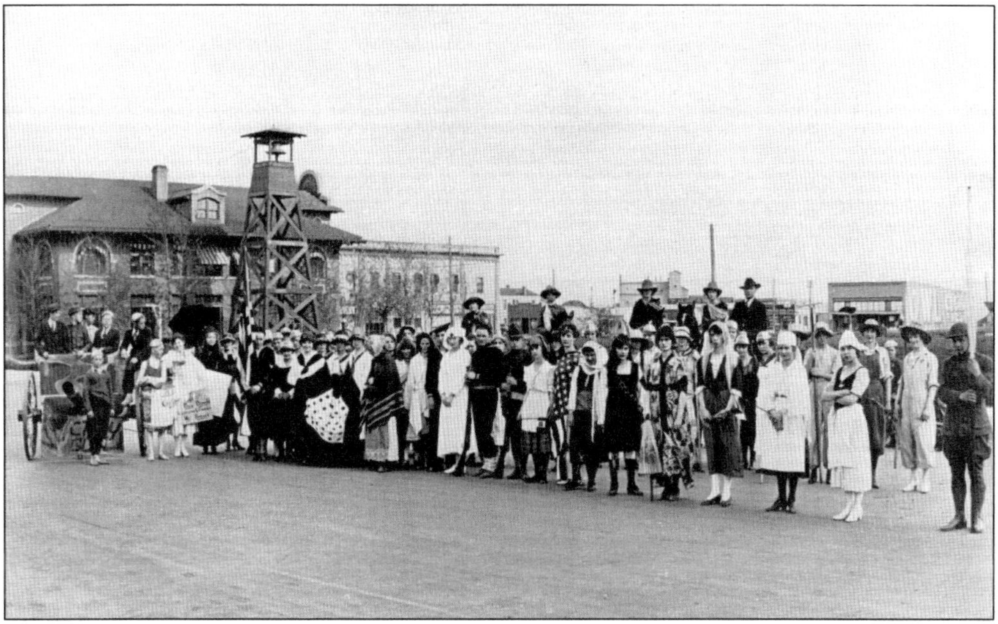

To celebrate the end of World War I, many communities threw large festivities. Pasco's Victory Bond Parade included students dressed up in costumes of various countries or military attire. Pasco's city hall and the fire bell can be seen in the background of this 1917 photograph. The poster held by the girl on the left says, "Buy bonds to promote freedom we earned." (Courtesy of FCHS.)

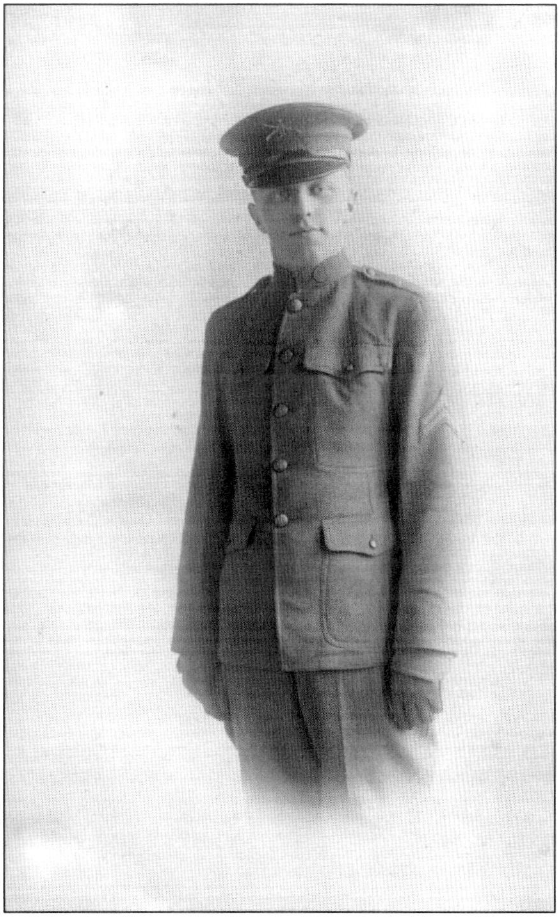

The American Expeditionary Forces started the American Legion in Paris in 1919. Allen Westby was one of at least 21 Pasco soldiers who joined the American Legion while they were on the battlefields of France. By 1925, Westby owned and operated Pasco Cleaners. He was politically involved in the Republican Party and served as city councilman in 1930. (Courtesy of FCHS.)

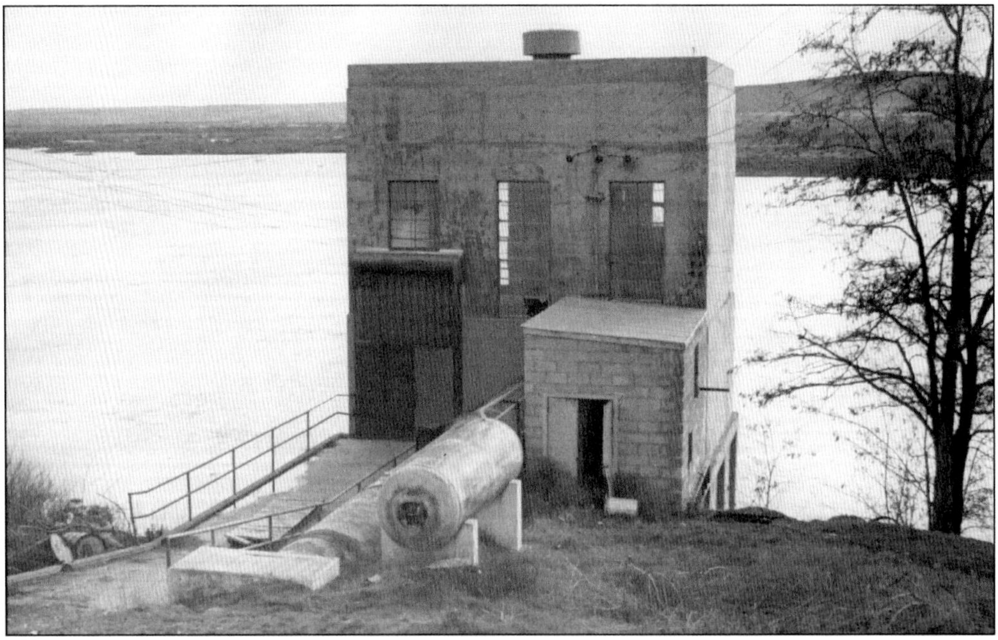

The Franklin County Irrigation District continued to experience financial problems through the 1920s and 1930s. Irrigation was extremely important to the survival of farming in Pasco. Landowners and bondholders agreed to discount bonds in favor of success of the district. This photograph shows the Columbia River pump house built by the Franklin County Irrigation District in 1919. (Courtesy of the Franklin County Irrigation District.)

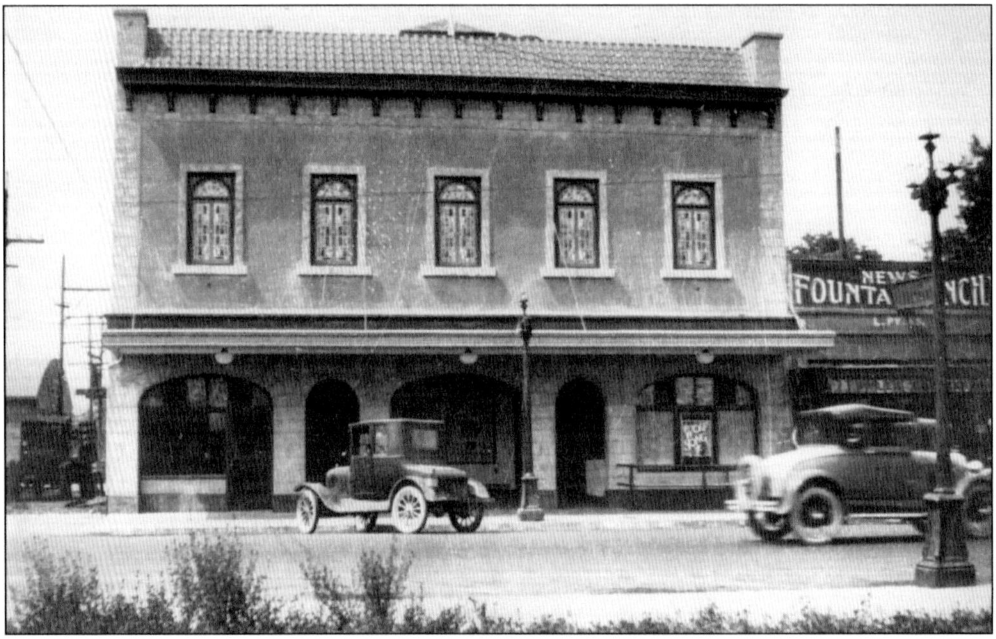

The Liberty Theatre, built on North Fourth Street before 1920, was an important part of life for Pasco citizens. Not only were movies shown nightly, but the stage was also used by the community for important events such as recitals and commencement exercises. In 1921, the Liberty Theatre acquired a pipe organ, which was used to accompany the silent movies. (Courtesy of FCHS.)

In 1924, the Liberty Theatre brought the silent movie *Turn to the Right* to the citizens of Pasco. Organ music was performed by George Nyckleceick to accompany the one-evening showing. *Turn to the Right* debuted in 1922 featuring Alice Terry, Jack Mulhall, Harry Myers, and George Cooper. The comedy was enjoyed, and many more silent movies would be played at the Liberty Theatre. (Courtesy of FCHS.)

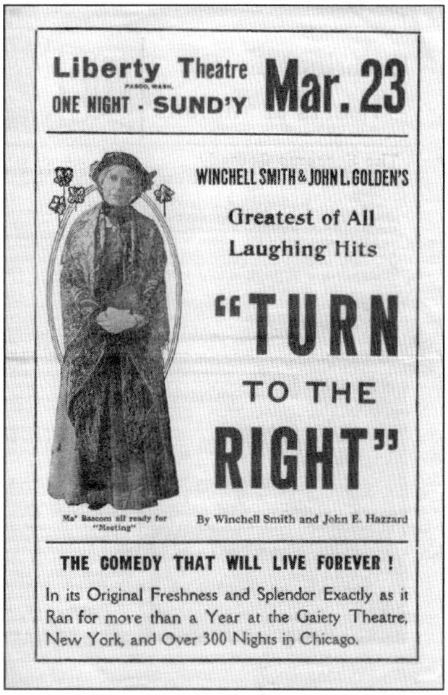

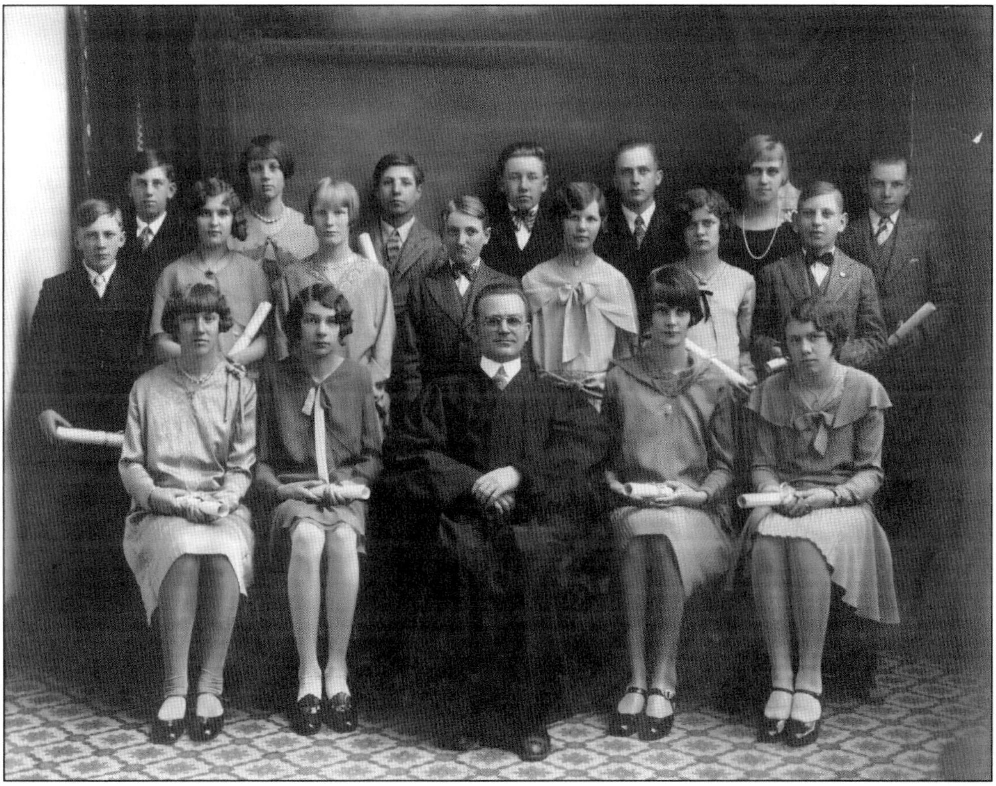

The 1919 *Sinewesah*, Pasco High School's annual, was a mere pamphlet with a statement written on the inside cover apologizing for the lack of volume. The apology went on to say that no *Sinewesah* had been planned because of the influenza pandemic. With no time to spare, the senior class of 1919 decided to publish one. This picture is of the 1920 senior class of Pasco High School. (Courtesy of FCHS.)

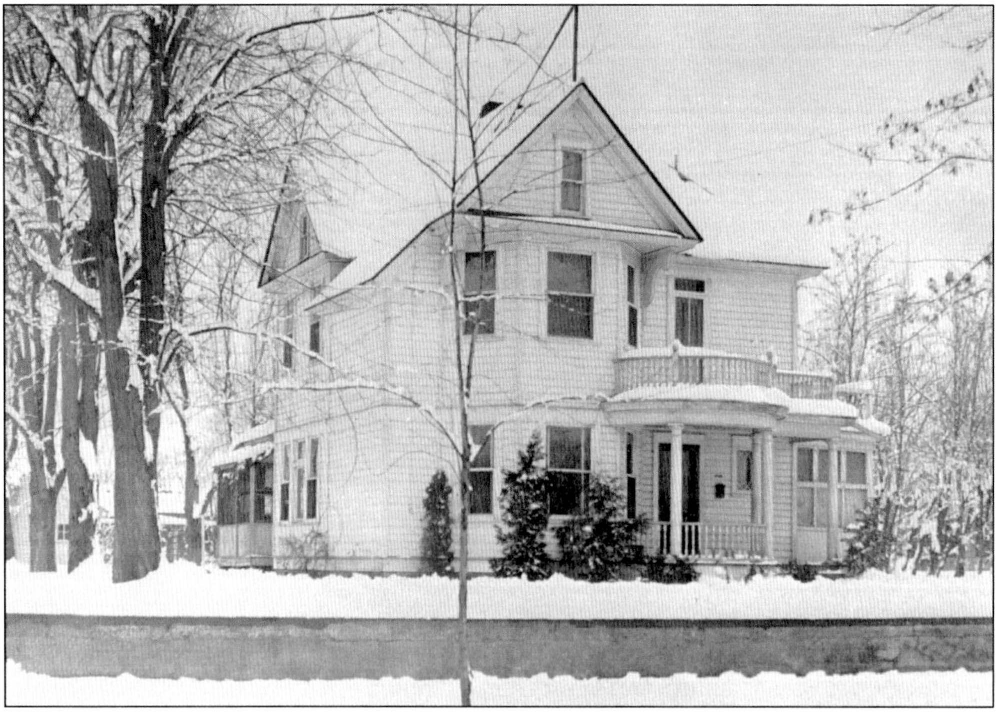

When attorney B. B. Horrigan married Bernice Crotty in 1907, they made this house at Seventh and Lewis Streets their home. They lived in the same home the remainder of their lives. Horrigan appreciated the hot and dry climate of southeast Washington. This 1920 photograph shows an unusual scene in Pasco, that of a snow-covered dwelling. (Courtesy of FCHS.)

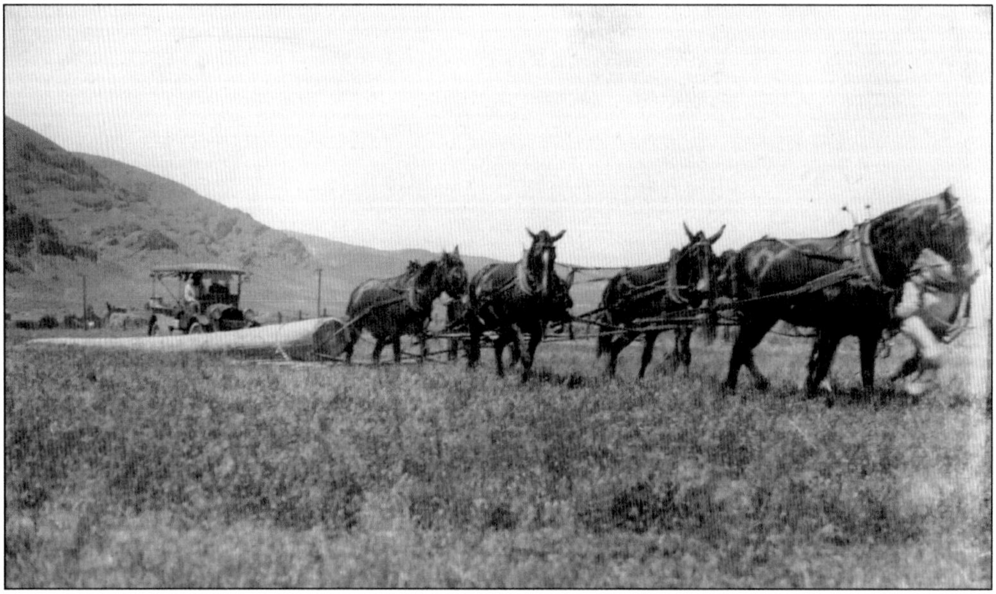

By 1920, Pasco was experiencing the luxuries of electricity and telephones. This photograph demonstrates how old and new technologies were working together in 1920. Here a team of horses is transporting large poles, examples of which can be seen in the background. Pasco's growth demanded a wider use of what had formerly been considered luxuries. (Courtesy of FCHS.)

Five

The Air above Pasco
1921 to 1930

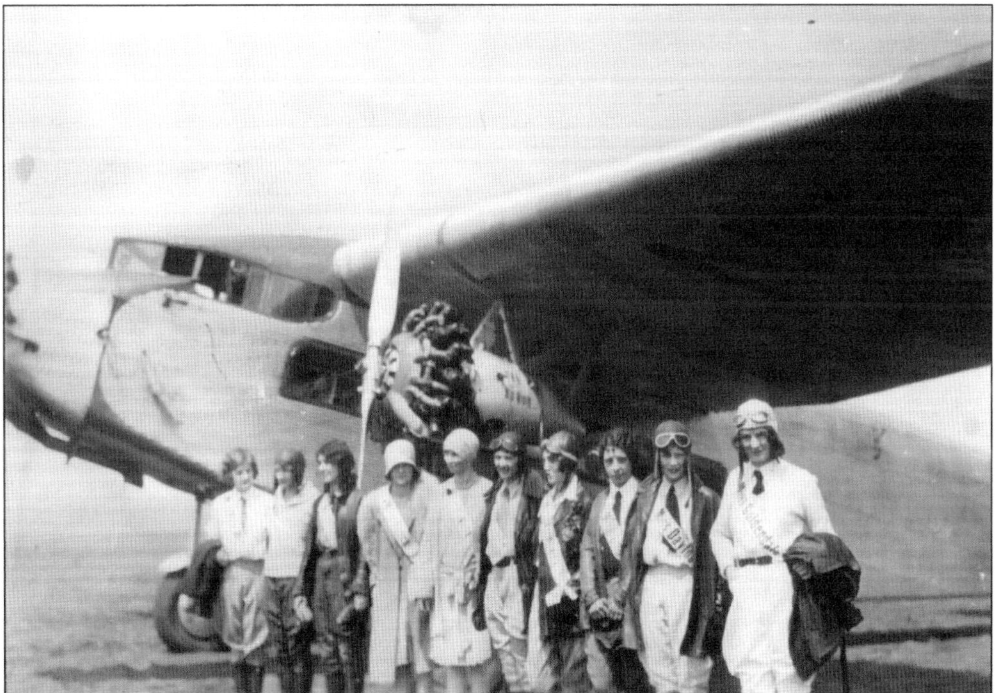

Princesses and maidens were a necessity of all celebrations in the 1920s. The Pasco Air Jubilee, held on May 18, 1929, was no different. Alice Collins of Goldendale (far right) was crowned Jubilee Queen. Her princesses were Margaret Witt of Kennewick (fourth from right), Agnes Hesseldenz of Pasco (seventh from right), and Velma Campbell (unidentified). (Courtesy of FCHS.)

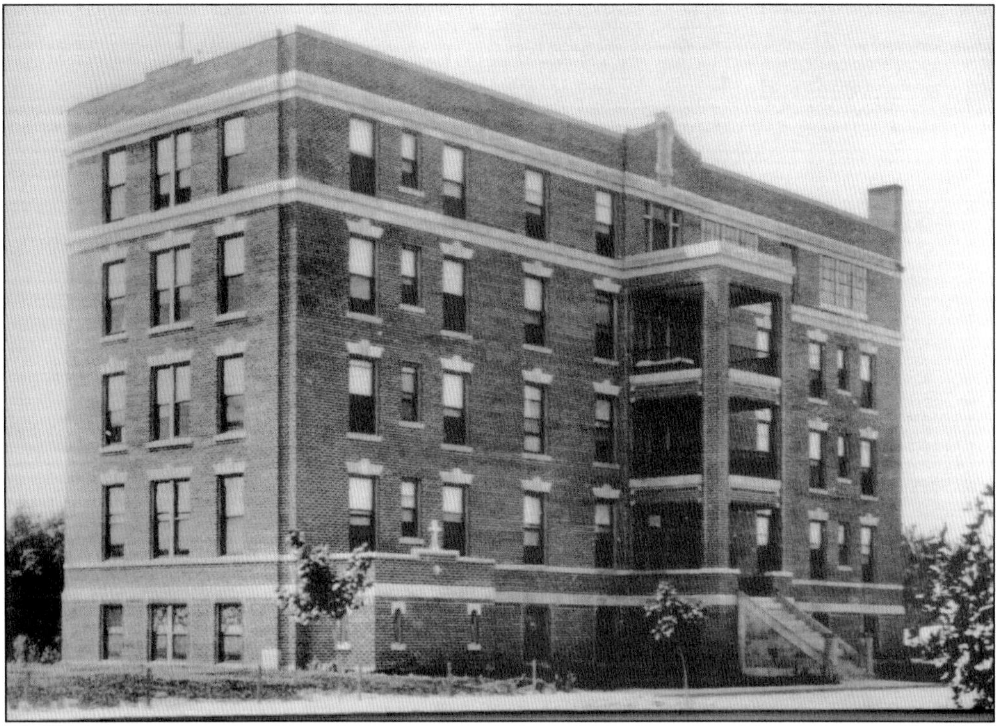

The new Our Lady of Lourdes Hospital was opened on July 29, 1921. Financial concerns and typical weather conditions plagued the new hospital from the beginning. Sisters typically needed to dust exterior windowsills before opening windows to prevent sand from entering the building. The fourth floor was left unfinished until finances improved. (Courtesy of Lourdes Health Network.)

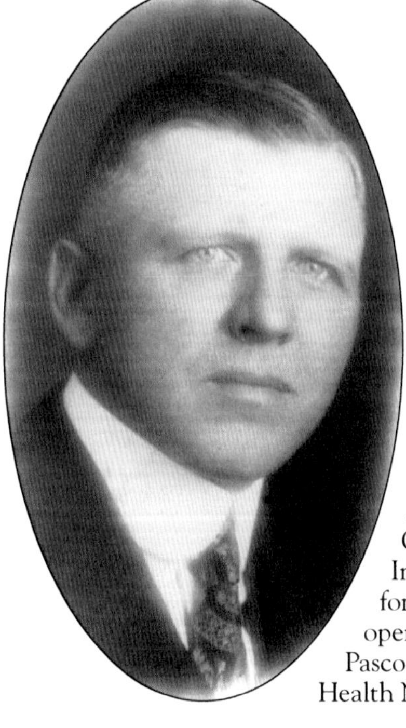

After obtaining his medical education from Rush Medical College in Chicago, Dr. Eugene Hamley settled in Sprague. In Sprague, he opened a medical practice where he worked for almost 20 years. When Our Lady of Lourdes Hospital opened their new facility in 1921, Dr. Hamley relocated to Pasco and took the position of chief of staff. (Courtesy of Lourdes Health Network.)

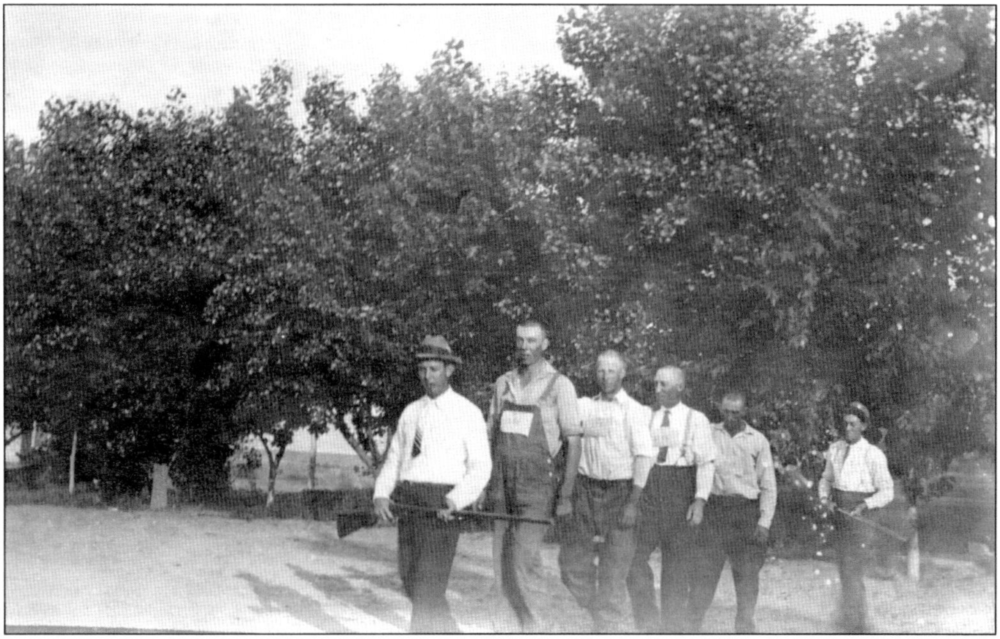

Fred Norling was Franklin County sheriff from 1923 to 1931. During this time, work release was granted to inmates. Not only did it allow inmates an opportunity for fresh air and exercise, it also helped fill the need for labor in the booming agricultural industry Pasco was experiencing. His deputy, Ralph McCotter, is shown here at the end of the line bringing work-release inmates out of the orchard. (Courtesy of FCHS.)

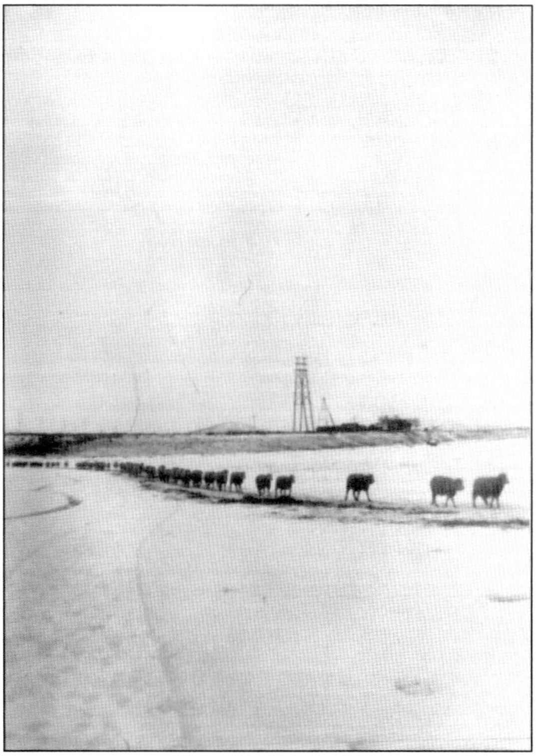

The winter of 1921–1922 was severe for the dry desert Pasco climate. Herbert Wexler needed to move his herd of 2,500 sheep from the depleted hay supply in Richland, across the river, to the Franklin County side of the river. The frozen Columbia River made it possible for the band to cross over the ice to their new feeding location. (Courtesy of FCHS.)

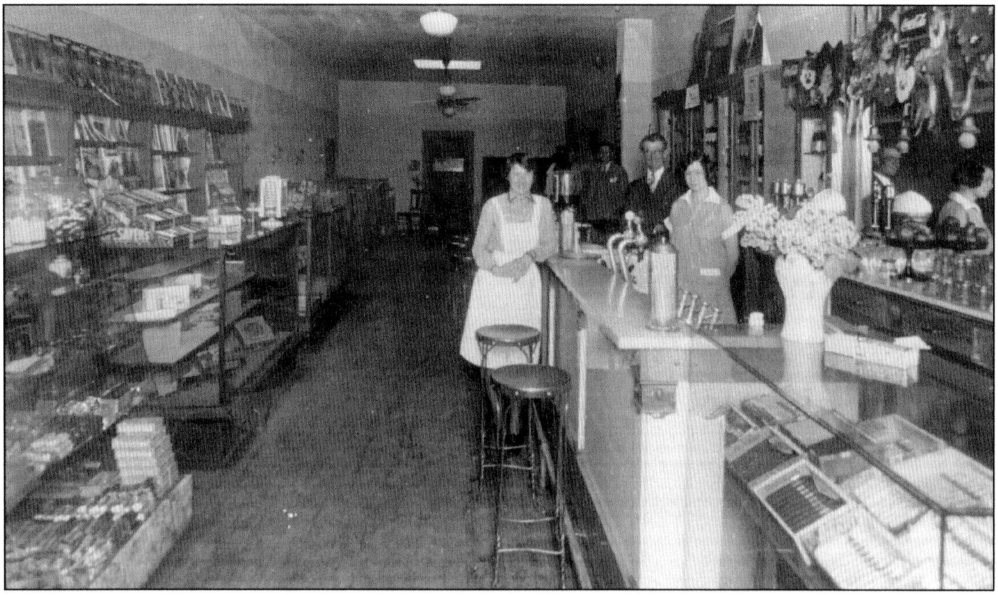

The Pyles News Stand started in the stairwell of the Pasco Hotel. As the Levi Pyles family grew, so did the store. By 1920, the Pyles News Stand built a small building next to the Liberty Theater. At the new location, it became known for its Sweet Shop in the front of the store and a restaurant hidden in the rear. (Courtesy of FCHS.)

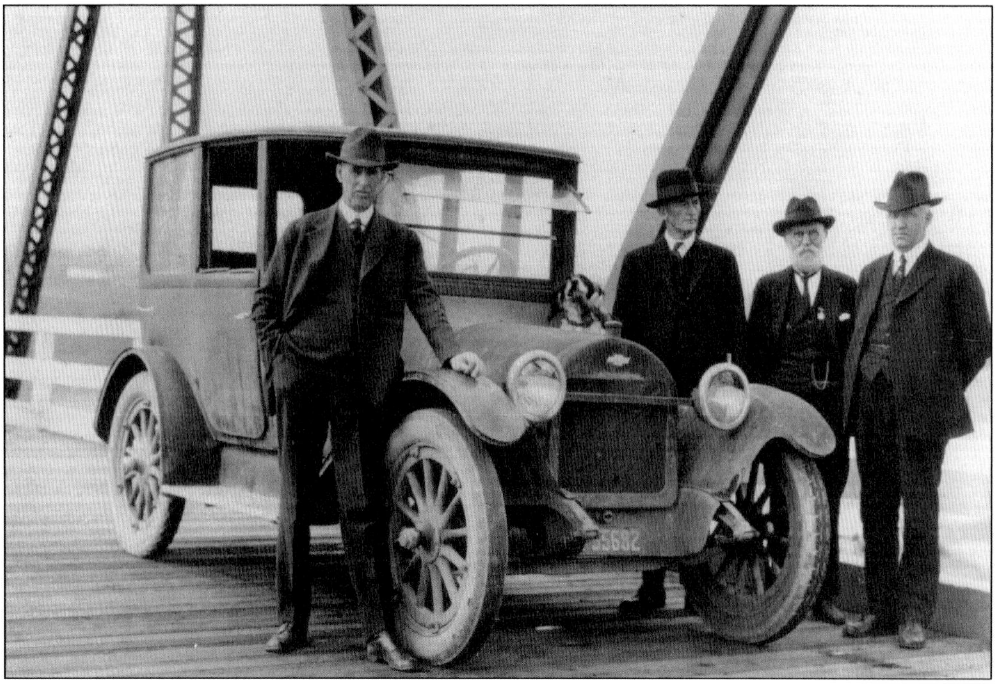

The Pasco-Kennewick Bridge opened for traffic on October 7, 1922, one month ahead of schedule. There were celebrations, complete with parades, speeches, and ribbon-cutting ceremonies. Tolls from that day brought in $237.60. Dignitaries who traveled in the first car to cross the bridge are identified as, from left to right, Sen. Wesley Jones from Yakima, Sen. Charles Franklin Stinson from Pasco, DeWitt Owens, and an unidentified man. (Courtesy of FCHS.)

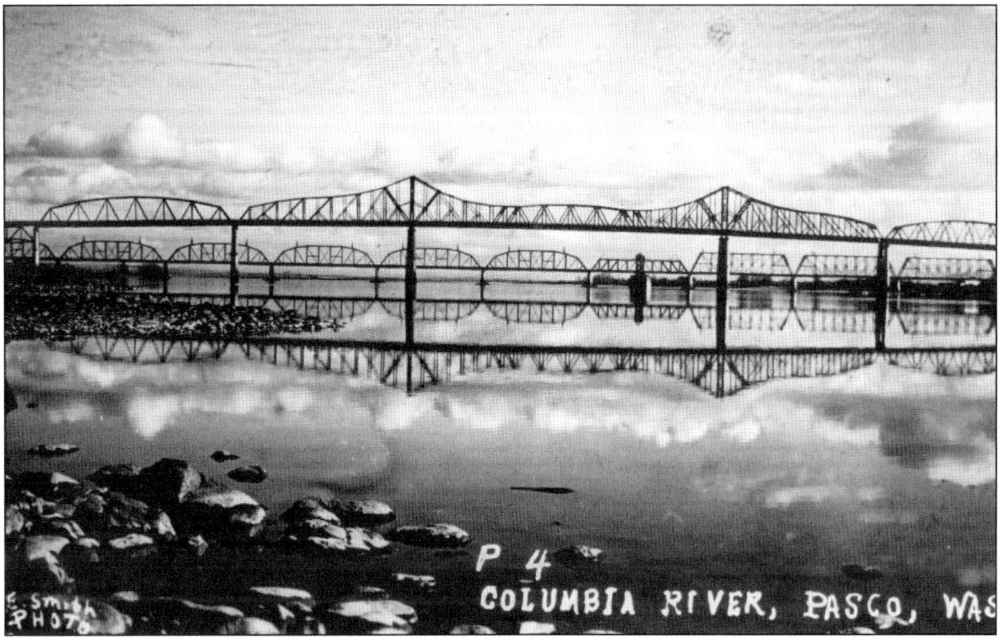

The Green Bridge, also known as the Pasco-Kennewick Bridge, was completed in 1922. It was a two-lane, wood-plank bridge, the first of three cantilever bridges built to cross the Columbia River. The Columbia River railroad bridge can also be seen in the background, with each bridge mirrored on the Columbia River. (Courtesy of Dan Stafford.)

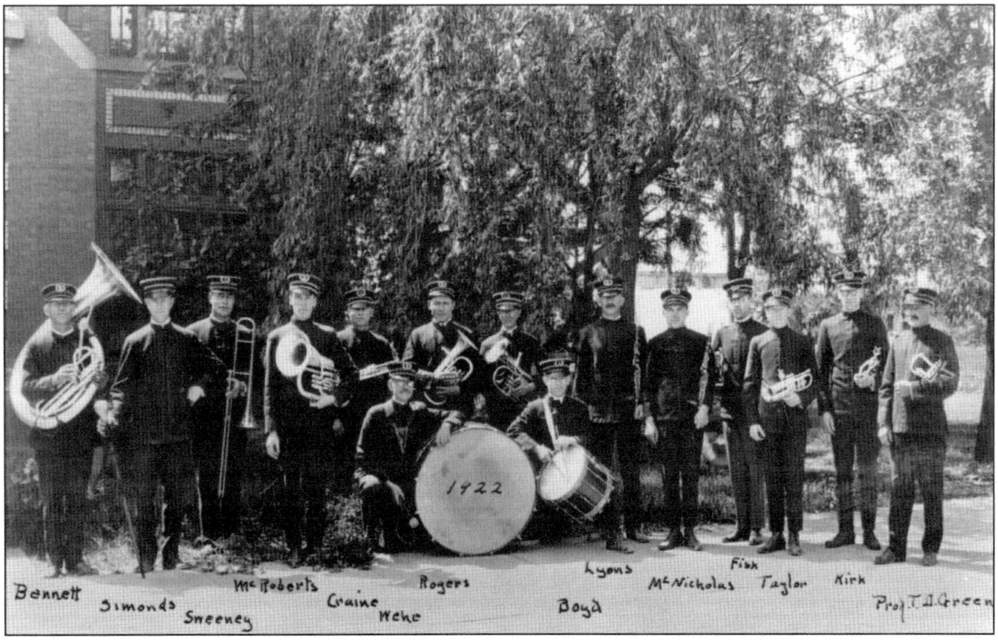

The Pasco marching band of the early 1920s was asked to play at many functions and celebrations. These celebrations included the Our Lady of Lourdes Hospital opening in 1921 and the Pasco-Kennewick Bridge completion in 1922. Members of the band were, from left to right, Bennett, Simonds, Sweeney, McRoberts, Craine, Wehe, Rogers, unidentified, Boyd, Lyons, McNicholas, Fisk, Taylor, Kirk, and Prof. T. D. Green. (Courtesy of FCHS.)

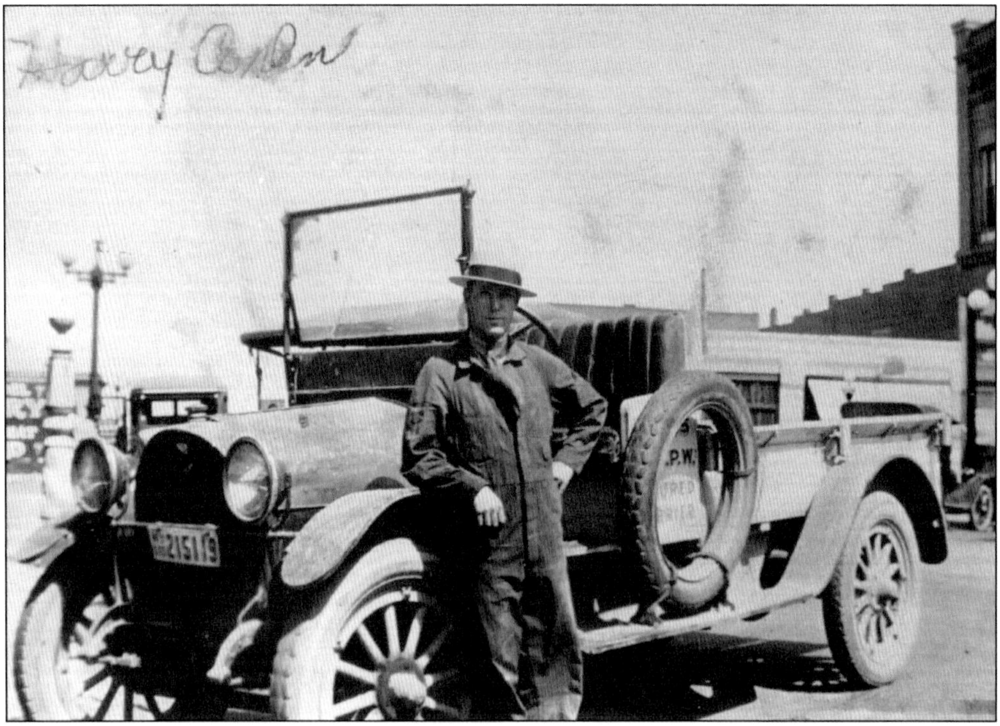

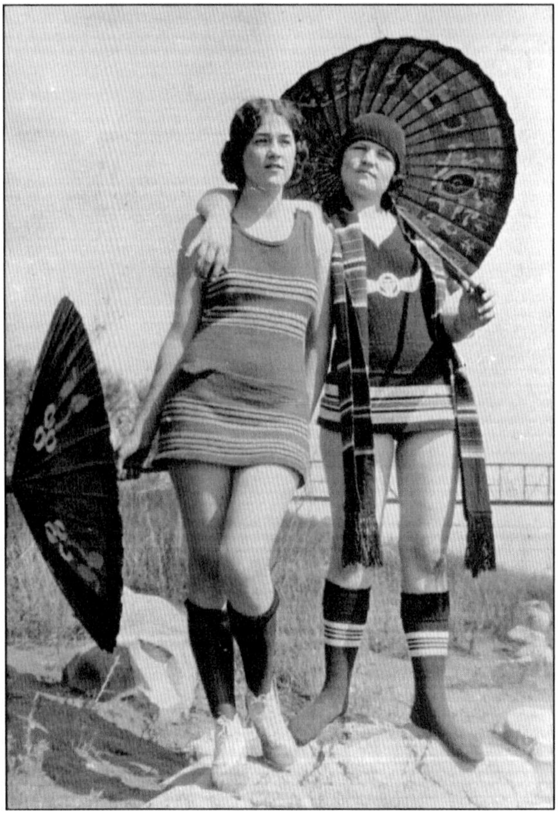

Harry and Edward Conlen were brothers who emigrated with their parents from Canada in 1909. In the 1920s, the Conlen brothers began selling automobiles and farming implements. The toll bridge between Kennewick and Pasco was completed in 1922, and the Conlen brothers offered their bus-limousine service, which delivered individuals and goods over the river. (Courtesy of FCHS.)

These two young Pasco girls are showing off the latest swimwear on the Columbia River in the early 1920s. The girl on the left is identified as Wren Pyles. The other is not identified. The Columbia River Green Bridge can be seen in the distance behind them. (Courtesy of FCHS.)

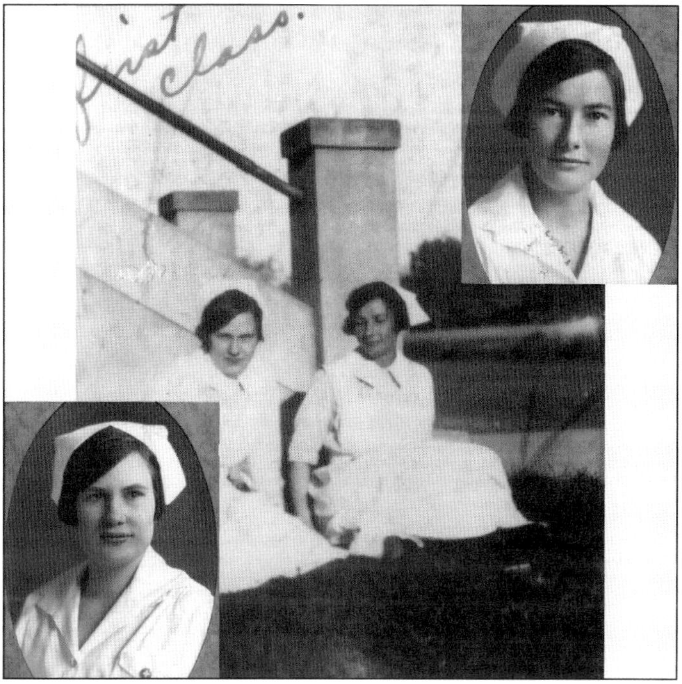

Beatrice Miller and Margaret Armour were the first to graduate from Our Lady of Lourdes Nursing School in 1924. Margaret married Harold Sonnichsen and moved to Coeur d'Alene. Beatrice married Harvey Huston and stayed involved with the nursing activities in Pasco. The American Nurses Association formed in Pasco in 1934, with Beatrice Huston as its president. (Courtesy of Lourdes Health Network.)

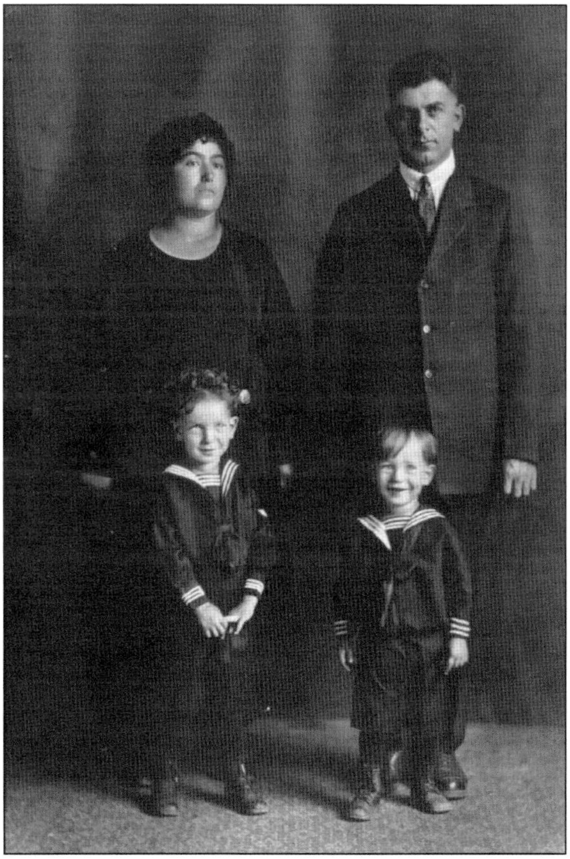

The Pontarolos were one of the only Italian families in Pasco in 1925. Joseph Pontarolo immigrated in 1913 and sent for Italia, his fiancée, seven years later. Pontarolo spent the rest of his life working in the Pasco railroad yard. His sons, Frank (on the left) and Albert (on the right), also made careers working with the Northern Pacific Railway. (Courtesy of Frank Pontarolo.)

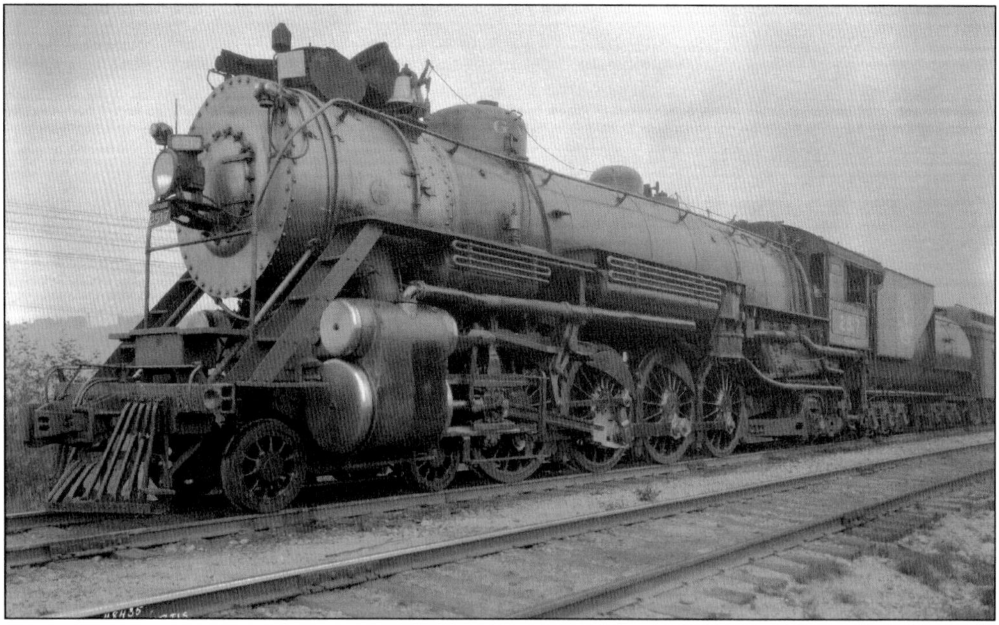

Raw silk was shipped to Seattle from the Orient and then railroaded to silk mills in Illinois and New Jersey. Redesigned passenger cars transported the silk, which could be valued in millions of dollars per train. Due to the high security risks of such valuable loads, silk trains were heavily guarded and given priority over all other trains. Pasco citizens witnessed these fast-moving trains as they passed through town in the late 1910s and 1920s. (Courtesy of the Washington State Historical Society.)

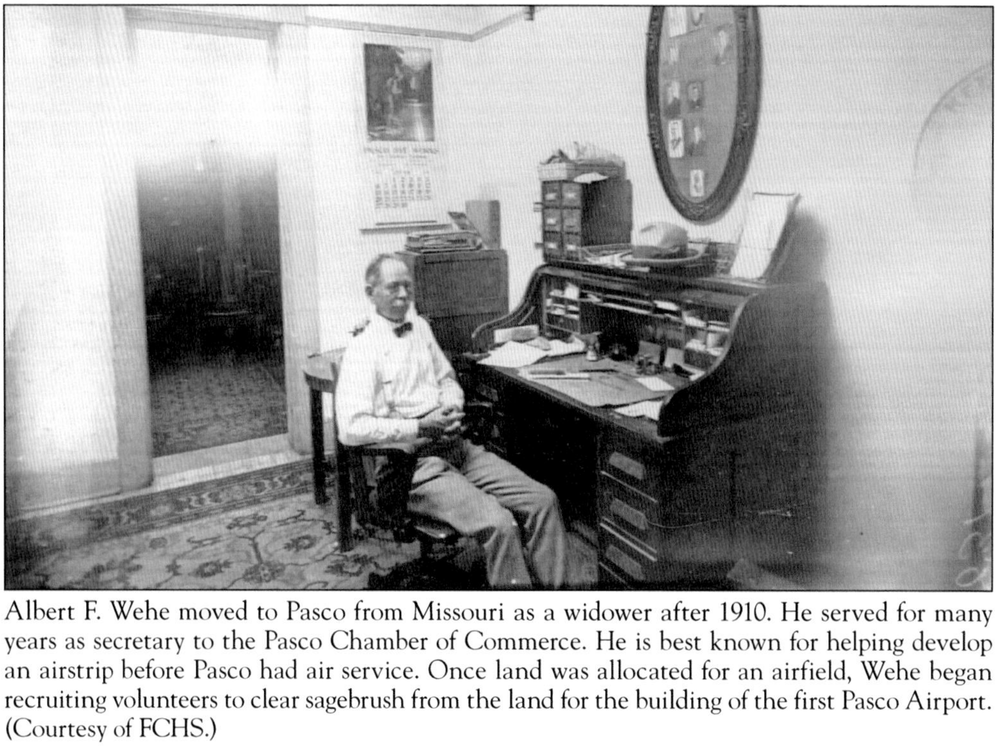

Albert F. Wehe moved to Pasco from Missouri as a widower after 1910. He served for many years as secretary to the Pasco Chamber of Commerce. He is best known for helping develop an airstrip before Pasco had air service. Once land was allocated for an airfield, Wehe began recruiting volunteers to clear sagebrush from the land for the building of the first Pasco Airport. (Courtesy of FCHS.)

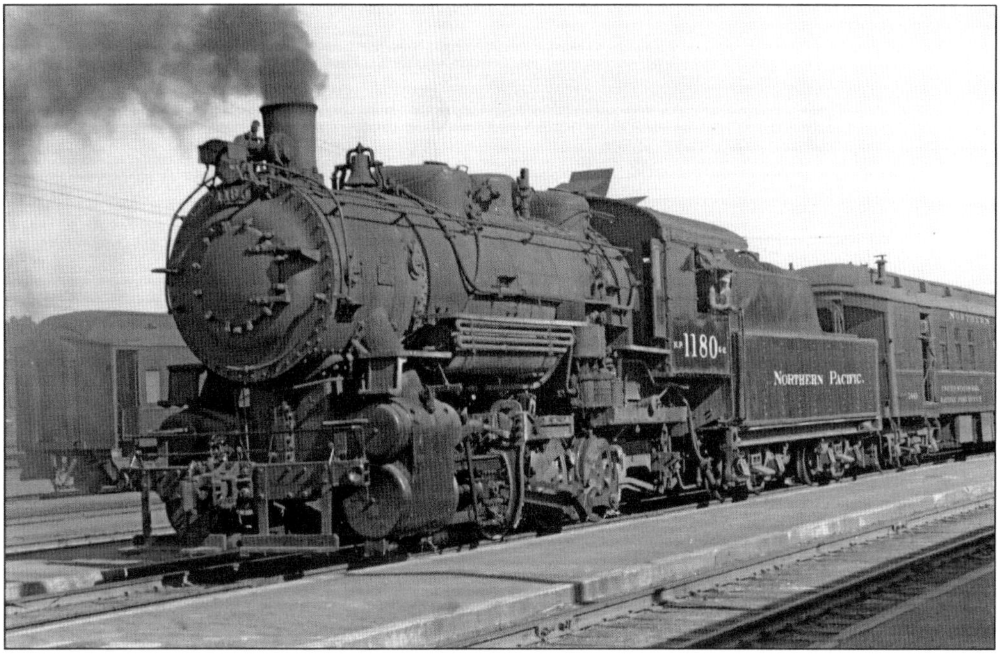

This Northern Pacific Engine No. 1180, built in 1920, hauled U.S. Mail Railway Post Office cars through the Pasco railroad yards. Railway Post Office routes were established in the 1880s and operated on a majority of passenger train routes. Mail would not only be gathered and delivered to and from the train, but the necessary sorting was also done while the train was traveling. The post office clerk would lean out of the car and, using a large hook, transfer mail from a pole in the railroad yard. Below is a postmarked postcard showing the Spokane, Portland, and Seattle Railway RPO seal from Pasco. (Above courtesy of Jim Frederickson; below courtesy of Dan Stafford.)

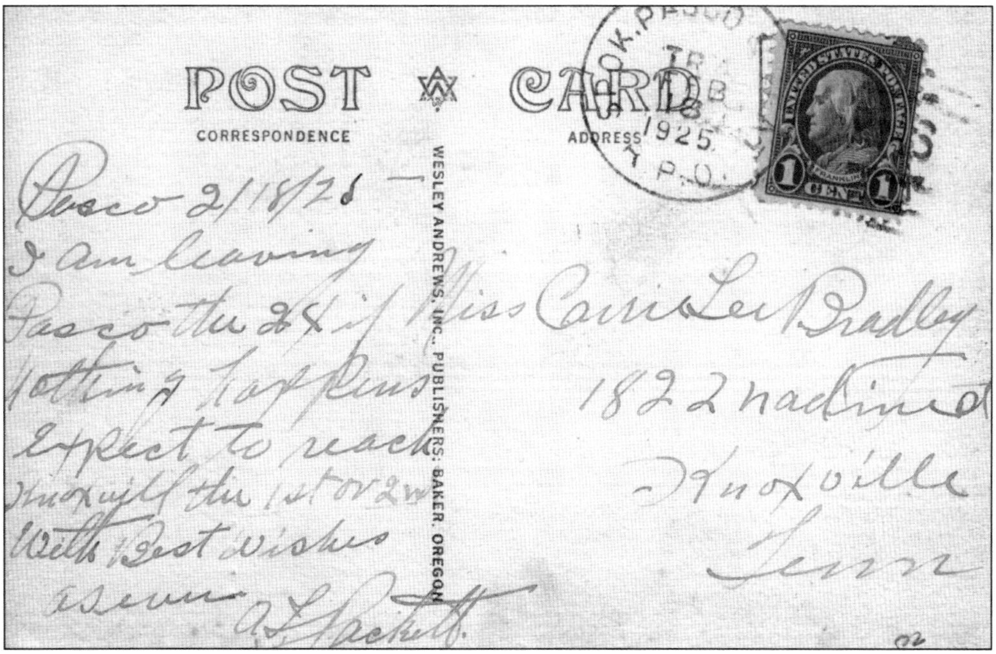

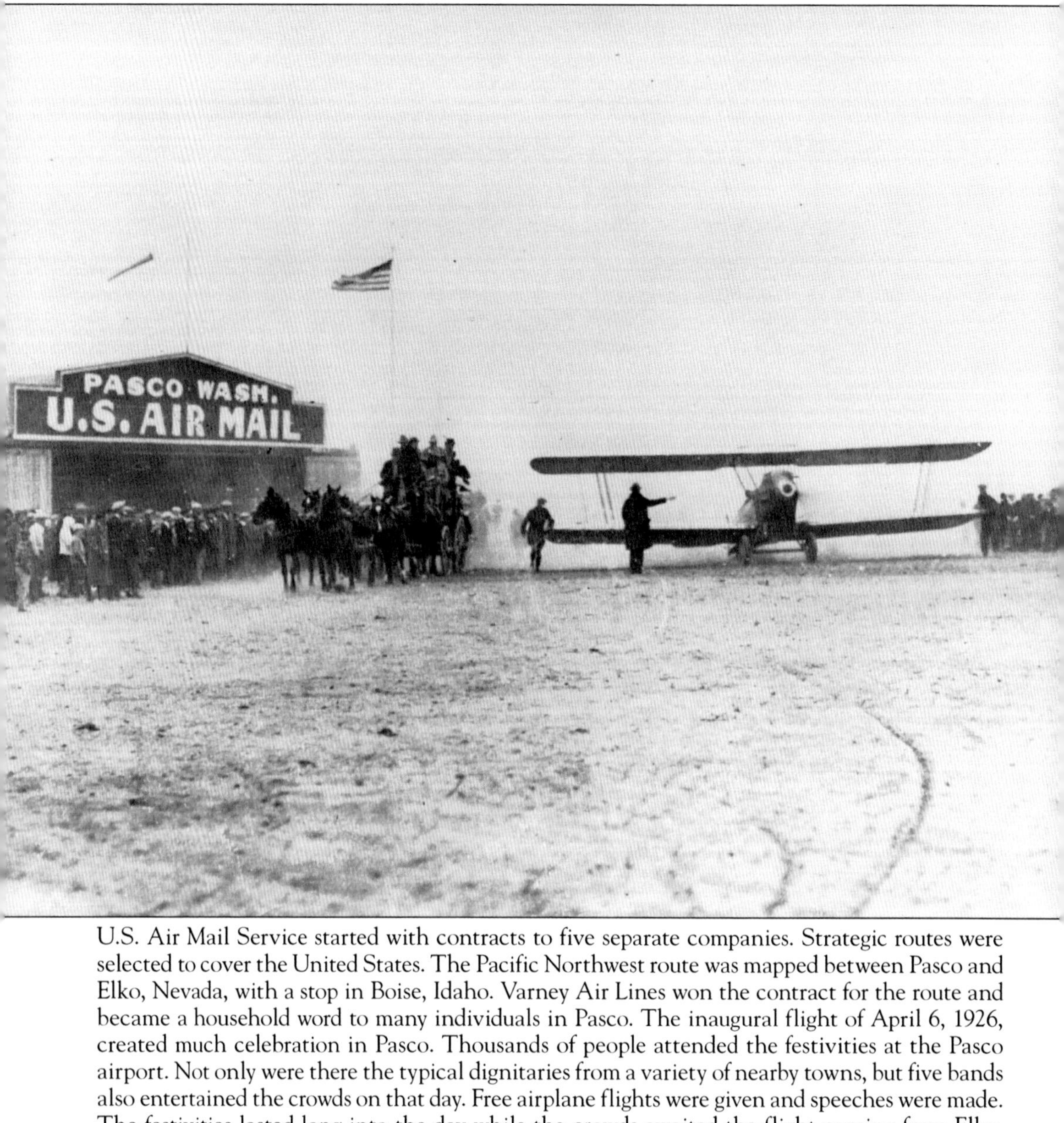

U.S. Air Mail Service started with contracts to five separate companies. Strategic routes were selected to cover the United States. The Pacific Northwest route was mapped between Pasco and Elko, Nevada, with a stop in Boise, Idaho. Varney Air Lines won the contract for the route and became a household word to many individuals in Pasco. The inaugural flight of April 6, 1926, created much celebration in Pasco. Thousands of people attended the festivities at the Pasco airport. Not only were there the typical dignitaries from a variety of nearby towns, but five bands also entertained the crowds on that day. Free airplane flights were given and speeches were made. The festivities lasted long into the day while the crowds awaited the flight coming from Elko, Nevada, to Pasco. (Courtesy of United Airlines Historical Foundation.)

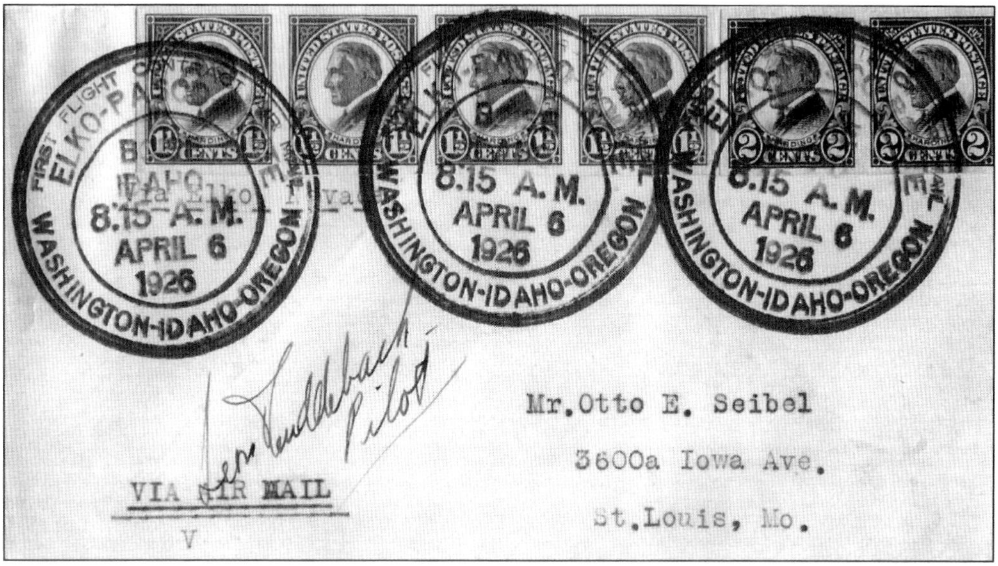

The Contract Air Mail Act of 1925 established airmail service contracts between the U.S. Post Office and private aviation companies. Varney Air Lines won the competitive bid for the route from Pasco, Washington, to Elko, Nevada. The inaugural flight carried 207 pounds of mail, which included 9,285 pieces. Mail came from as far away as Shanghai, China, and continued on to destinations in New York City, San Francisco, Elko, Boise, Salt Lake City, Chicago, and many foreign countries. The contents included not only correspondence but also grape juice and Kennewick asparagus. In addition to the "First Flight Air Mail" cancellation stamp (above), a stamp was affixed to the back of envelopes announcing the "Air-Mail Jubilee" (below). (Both courtesy of the United Airlines Historical Foundation.)

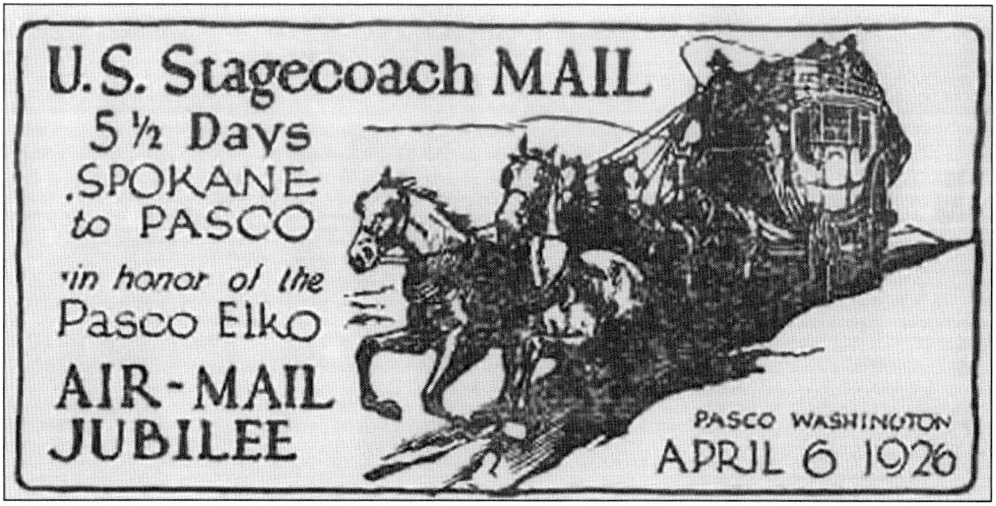

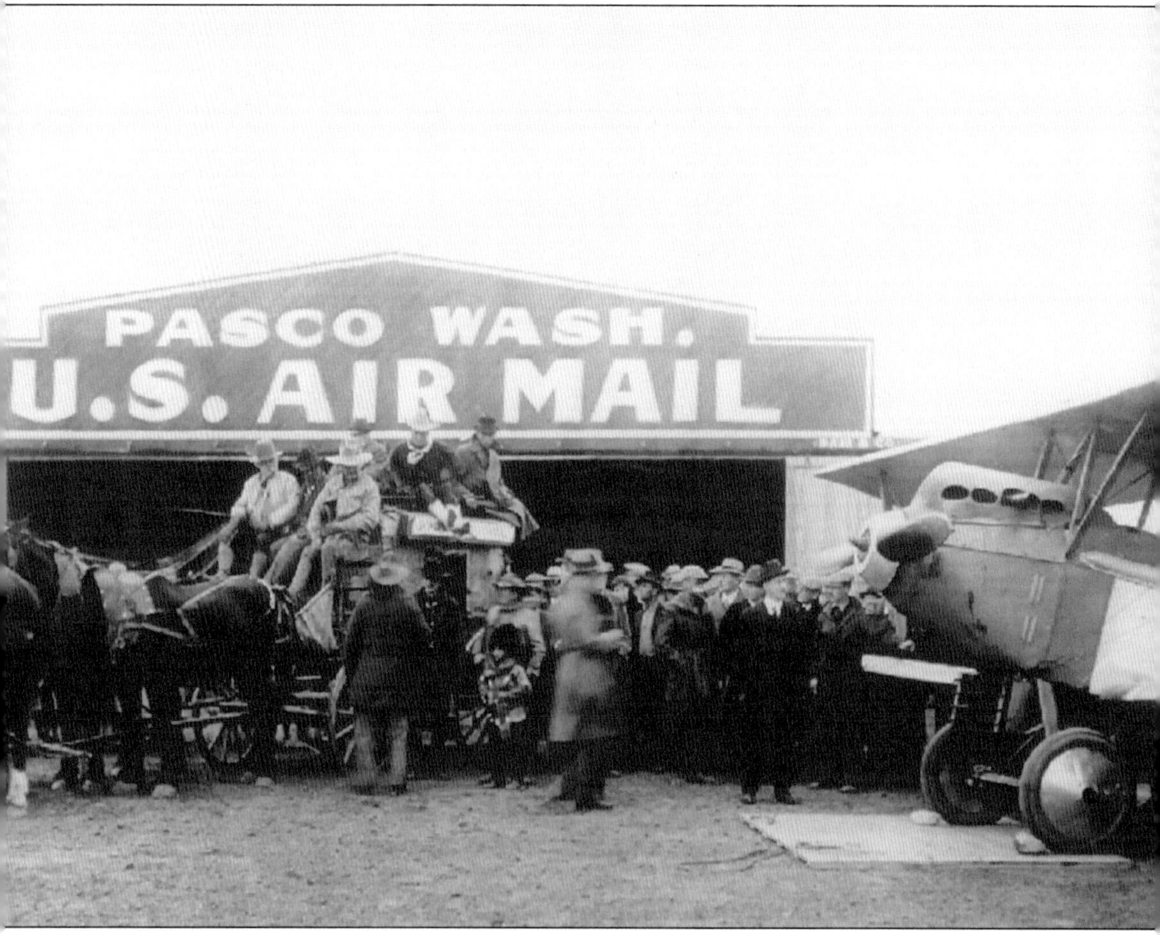

Felix Warren, a veteran stagecoach mail-delivery runner, brought a stagecoach to Pasco from Spokane for the airmail flight celebrations. The trip from Spokane took five days, but the airmail flight would travel over 400 miles in four hours. To signify the turnover in mail delivery, Warren delivered 207 pounds of mail to Leon Cuddeback's plane. The celebration included Felix Warren shooting blank cartridges in a playful display of the Old West. (Courtesy of the United Airlines Historical Foundation.)

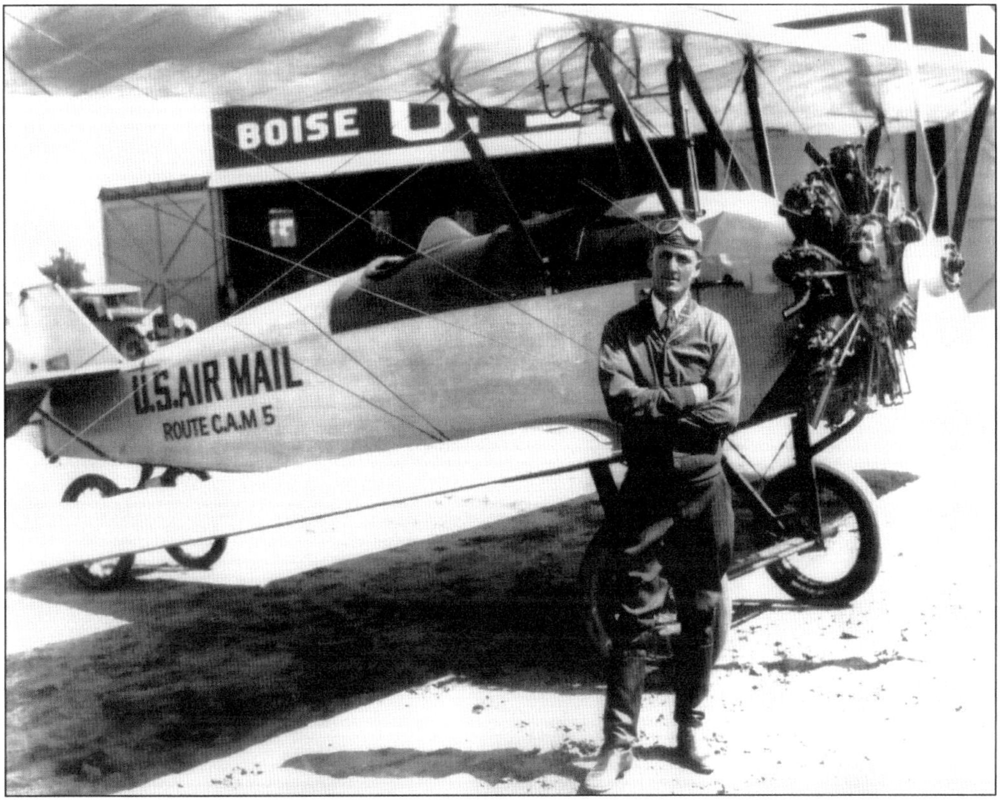

Leon Cuddeback was the pilot of the first successful airmail flight from Pasco to Elko, Nevada. Joe Taff and George Buck were to ceremoniously flip a coin for the honor to pilot the Swallow plane. However, flying to Pasco the previous day, they were forced to glide into a sand dune. Neither was hurt badly, but the accident cost them the flight. Varney's chief pilot, Cuddeback, was enlisted by default. (Courtesy of the United Airlines Historical Foundation.)

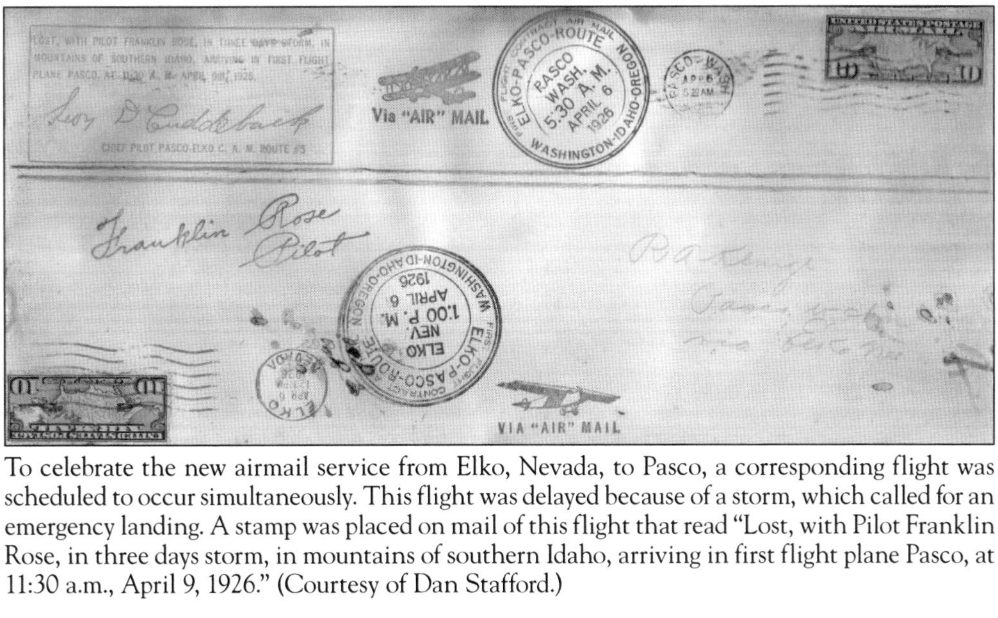

To celebrate the new airmail service from Elko, Nevada, to Pasco, a corresponding flight was scheduled to occur simultaneously. This flight was delayed because of a storm, which called for an emergency landing. A stamp was placed on mail of this flight that read "Lost, with Pilot Franklin Rose, in three days storm, in mountains of southern Idaho, arriving in first flight plane Pasco, at 11:30 a.m., April 9, 1926." (Courtesy of Dan Stafford.)

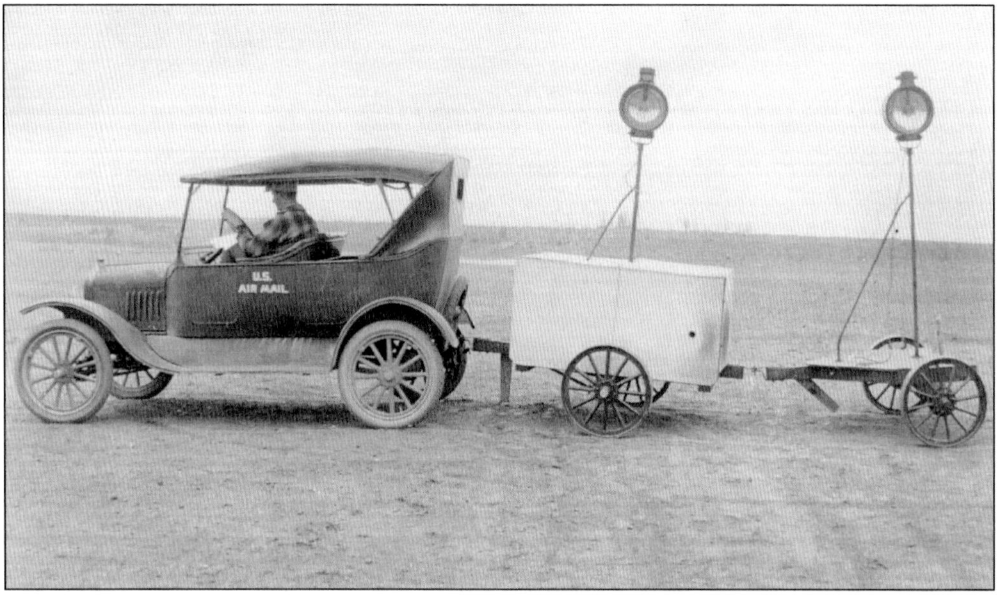

Cecil Downey, an electrician by trade, is shown towing airport lighting equipment for Varney Airlines in 1926. This equipment was all that was available to aid pilots during their landing approaches. Radios, beacons, weather reports, and other tools would be developed later. Due to the amount of aeronautical accidents during this time, the U.S. Department of Commerce determined locations for emergency landing fields, which were spaced 30 miles apart. (Courtesy of FCHS.)

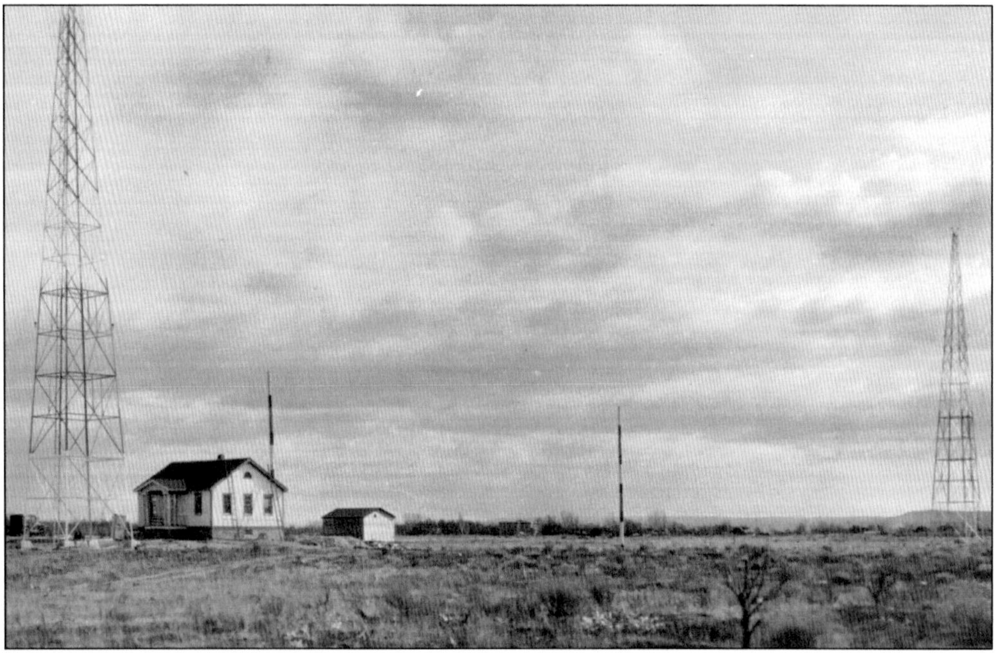

The first airport radio transmitter was run from the Cartmell house between Eighteenth and Nineteenth Avenues on Cartmell Street. Before radio transmitters were used, flares were manually placed on the runways to guide pilots to the ground. The need for better air traffic communication was evident after an airplane ran into a Model T that was placing needed flares. (Courtesy of FCHS.)

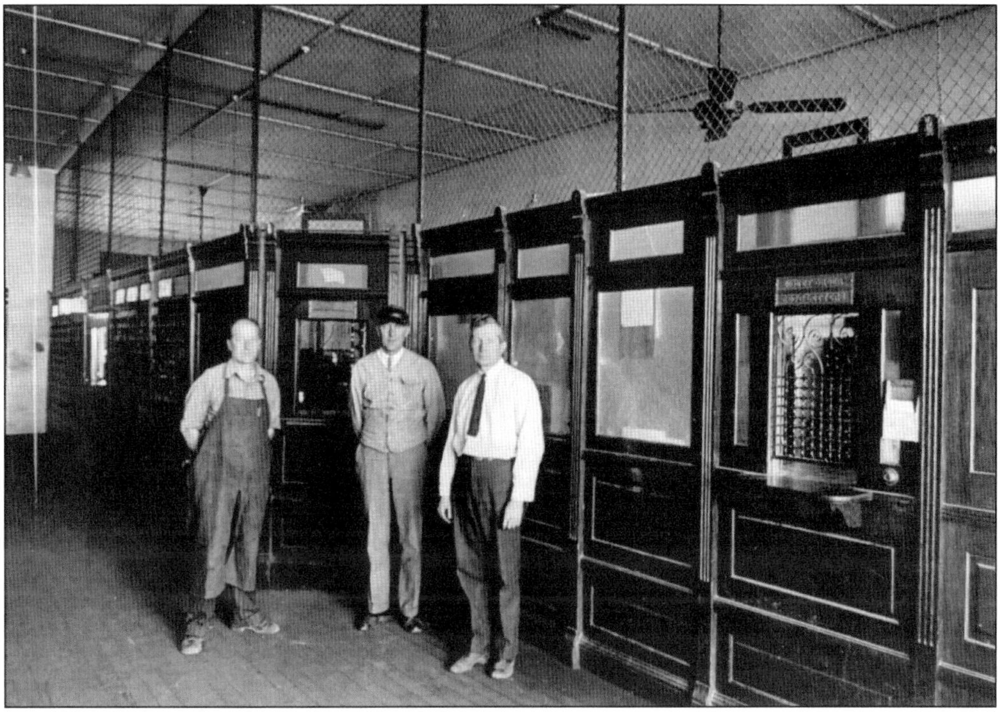

The Pasco Post Office was located on Second Street in 1926. From left to right are Sam Davenport, Arch Churchman, and William Russell Cox. Cox was the postmaster from 1923 to 1935, at which time the position of postmaster alternated with national political party preference. A. A. Barnes (not pictured) served as postmaster from 1914 to 1923 and again from 1935 to 1946. (Courtesy of FCHS.)

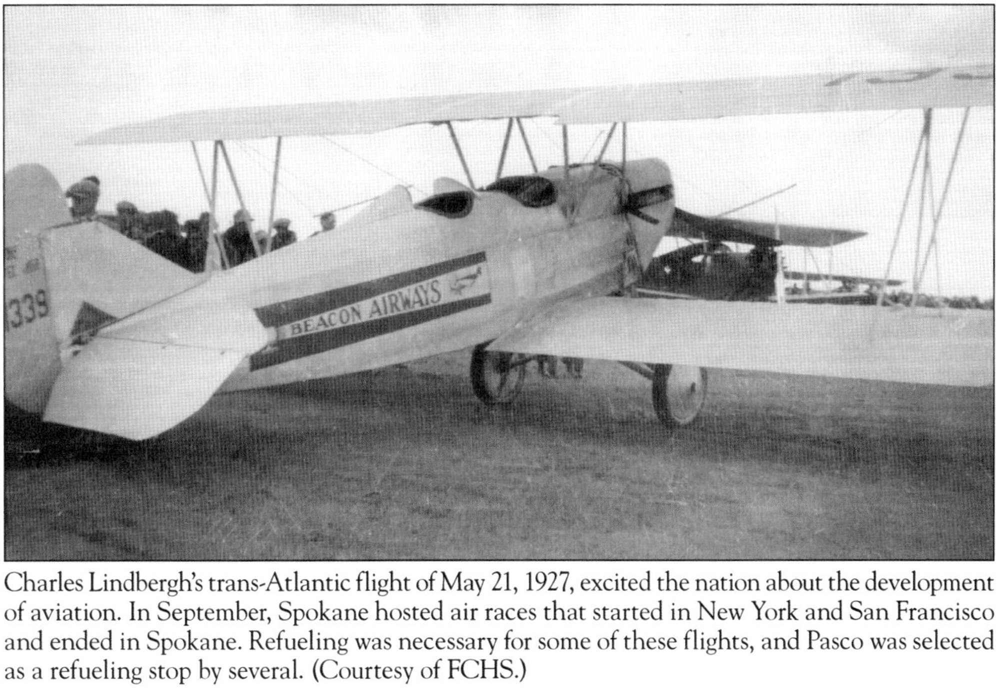

Charles Lindbergh's trans-Atlantic flight of May 21, 1927, excited the nation about the development of aviation. In September, Spokane hosted air races that started in New York and San Francisco and ended in Spokane. Refueling was necessary for some of these flights, and Pasco was selected as a refueling stop by several. (Courtesy of FCHS.)

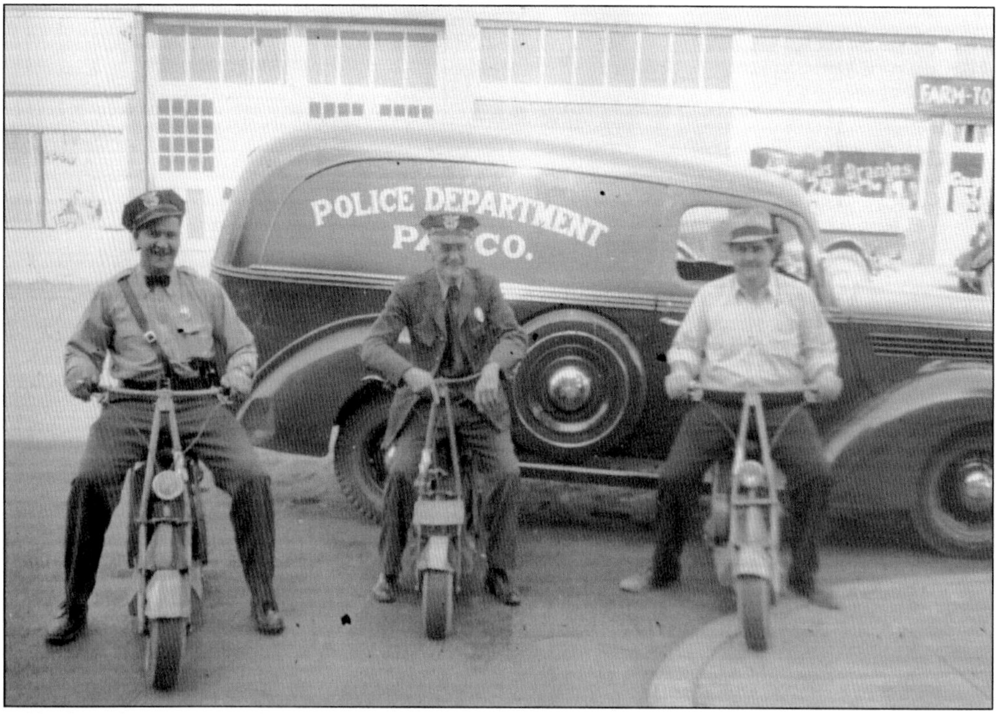

Alfred Buchanan moved to Pasco from Ainsworth in 1885 when his mother, Dora, relocated her restaurant. By 1907, Buchanan held the position of marshal, which he did again in 1909. He served the Pasco Police Department for over 30 years, including serving as police chief. Buchanan was well thought of, especially in mentoring young men in the community. He is pictured here between Paul Schlagel (left) and Melvin Schlagel (right). (Courtesy of FCHS.)

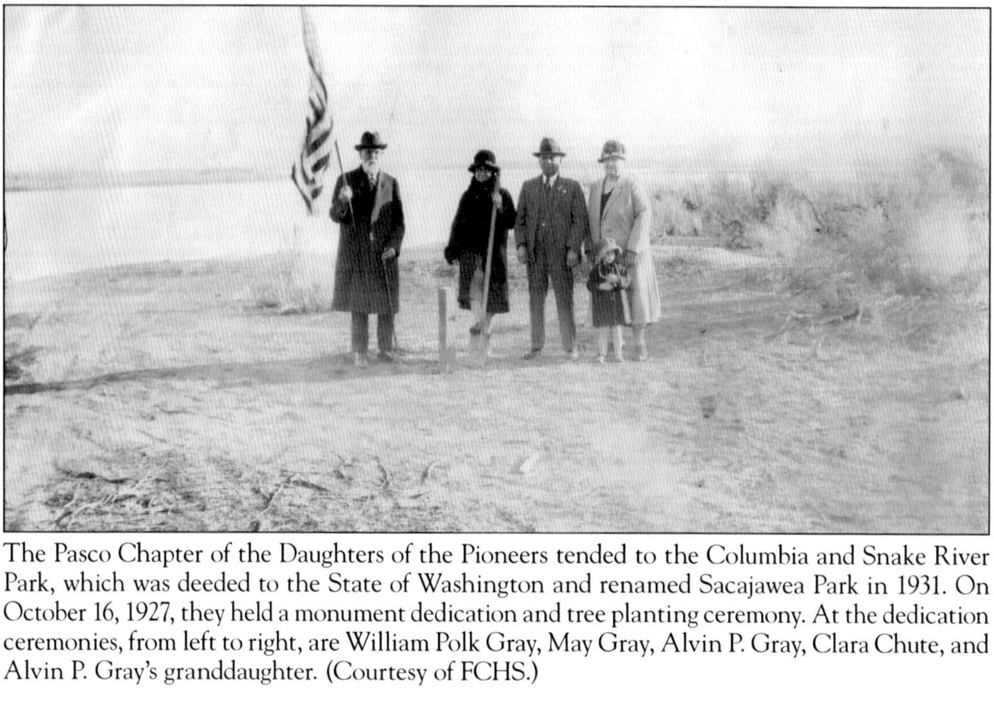

The Pasco Chapter of the Daughters of the Pioneers tended to the Columbia and Snake River Park, which was deeded to the State of Washington and renamed Sacajawea Park in 1931. On October 16, 1927, they held a monument dedication and tree planting ceremony. At the dedication ceremonies, from left to right, are William Polk Gray, May Gray, Alvin P. Gray, Clara Chute, and Alvin P. Gray's granddaughter. (Courtesy of FCHS.)

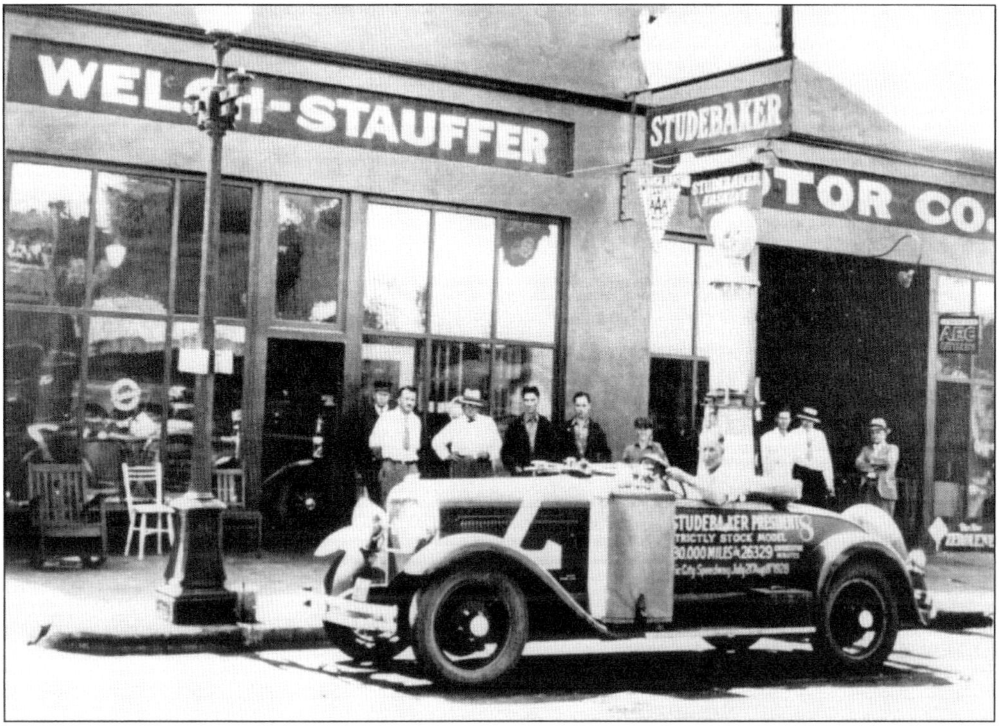

Welch-Stauffer Motor Company, located on Lewis Street, was proud to show off the latest Studebaker President 8 open-body model in 1928. The railroad in Pasco made it possible to have and display America's newest commercial items. The men pictured from left to right are unidentified, Ed Welch, Bill Chute, Myron Radelmiller, George Austin, unidentified, Elmer Yaden, Frank Hays, unidentified, and E. W. Landt. (Courtesy of FCHS.)

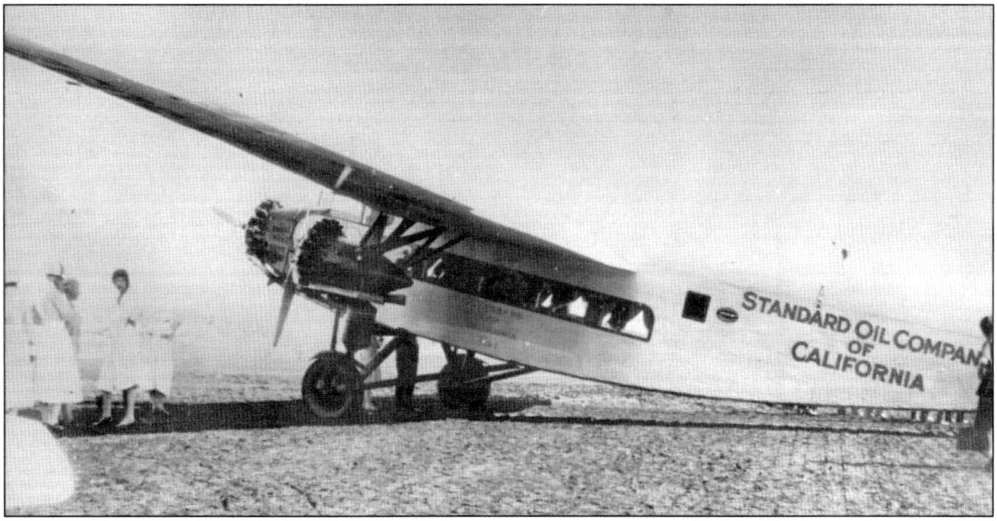

The 1929 Pasco Air Jubilee was a huge success and a large celebration. Approximately 10,000 people attended from various communities to watch aerial stunts and contests. Many took their first airplane rides that day. Standard Oil Company brought this three-engine Fokker that was equipped with loudspeakers to broadcast to the crowd below while it was in flight. (Courtesy of FCHS.)

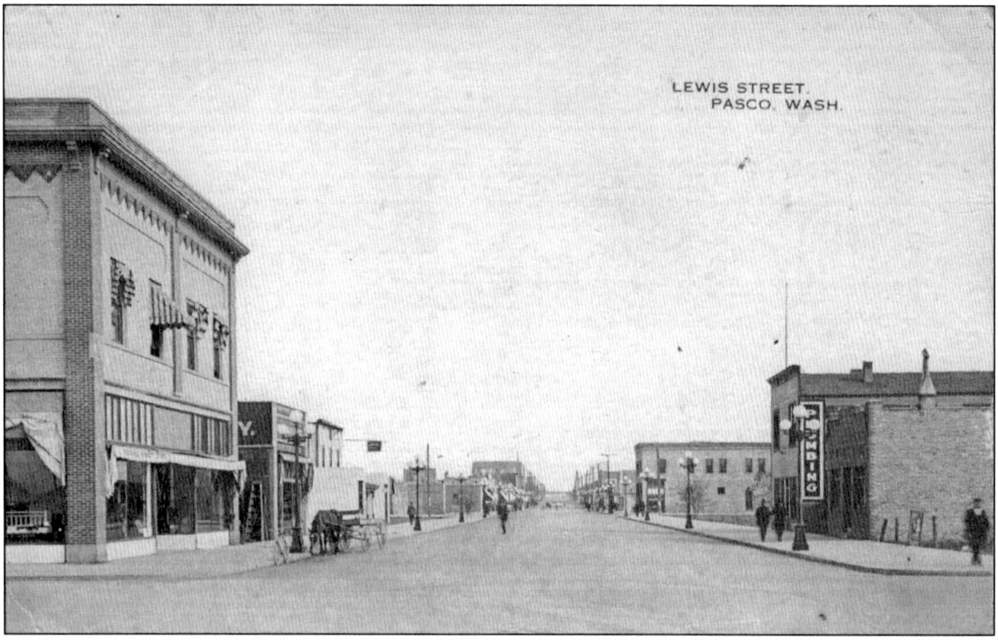

Lewis Street was one of the more popular business streets in Pasco during the late 1920s. During this time, there were mixed modes of transportation: automobiles, horses, bicycles, and pedestrians. Lewis Street stretched to include the Knights of Pythias Hall, Pasco Plumbing, Central Sanitation District, Sylvester's Pool Hall, and the Pasco Bank looking west. Looking west from the Tacoma Avenue intersection, there was the Hotel Cunningham, a barbershop, various liquor stores, and bars. This intersection included the railroad track with the depot nearby. In many ways, Pasco represented the all-American town of the late 1920s. (Both courtesy of Dan Stafford.)

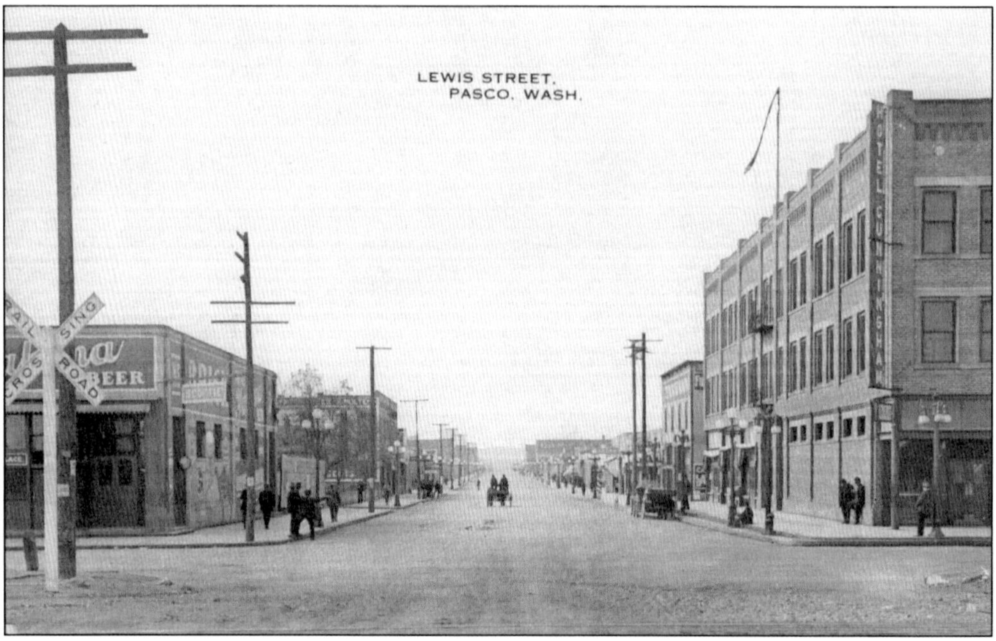

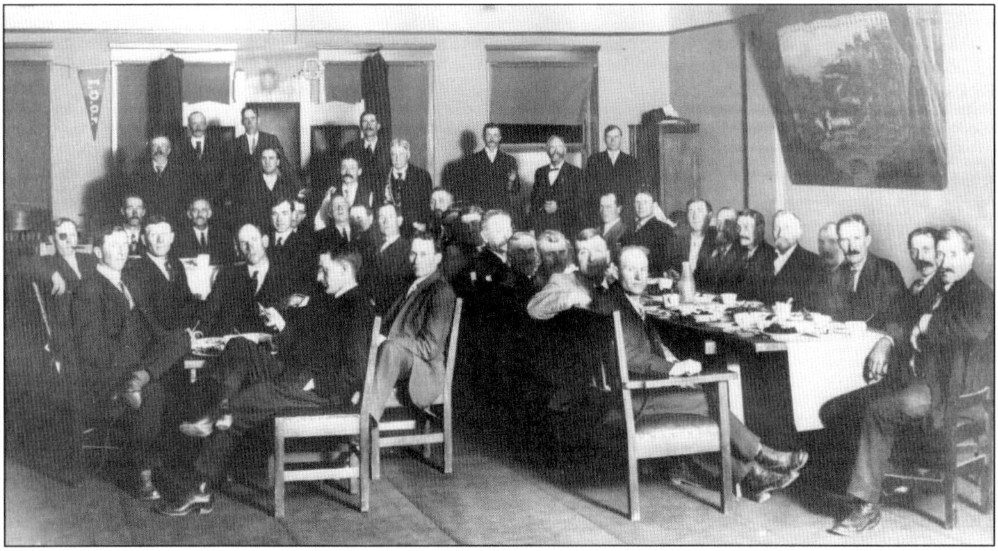

Societies and fraternal organizations were a very important part of most communities in America, especially in the late 1800s and early 1900s. These two photographs show the Independent Order of Odd Fellows (IOOF) and the affiliated women's group, the Rebekahs. The IOOF was started in America in 1819 on the principles of friendship, love, and truth. The three linked circles symbolize these principles. The photograph with the men is undated, but the ladies were photographed in 1930. Seated from left to right are (first row) Bertha McGhee, unidentified, Betty Bagley, two unidentified, and ? Peterson; (second row) unidentified, Opal Rowe, Edith Bergman, Matilda Richardson, Frances Pangle, unidentified, and Erma Hutchinson; (third row) unidentified, Ina Lewis, Cora Nogle, three unidentified, and Oda Cox; (fourth row); Effie Holbrook, Esther Wellman, Lulu Churchman, Beulah Myklebost, Lyla Clemens, and unidentified. (Both courtesy of FCHS.)

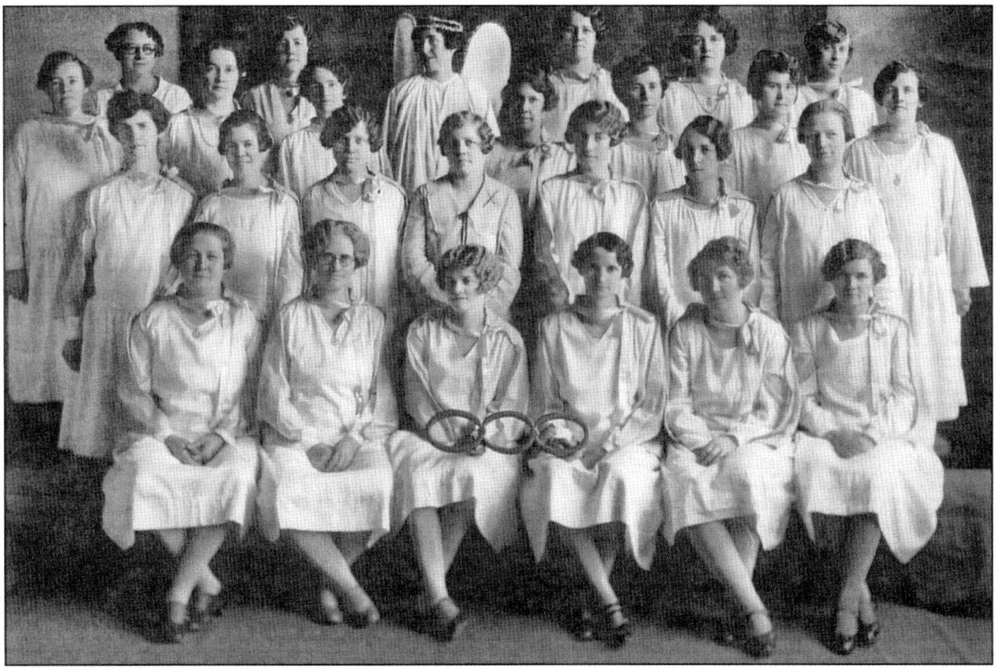

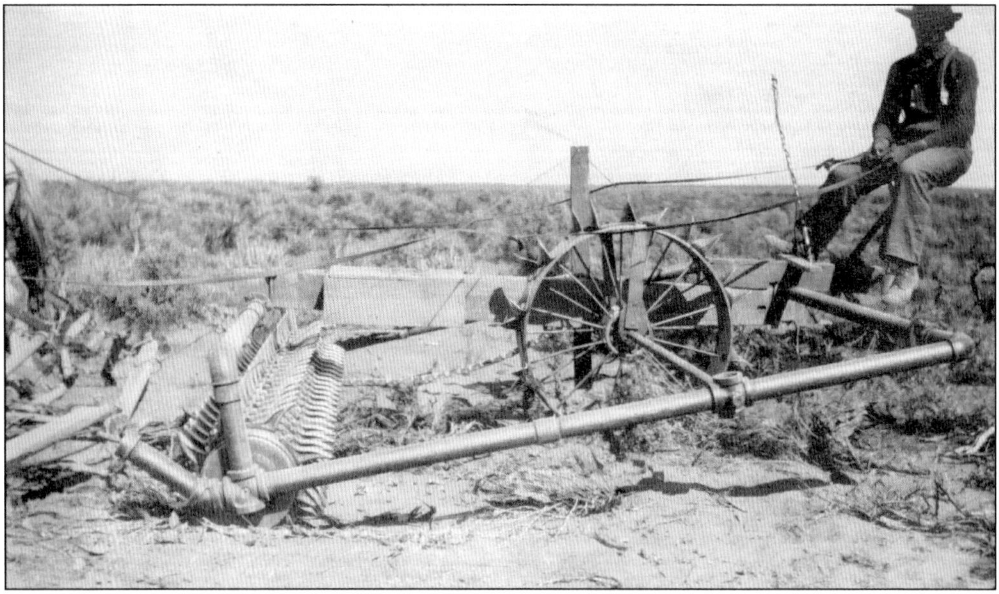

Sagebrush grew abundantly in the arid ground of Pasco. Clearing the land so that it could be used for farming took considerable time and effort. Sagebrush grubbers were used to help till the soil and extract the roots of these pesky bushes. These grubbers were pulled by a horse and needed only one man to guide their blades. This was definitely a time-saving piece of equipment. (Courtesy of FCHS.)

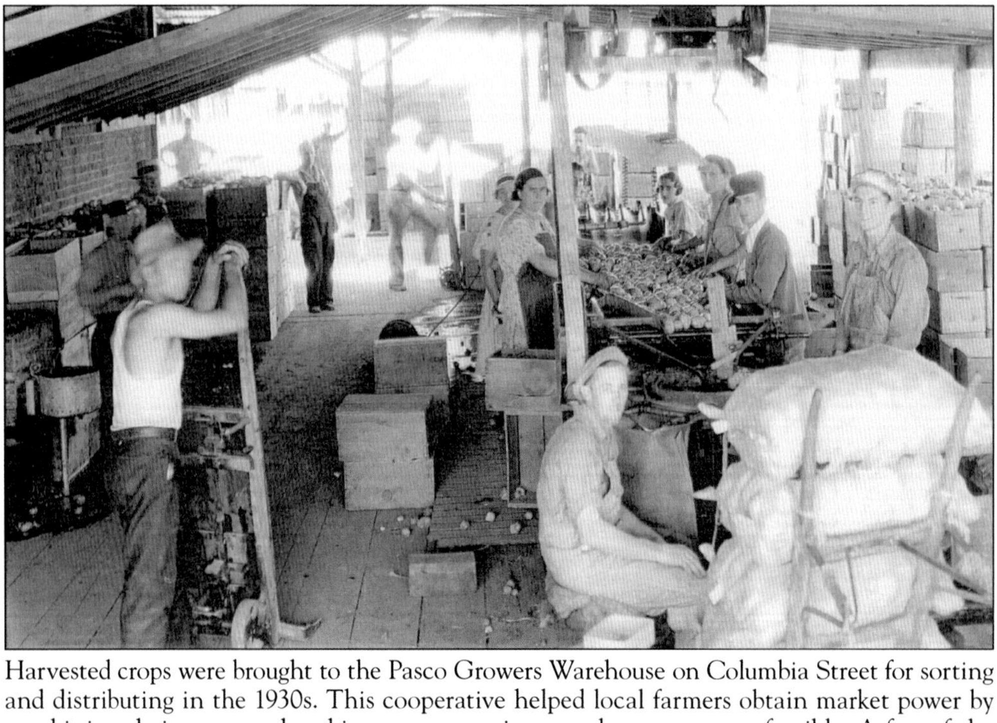

Harvested crops were brought to the Pasco Growers Warehouse on Columbia Street for sorting and distributing in the 1930s. This cooperative helped local farmers obtain market power by combining their crops and making transportation to other areas more feasible. A few of the workers in this photograph are Ina Wines, Wilbur Myerhoffer, Sophie Job, Claude and Raleigh Carr, and Albert Sperline. (Courtesy of FCHS.)

Six

Pasco and the Great Depression 1931 to 1940

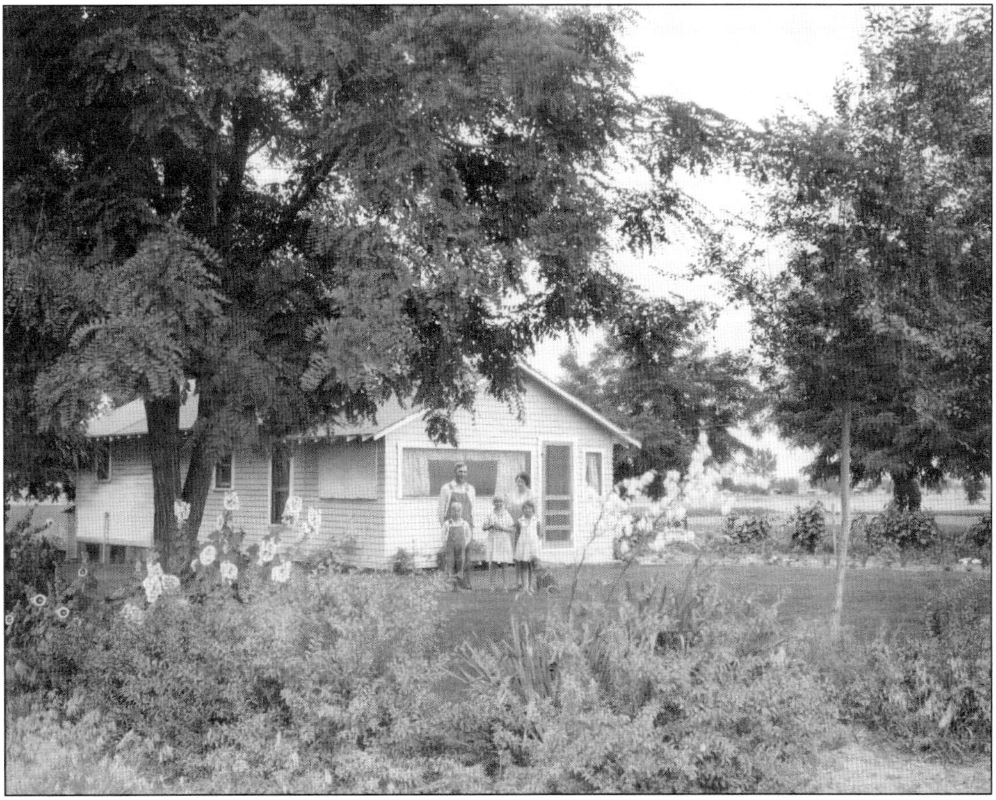

Charles Bell, also known as Sandy, a railroad switchman, moved to Pasco from Indiana in the mid-1920s. By the early 1930s, he had left the railroad and became a water master for the Franklin County Irrigation District. His home became a showcase of the Northern Pacific Railway to encourage other individuals to move to Pasco. The children from left to right are James, Dorothy, and Myrtle. Bell and his wife, Helen, are standing behind the children. (Courtesy of FCHS.)

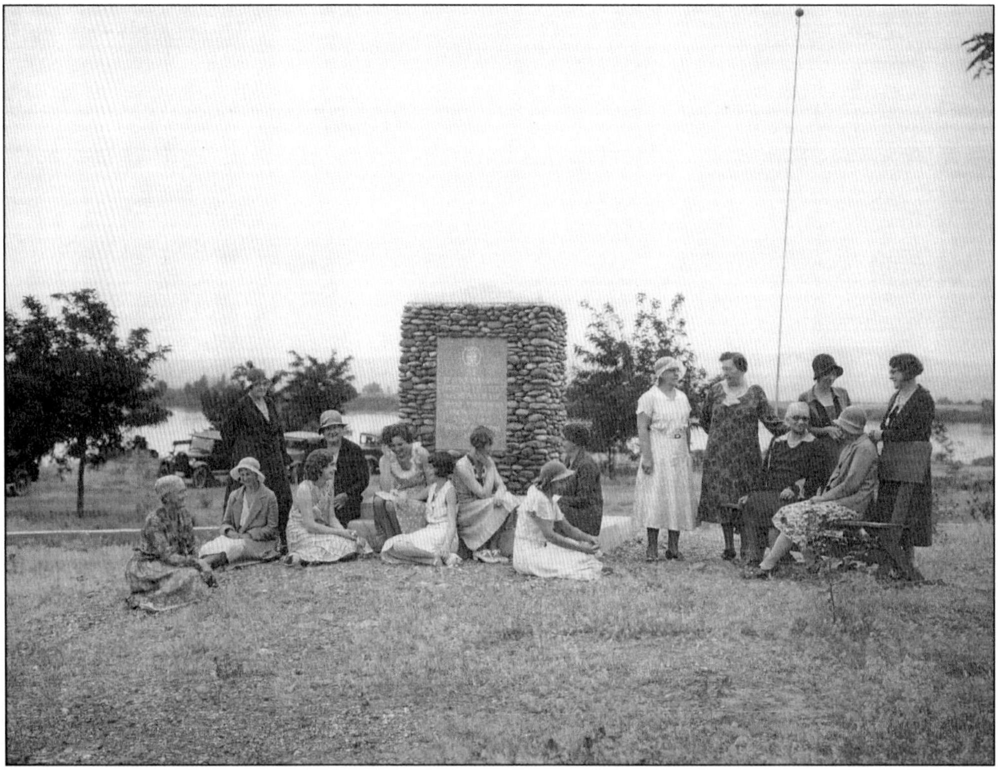

The Daughters of the Pioneers were dedicated to protect, preserve, and make known historical spots, documents, relics, records, and incidents of early days. In 1931, this organization donated land where Lewis and Clark had camped in the state of Washington. The Daughters of the Pioneers tended the area for years by planting trees and moving rocks to make a pleasing park. The park was renamed Sacajawea Park. (Courtesy of FCHS.)

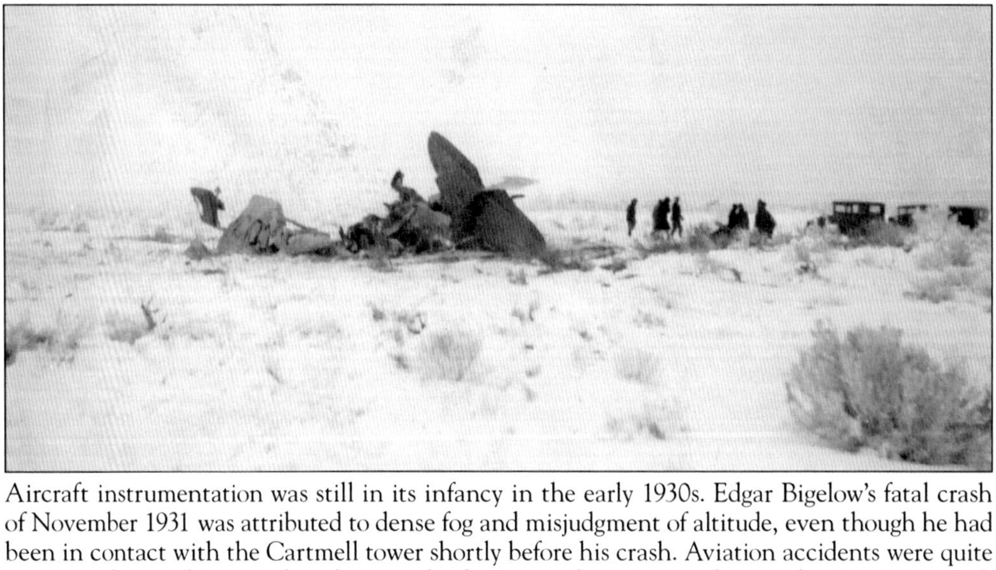

Aircraft instrumentation was still in its infancy in the early 1930s. Edgar Bigelow's fatal crash of November 1931 was attributed to dense fog and misjudgment of altitude, even though he had been in contact with the Cartmell tower shortly before his crash. Aviation accidents were quite common during this time, but this was the first airmail carrier accident at the Pasco terminal. (Courtesy of FCHS.)

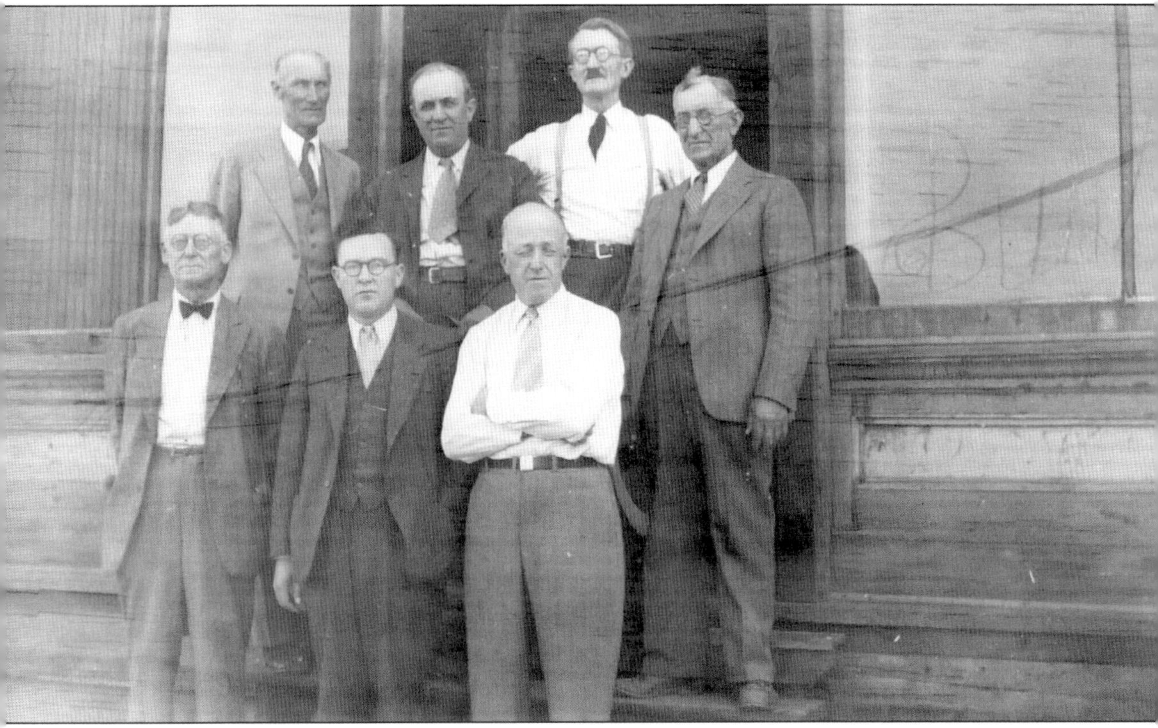

Communities in Franklin County in 1930 were, from largest to smallest, Pasco, Kahlotus, Connell, Eltopia, and Mesa. Pasco was the county seat, which meant that much of the surrounding communities' business was done in Pasco. In front of the courthouse in this 1932 photograph are, from left to right, (first row) E. F. Redd (county auditor and treasurer), Carl Wommack, and William Burns; (second row) H. B. Jensen (county commissioner), Frank Lamb (county commissioner), Levi Pyles, and D. C. W. Neff (county commissioner). (Courtesy of FCHS.)

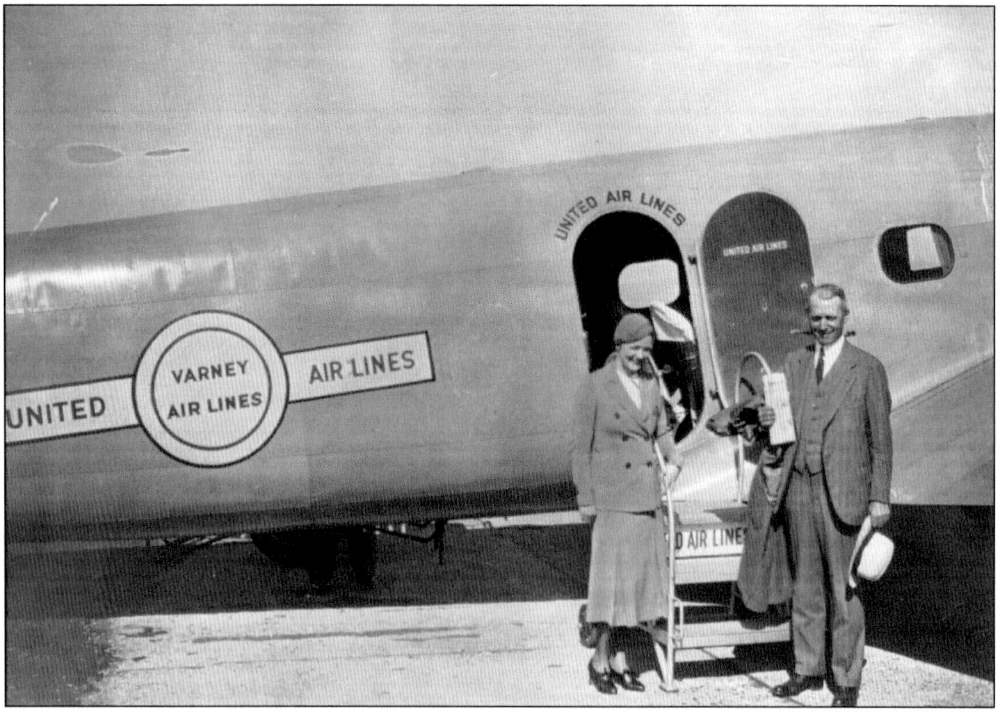

In 1931, Varney Air Lines merged with Boeing Air Transport, Pacific Air Transport, and National Air Transport. The name of the new company was United Air Lines. The sign on this airplane shows how the Varney Air Lines name was still used under the United Air Lines label. This photograph was taken as Washington State College president Ernest O. Holland boarded a plane for Chicago in 1933. (Courtesy of FCHS.)

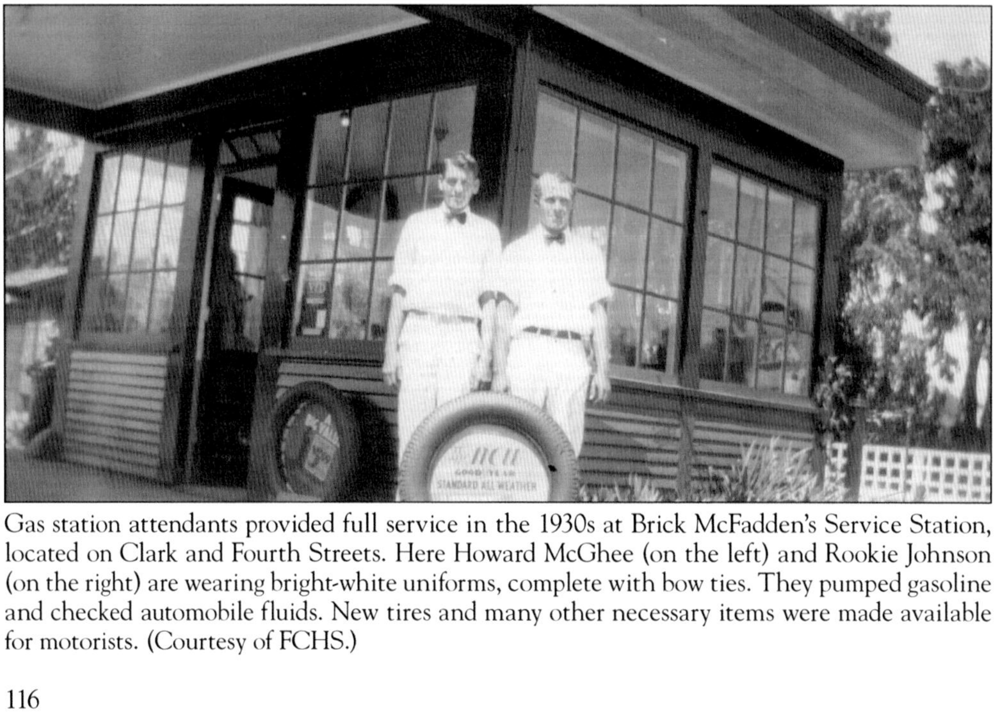

Gas station attendants provided full service in the 1930s at Brick McFadden's Service Station, located on Clark and Fourth Streets. Here Howard McGhee (on the left) and Rookie Johnson (on the right) are wearing bright-white uniforms, complete with bow ties. They pumped gasoline and checked automobile fluids. New tires and many other necessary items were made available for motorists. (Courtesy of FCHS.)

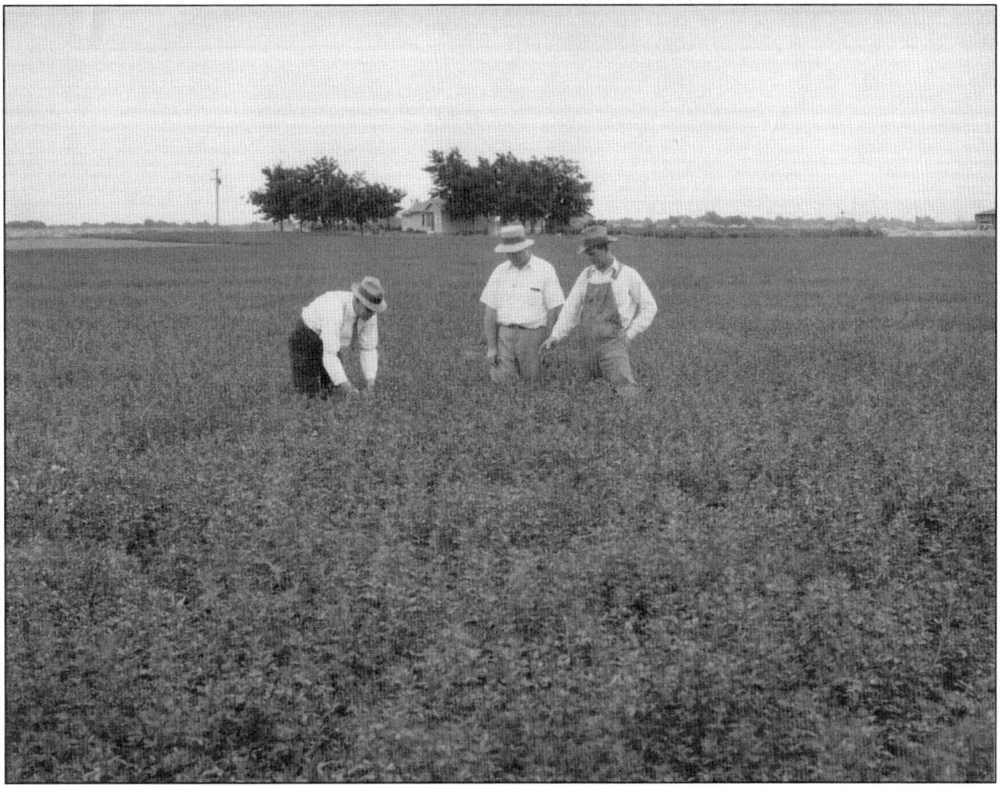

The Northern Pacific Railway hired W. C. Larsen as an immigration agent to influence families to move to Pasco in the mid-1930s. He would show photographs of Pasco in various communities while he explained the possibilities that the area provided. This healthy crop of alfalfa is an example of farming opportunities he boasted. From left to right are C. A. Bell (farmer), I. M. Ingham (county agent), and W. C. Larsen. (Courtesy of FCHS.)

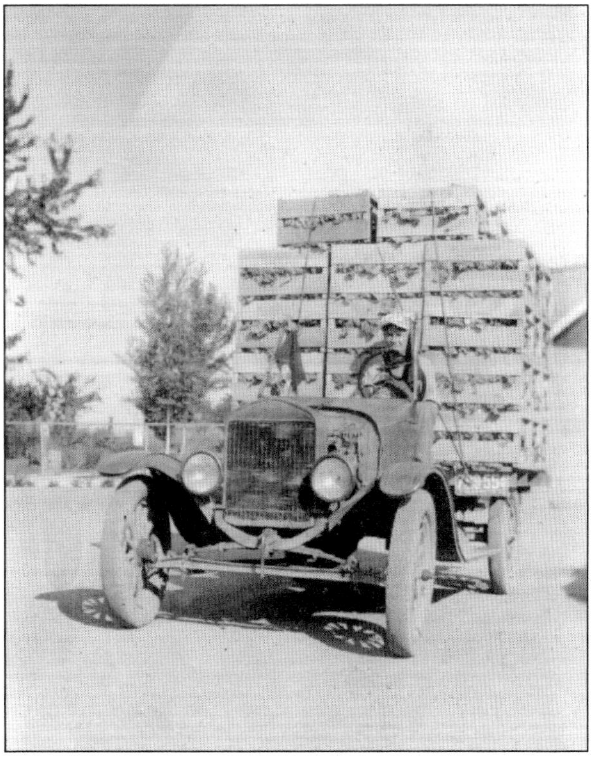

Products from the Diversity Farm were delivered to customers' doors, local markets, and neighboring communities. Wallace Harris was the primary delivery driver for many years. In this photograph, Harris is hauling lettuce to Kennewick. Harris's contribution to the community was considered so vital that he was exempted from serving in World War II. (Courtesy of the Harris family.)

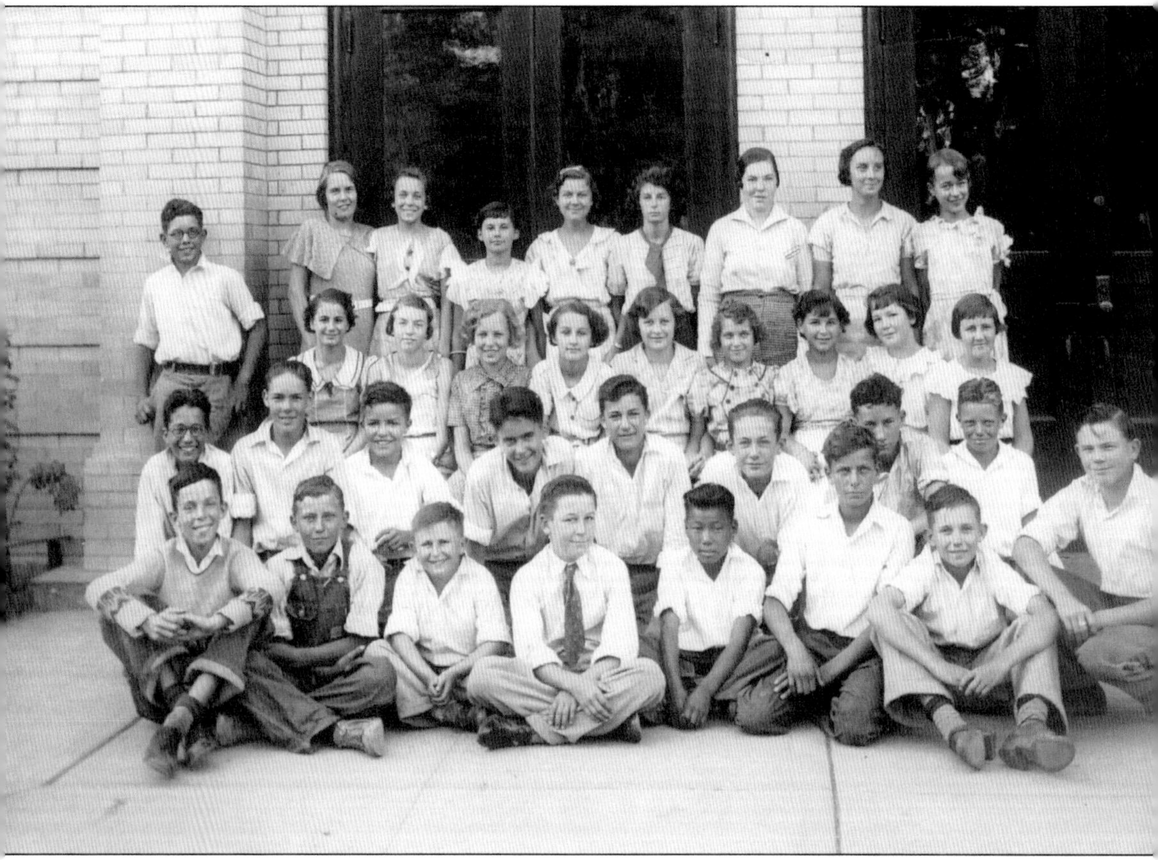

In the 1930s, Whittier School was used only for elementary grade classes. Students from Whittier School were then transferred to the larger Longfellow School after completing their elementary grades. Pasco High School was the only high school available in the area for many years. In 1935, one of the eighth-grade classes of Longfellow School included, from left to right, (first row) Norman Lance, Merle Rogers, Billy LeRoux, Don Hales, Bobby Yamauchi, Frank Pontarolo, Myrt Hastings, and unidentified; (second row) ? Buckley, Dave Pullium, Bob Skill, Art Burke, Howard Hales, Bill Jewell, Bill Parkhurst, and Pete Green; (third row) Darlene Haven, Roberta McCabe, Bonnie Mykelbost, Lois Roberts, Wilma Bailey, Evelyn Reardon, Carmen Newlun, Edith Potter, and Ruth Merritt; (fourth row) unidentified, Margaret Cook, Elizabeth Eaton, ? Kissler, Barbara Smith, LaVonne Robbins, Bette Leonard, Joy Haag, and Grace Kison. (Courtesy of FCHS.)

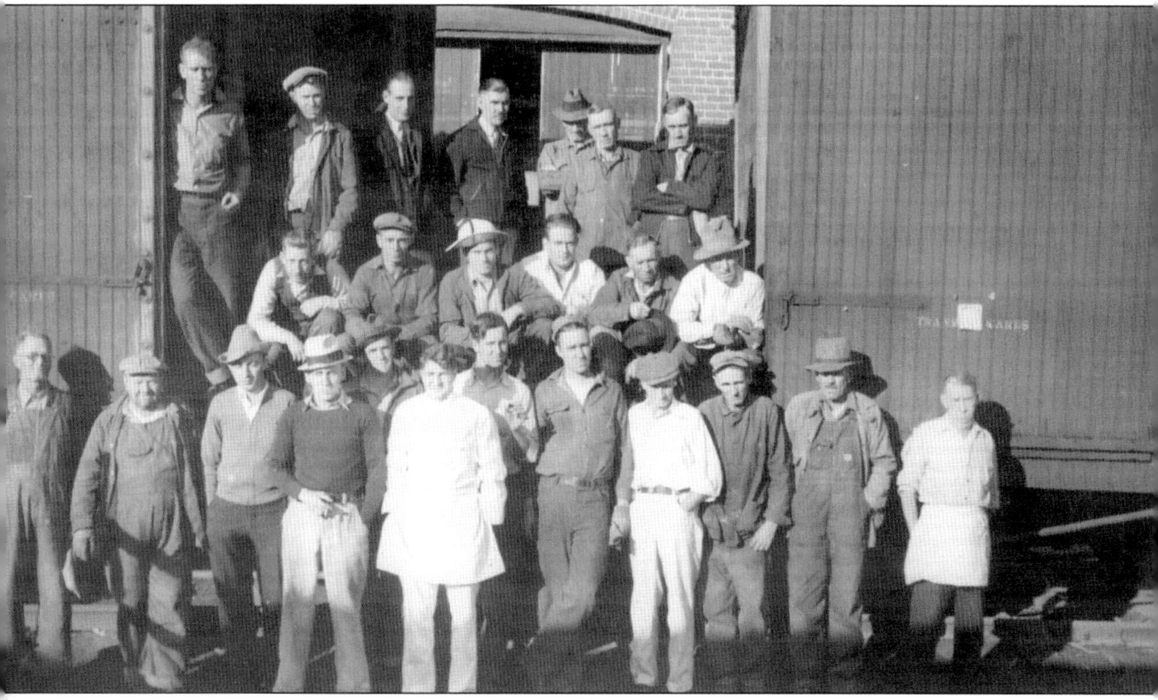

The Great Depression plagued the country with homeless men and women looking for work and security. Many of these people traveled west to find their dreams empty. In 1933, the federal government established the Federal Transient Service, which gave a matching $1 to every $3 in local direct relief for the homeless. The Federal Transient Shelter at Pasco was established in 1934 to provide shelter, food, job training, and education. In the 15 months the shelter was open, over 43,000 people were registered with the shelter. Many of these individuals stayed for more than one night, and a micro-community was established. A representative government, including campaign parades and promises, was created at the shelter. The shelter published a weekly newspaper titled the *Pasco Manifest*, which covered not only local shelter news but also national and regional news. Entertainment consisted of boxing and wrestling matches, amateur nights, and card tournaments. Basketball and baseball were other activities enjoyed by the guests of the shelter, who built a city ball field at the corner of First and Columbia Avenues. (Courtesy of FCHS.)

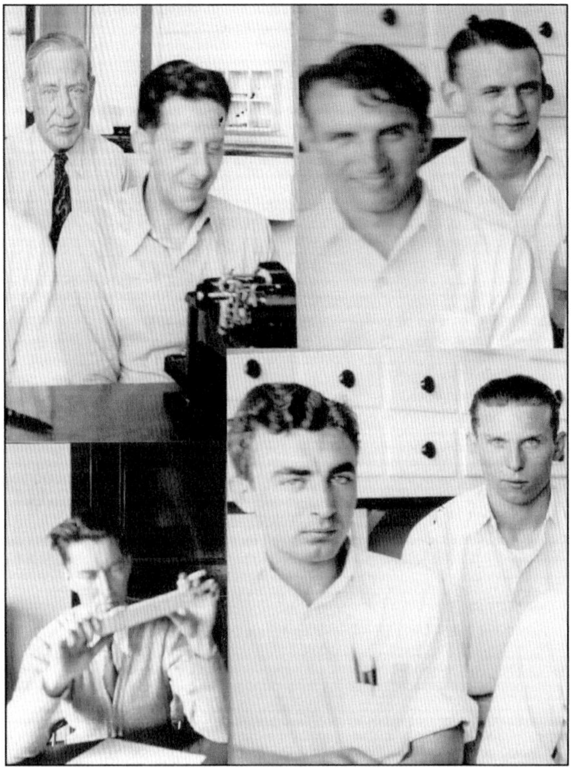

Educational classes were offered to transients while staying at the Federal Transient Shelter at Pasco. English classes covering topics such as public speaking, business correspondence, and spelling were very popular. Trade skills were also taught in mechanical drawing and electrical classes. These classes offered an education in varied aspects of the history, terms, and laws of electricity and covered subjects like single-phase circuits, meters, and motors. (Courtesy of FCHS.)

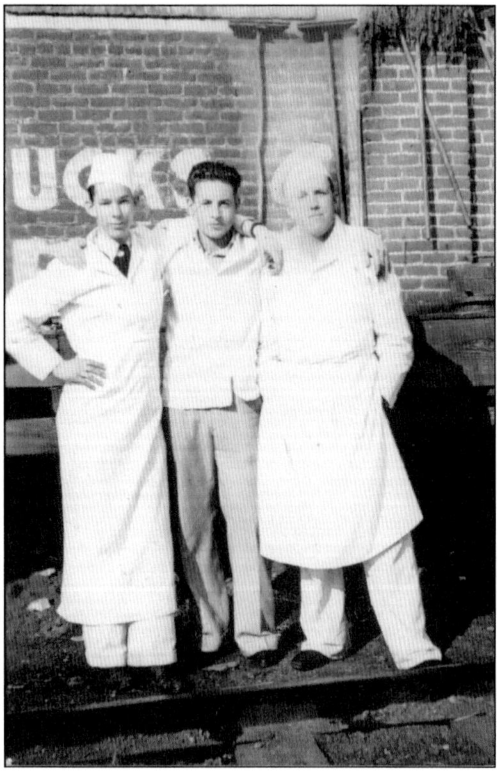

The Federal Transient Shelter at Pasco maintained an average of 150 permanent guests. Half of these worked for the shelter in jobs such as tailor, barber, launderer, nurse, teacher, dining room attendant, or office staff. The other half worked in the Pasco community helping with cleanup and repair work. The dining room was greatly appreciated by the shelter guests and provided an average of 725 meals a day. (Courtesy of FCHS.)

The Federal Transient Shelter at Pasco was supervised and actively run by Joseph Werner, a young man from Yakima. Before coming to Pasco to run the shelter, Werner worked for the YMCA in Yakima. When the shelter closed, Werner moved to Alaska to work for the U.S. Forest Service. He later became a successful accountant in Juneau, Alaska. (Courtesy of FCHS.)

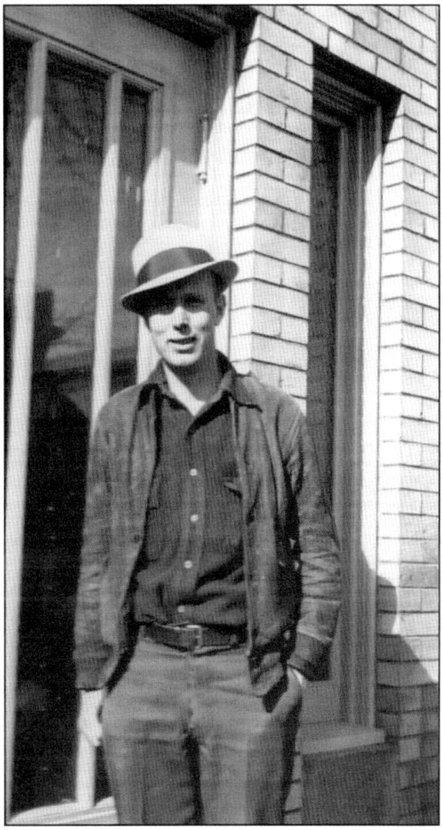

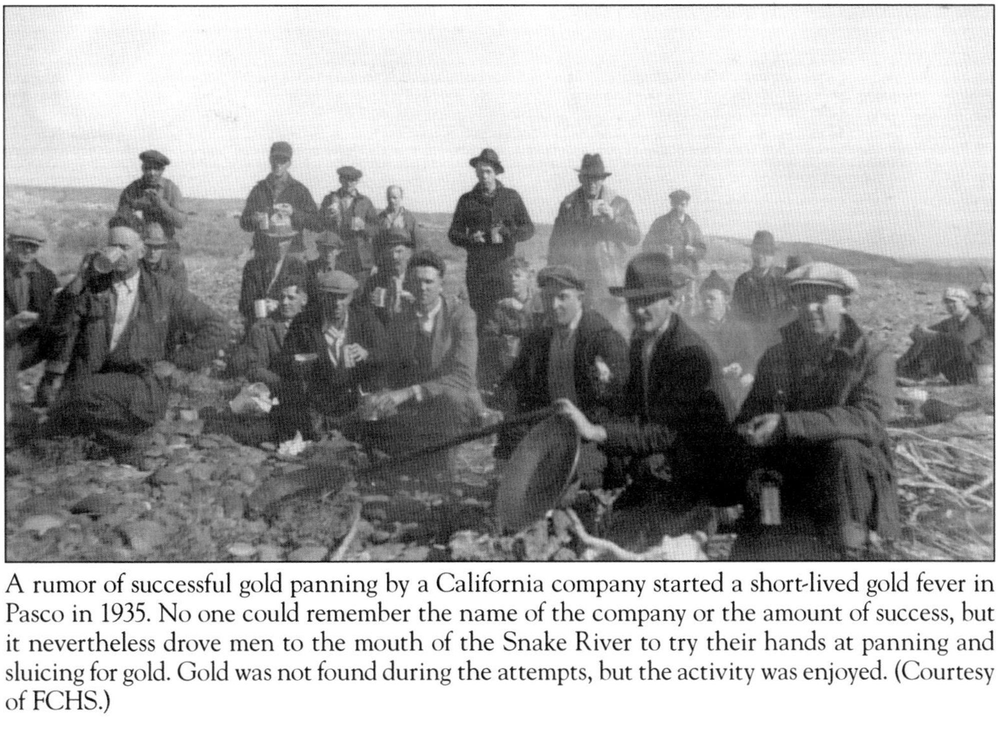

A rumor of successful gold panning by a California company started a short-lived gold fever in Pasco in 1935. No one could remember the name of the company or the amount of success, but it nevertheless drove men to the mouth of the Snake River to try their hands at panning and sluicing for gold. Gold was not found during the attempts, but the activity was enjoyed. (Courtesy of FCHS.)

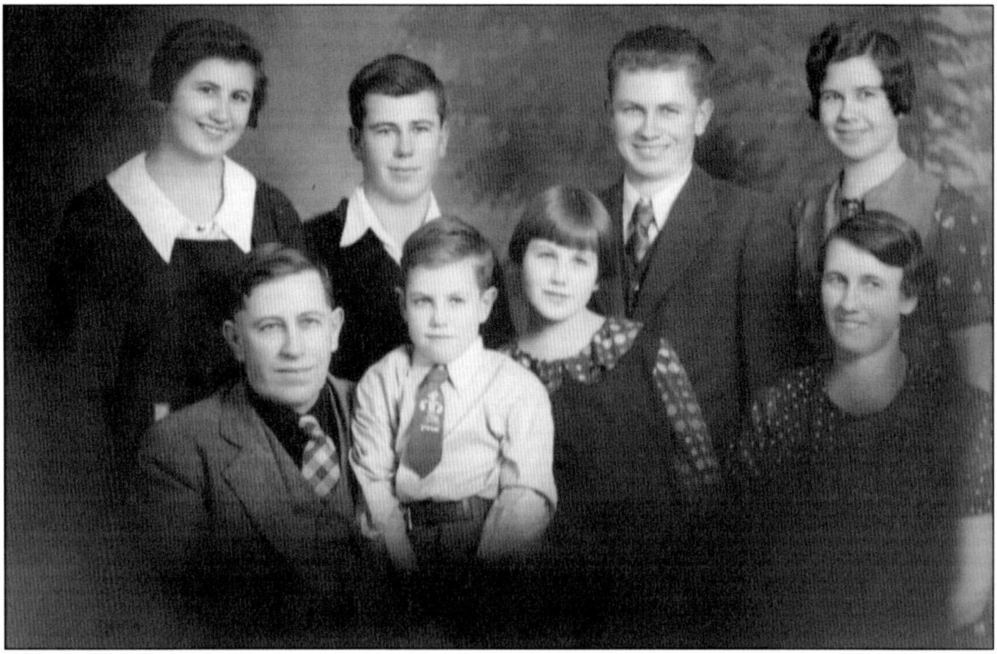

The Harris family members were true Pasco pioneers. Fred Harris came to Pasco in 1889 from Iowa. Lura Wallace Harris was born in Pasco in 1891. They married in 1912 and started working to build their farm. It became well known as the Diversity Farm. This picture of the Harris family was taken in 1935. From left to right are (first row) Fred, Alvin, Mary, and Lura; (second row) Gertrude, William, Wallace, and Lucille. (Courtesy of the Harris family.)

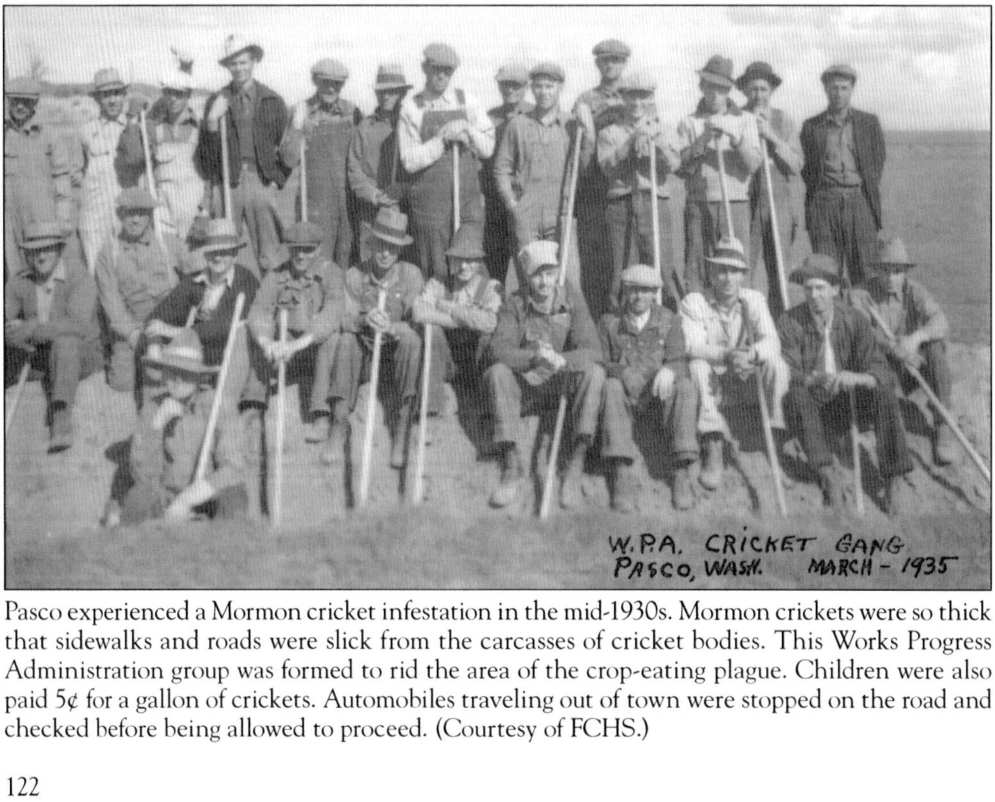

Pasco experienced a Mormon cricket infestation in the mid-1930s. Mormon crickets were so thick that sidewalks and roads were slick from the carcasses of cricket bodies. This Works Progress Administration group was formed to rid the area of the crop-eating plague. Children were also paid 5¢ for a gallon of crickets. Automobiles traveling out of town were stopped on the road and checked before being allowed to proceed. (Courtesy of FCHS.)

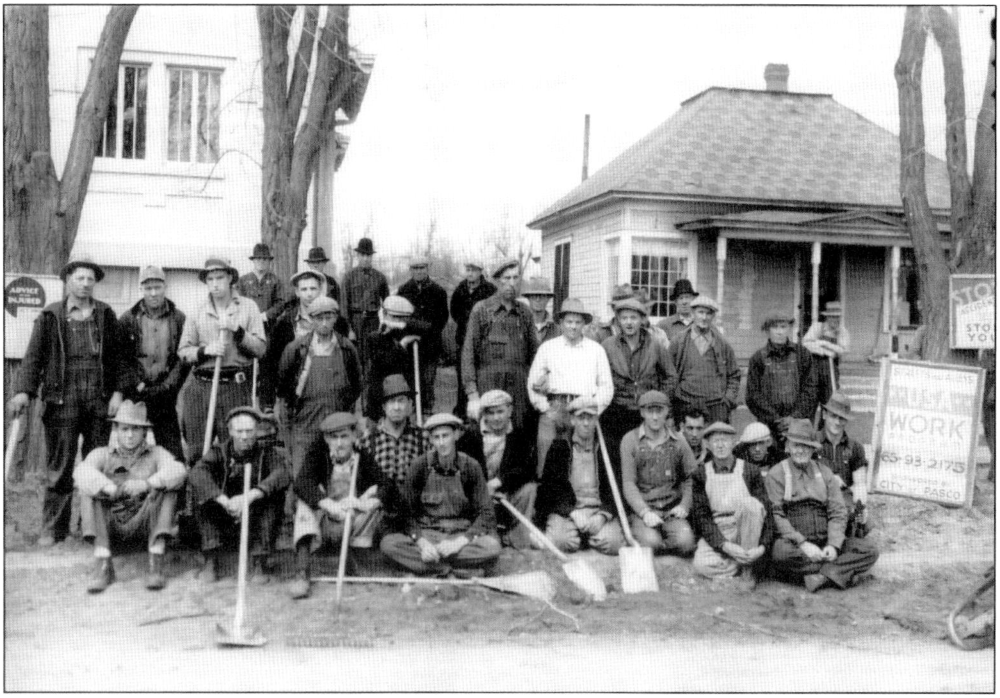

The Works Progress Administration (WPA) was created in April 1935 by President Roosevelt in an attempt to provide recovery and relief from the Great Depression. Over a million public work projects were created, which employed more than eight million people. This photograph was taken in April 1938 to celebrate the third anniversary of the WPA. This Pasco group was employed to work on the streets and alleys in the town. (Courtesy of FCHS.)

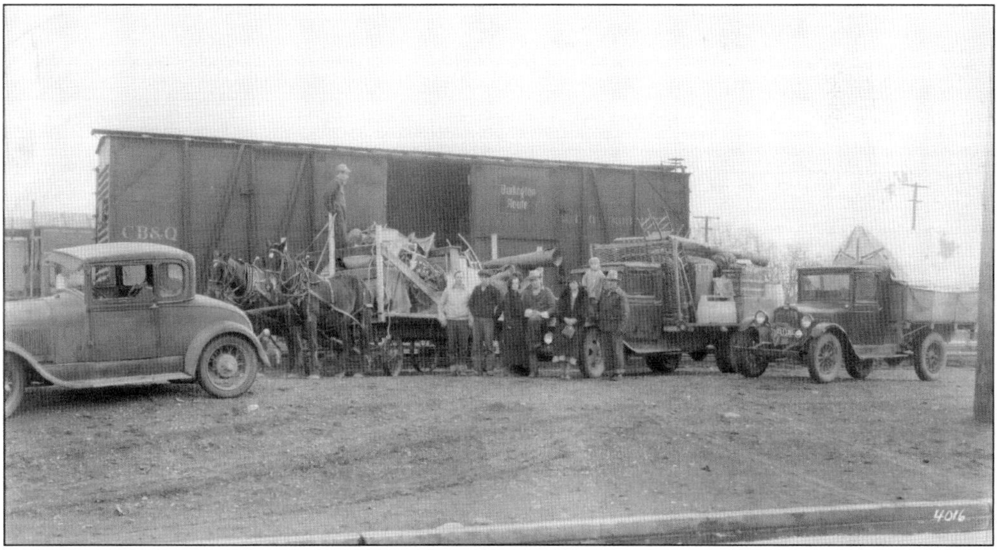

Railway transportation of household goods was provided by the Northern Pacific Railway to families that were willing to relocate to Pasco. The Franklin County Irrigation District had been recently reorganized, and success was on the horizon. Individuals willing to work the soil were desperately needed. These families have just arrived from the Dust Bowl–stricken area of Scotts Bluff, Nebraska, in the mid-1930s. (Courtesy of FCHS.)

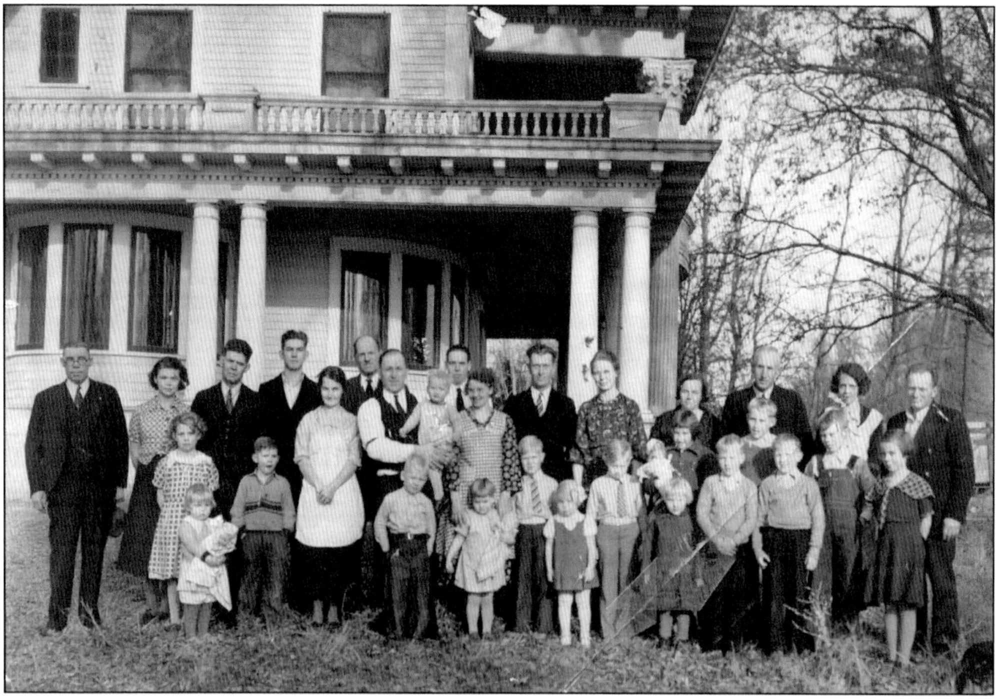

The Northern Pacific Railway hired W. C. Larsen to promote Pasco to families that would be willing to relocate and farm the land. By 1937, an estimated 488 families had immigrated. A majority of these families were from areas impacted by the Dust Bowl. This picture, taken December 25, 1936, shows five new families from North Dakota, Minnesota, Idaho, Nebraska, and Oregon. (Courtesy of FCHS.)

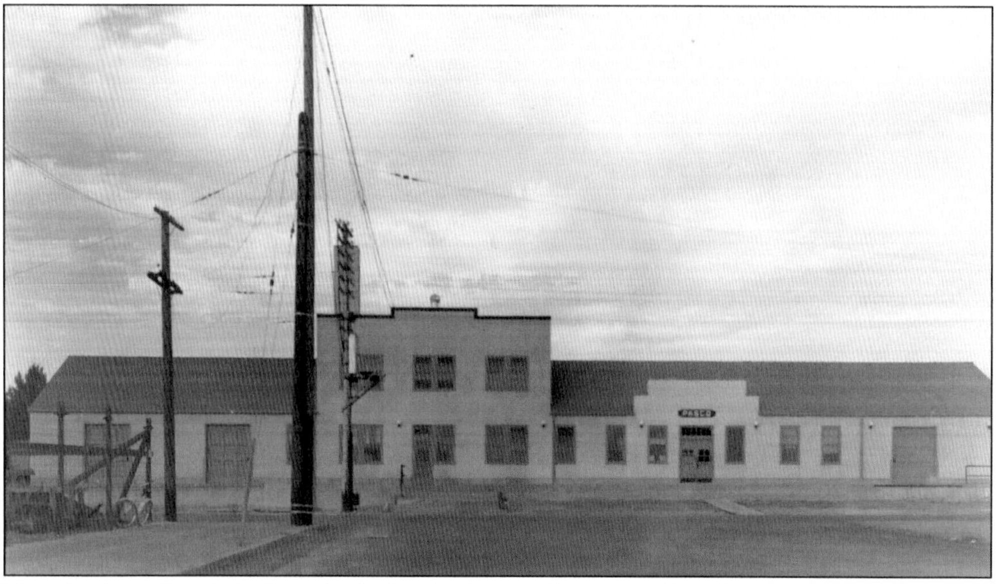

The Northern Pacific Railway built the third Pasco depot in 1936. The second depot was built a distance from the freight yard. The third depot was advantageously built in the same location as the first depot so that the freight yard and passenger depot could be serviced more efficiently. (Courtesy of the Washington State Railroads Historical Society.)

In 1939, America was starting to pull out of the Great Depression. Jobs were highly valued, and the railroad was still one of Pasco's largest employers. This photograph shows one of the many work teams employed by the railroad. From left to right are J. D. Wallace (brakeman), J. J. Mottner (engineer), H. A. Terrell (switchman), A. W. Bennke (switchman), and M. A. Houser. (Courtesy of the Washington State Railroads Historical Society.)

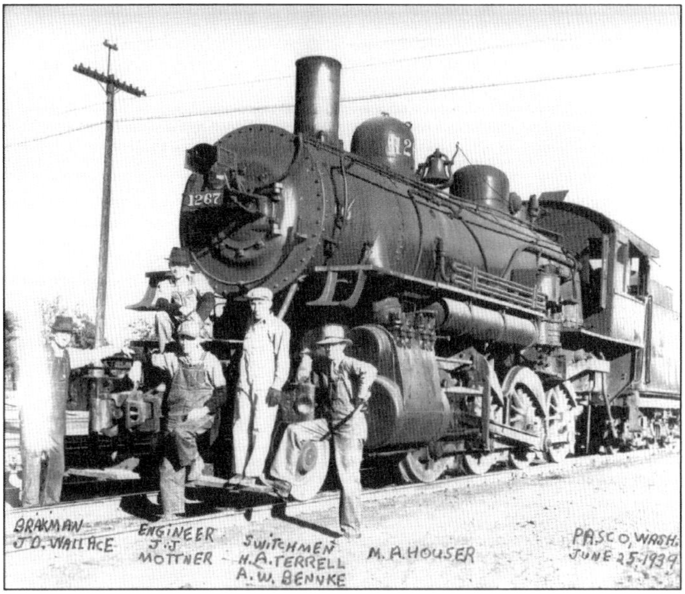

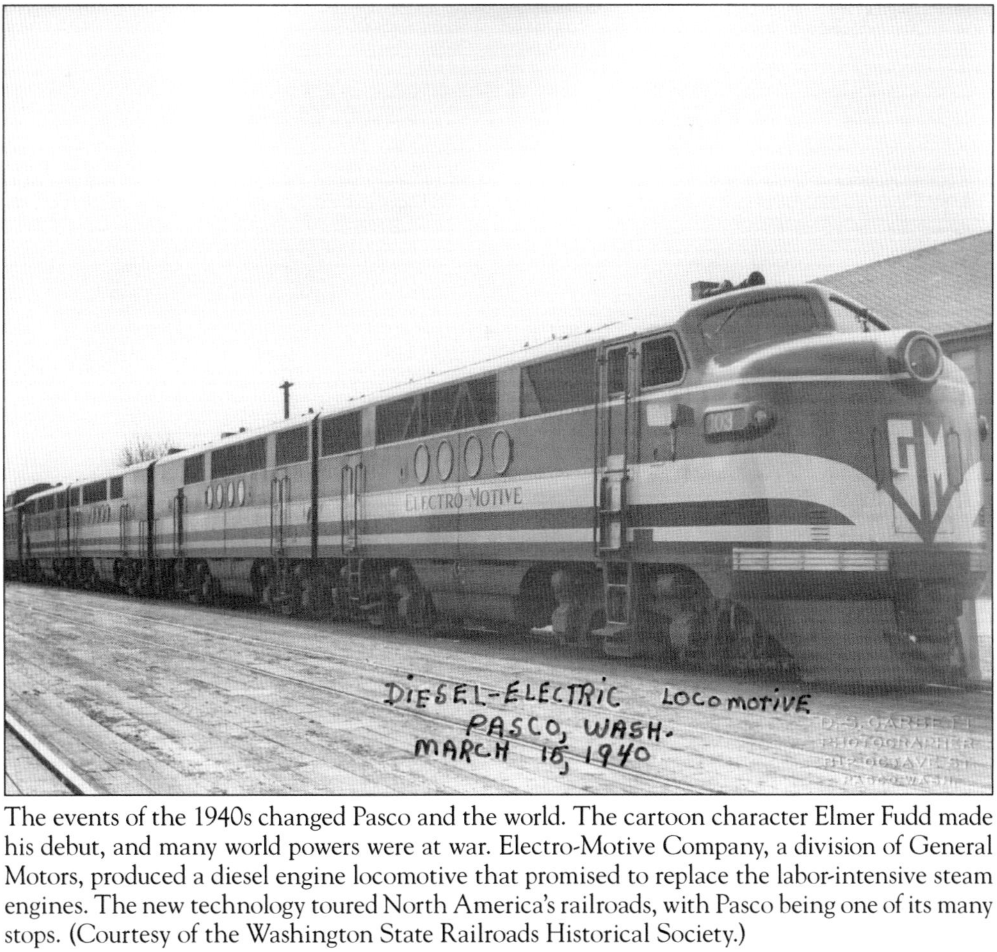

The events of the 1940s changed Pasco and the world. The cartoon character Elmer Fudd made his debut, and many world powers were at war. Electro-Motive Company, a division of General Motors, produced a diesel engine locomotive that promised to replace the labor-intensive steam engines. The new technology toured North America's railroads, with Pasco being one of its many stops. (Courtesy of the Washington State Railroads Historical Society.)

Bibliography

Berryman, Marvin E. "Varney Air Lines." The United Airlines Historical Foundation. Denver, CO: www.uahf.org/united_history.asp (accessed June 18, 2009).

Bureau of Land Management. *Government Land Office Homestead Records*. Springfield, MA: www.glorecords.blm.gov/PatentSearch (accessed June 18, 2009).

Franklin County Historical Society. *The Franklin Flyer, May 1968–January 1977*. Pasco, WA: self-published, 1978.

History Ink/History Link. *The Free Online Encyclopedia of Washington State History*. www.historylink.org (accessed June 18, 2009).

An Illustrated History of the Big Bend Country, Embracing Lincoln, Douglas, Adams, and Franklin Counties, State of Washington. Spokane, WA: Western Historical Publishing Company, 1904.

Lourdes Foundation. "Our History." Lourdes Health Networks. www.lourdeshealth.net/history.html (accessed June 18, 2009).

Meyer, Bette Eunice, and Barbara Kubik. *Ainsworth: A Railroad Town*. Fairfield, WA: Ye Galleon Press, 1983.

Newmeier, Franz. *Steamboats.org: Steamboating the Rivers*. Munich, Germany: www.steamboats.org (accessed June 18, 2009).

Oberst, Walter A., and Ralph Smith. *Pasco, 100 Years in Pictures*. Pasco, WA: Franklin County Historical Society, 2002.

Oberst, Walter A. *Railroads, Reclamation and the River: A History of Pasco*. Pasco, WA: Franklin County Historical Society, 1978.

Pasco Reclamation Company's Project. Pasco, WA: Pasco Reclamation Company, 1911.

U.S. Census Bureau. *United States Federal Population Schedule, 1870–1930*. Washington, D.C.: Ancestry.com (accessed June 18, 2009).

U.S. Selective Service System. *World War I Draft Registration Cards, 1917–1918*. Provo, UT: Ancestry.com (accessed June 18, 2009).

Washington State Digital Archives. *Birth, Marriage and Death Index*. Cheney, WA: Washington Secretary of State (accessed June 18, 2009).

Werner, Joseph. "Federal Transient Shelter." (Scrapbook, n.d.)

Washington State Railroads Historical Society. *Washington State Railroads Historical Society Museum*. www.wsrhs.org (accessed June 18, 2009).

Index